CIRCLE OF FRIENDS

ALSO BY CHARLES GASPARINO

King of the Club

The Sellout

Bought and Paid For

Blood on the Street

CIRCLE OF FRIENDS

The Massive Federal Crackdown on Insider Trading—and Why the Markets Always Work Against the Little Guy

CHARLES GASPARINO

HARPER
BUSINESS

An Imprint of HarperCollins*Publishers*
www.harpercollins.com

HarperCollins books may be purchased for educational, business, or sales promotional use. For information, please e-mail the Special Markets Department at SPsales@harpercollins.com.

FIRST EDITION

Designed by Ruth Lee-Mui

Library of Congress Cataloging-in-Publication Data has been applied for.

ISBN: 978-0-06-209606-7

13 14 15 16 17 DIX/RRD 10 9 8 7 6 5 4 3 2 1

To Don Ryan, my friend,
my professor who taught me the world

ACKNOWLEDGMENTS

I could not have written this book without the help of numerous people. They include government officials directly involved in the insider trading investigations who have taken time out from their busy schedules to help me get my facts right. Some of these folks are currently employed by the government, while others have left for the private sector. All of them would like to remain anonymous because investigations remain ongoing.

Jonathan Gasthalter, the chief spokesman for SAC Capital Advisors, went out of his way to confirm facts and figures about the hedge fund. Nancy Condon, the spokeswoman for the Financial Industry Regulatory Authority, Judy Burns and John Nester, press officials for the SEC, Peter Donald from the FBI's press office, and Ellen Davis, of the Manhattan U.S. attorney's office, were invaluable in helping me understand key aspects of the insider trading crackdown.

Hollis Heimbouch of HarperCollins deserves special thanks, not just for guidance and support but also for patience; *Circle of Friends* took more than two years to finish as the size and shape of the insider trading probe grew, and the book changed to reflect that new reality.

Ethan Friedman worked long and hard to shape the manuscript and Max Meyers was a source of great insight. My longtime literary agent Todd Shuster must curse the day he took me on as a client. I, on the other hand, owe him many thanks for helping with this project and others.

I also would thank some people at Fox News, including Kevin Magee, Brian Jones, Dianne Brandi, Sital Patel, and my television agent, Wayne Kaback. Bruce Levy, my old friend from the *Wall Street Journal*, deserves special thanks for fact-checking much of the material in this book. Last but not least, I want to thank my wife, Virginia Juliano, for putting up with my book writing and much more.

CONTENTS

CIRCLE OF FRIENDS

INTRODUCTION

"I know this guy who's got an ironclad way to make money. I can't lose and I can't get hurt."

—Bud Fox, *Wall Street*

I can't believe this is happening to me," David Slaine thought one morning in mid-2007 as special agent David Makol of the FBI explained to him that his life as he knew it had changed. Slaine, he said, should be prepared to spend "a long time in jail," unless that is, he confessed to his crimes and agreed to help the government catch others engaged in the same dirty dealings.

Slaine had been nabbed for a crime the veteran stock trader knew all too well: insider trading. Slaine worked two decades on Wall Street for a variety of firms and made a lot of money. He wasn't a household name, but many of the market's successful traders aren't—and they like it that way. To invite press attention is to draw attention to the way they earn their money, which government investigators increasingly believed involved trading on confidential, top-secret information about companies, also known as *insider trading*.

Slaine is a tall man with broad shoulders and a macho temperament. He was known both as a skilled and intense trader but also as a brawler—someone who had at least one trading-floor fight. He also was a man known to Federal investigators as something else: a fat cat willing to skirt the rules, looking for edges over his competition, even if that edge involved an inside tip about a stock before it had been made public.

Slaine came onto the radar screen of the FBI the way most people do—from another cooperator. The feds had busted a ring of traders—a circle of friends—at UBS, Bear Stearns, and Morgan Stanley, one of the firms, where Slaine had worked, for passing inside information to each other, mainly tips about upcoming deals that are supposed to be kept secret—or at least not acted upon—until they're made public. One of those friends, not unlike a mob rat looking for leniency, ratted out Slaine for allegedly doing the same thing. As his name circulated through the FBI, agents realized he had worked with one of their main targets in the burgeoning probe, Galleon Group founder Raj Rajaratnam. FBI agents, skilled at putting together connections and relationships, soon thought they were on to something huge.

Based on the initial pieces of information they were receiving from informants and witnesses, investigators became convinced that a massive circle of friends existed on Wall Street; that men and a few women, mainly at some of Wall Street's biggest trading outfits, known as *hedge funds*, were using and trading on insider information with impunity.

It was a sea change in the thinking of the federal regulatory apparatus designed to monitor and prosecute insider trading. For years the operating assumption in the law enforcement community was that the illegality was contained largely among boiler rooms—small firms that operated on the fringes of the more established Wall Street companies—or the occasional dumb (and greedy) celebrity and a few sharks who know how to game the system. But what they were finding now was that insider trading was more systemic; almost daily, regulators noticed massive trading volume preceding mergers and other market-moving corporate announcements, with the suspicious trading patterns emanating like a bad odor from the fastest-growing part of the investing business—hedge funds. Once a backwater business catering to "accredited investors," meaning those with more than $1 million in assets, both the size and the importance of the hedge funds had grown enormously in recent years. Because it catered to the rich, the hedge fund industry has until recently evaded the regular supervision of investment banks or even mutual funds, which count as their customers the average investor and are known on Wall Street simply and somewhat derisively as "retail."

This exclusivity did little to hamper the hedge funds' growth, since the ranks of the millionaire class continued to expand through much of the 1990s and into the next decade. And it did something else: It made the hedge fund ripe for abuse. Hedge funds now controlled about $2 trillion in assets (and growing) and the pressure to raise money is intense with each fund bragging that it had an information "edge" over the other. Big funds like Raj Rajaratnam's Galleon Group or Steve Cohen's SAC Capital controlled much of the daily trading volume of stocks. They were Wall Street's best customers, meaning that they got early reads on research and other market intelligence—and maybe more.

That edge, regulators had come to believe, was code for trading on illegal insider information, passed along through various cliques and contacts that the funds had in corporate America, on Wall Street, in the hedge fund business, or in a combination of all three. The information was often paid for, government officials discovered, or passed along as part of a quid pro quo of traders sharing inside tips.

The question was how to break into this vast criminal conspiracy that regulators believed was baked into the business model of some of Wall Street's biggest and most profitable hedge funds.

Slaine represented immense possibilities in this regard. He worked for Galleon and two other major Wall Street firms and now worked for himself. He didn't rub shoulders with the likes of Steve Cohen, but Slaine knew some of Cohen's foot soldiers as well as those at other big hedge funds to be helpful to the feds if they could get him to flip.

The feds had named their investigation "Perfect Hedge" for its double meaning: Insider trading was the perfect hedge in making money in uncertain markets because the trader knows what's going to happen before the rest of the market. His cheating ensures a perfectly hedged trade that could never lose.

But its other meaning involved what people like Slaine represented if they cooperated: a perfect witness in creating the perfect case that broke the biggest insider trading ring in recent history.

Breaking such a case was not unlike breaking the mob, FBI officials reasoned, and it would take the same tactics: aggressive (albeit fully legal) pursuit of evidence and witnesses. Playing rough with witnesses was something the FBI agents were good at. One way they play rough is to lay out in stark terms what is waiting for the witness if he or she doesn't cooperate: a long jail term and all the dark consequences of spending a chunk of time living with career criminals.

Ironically, one of the men leading the FBI probe was anything but a tough guy. David Chaves was known as the "Velvet Fist" inside the bureau because he had both a soft touch with cooperators and because he truly believes in redemption—if, of course, the target is willing to cooperate first. If not, he'll throw them in jail like anyone else, where, as he is fond of saying, "you will have no friends to help you."

Chaves and his team spent months examining Slaine's trading patterns. Other teams simultaneously focused on the trading at Galleon and SAC Capital. The trades all had something in common: Each successful bet in the string occurred before key corporate events were made public. Moreover these guys produced investment returns that beat the market with regularity, something the vast regulatory apparatus designed to rid the markets of insider trading had come to believe is nearly impossible to do on a consistent basis—unless, of course, you know something the market doesn't.

Now they just needed to sell Slaine on the idea. Chaves believed Slaine was "flippable" despite his tough-guy reputation. Some of this judgment was just gut instinct on the part of the bureau; some of it was common sense. Slaine was in his mid-forties—not so young, particularly after adding a prison sentence that could span ten years or more for insider trading, based on the sentencing guidelines. He was married (though heading for divorce), with a young daughter, so the last thing he needed was a decade or more in prison.

But if he cooperated he was still young enough to start a new life, even if he was forced to serve a reduced sentence that often follows a plea deal. And Chaves's biggest selling point would be that Slaine could avoid jail altogether depending on how good a witness he turned out to be.

Chaves didn't handle the task of turning Slaine the crook into Slaine the cooperator. That would be handled by David Makol, considered one of the best "flippers" in the bureau, and Chaves's go-to guy on such matters. He was tough when he had to be, and soft when he thought the target would appreciate a gentle hand, at least according to colleagues. People who have experienced Makol's work have a less benign view. They describe him as manipulative, and at times, abusive, someone who while staying within the limits imposed on him by the bureau will use threats and intimidation to achieve his overarching goal of flipping witnesses and making them compliant in every possible way.

Makol decided to pay a surprise visit to Slaine outside his apartment on Manhattan's Upper East Side. Standing with a fellow agent on 80th Street and Park Avenue, he flashed his badge, introduced himself, and invited Slaine to grab a cup of coffee at a nearby diner. Slaine, seemingly unnerved, agreed.

After they sat down, Makol, in a firm but direct manner, explained the situation: Slaine wasn't the upstanding citizen he wanted everyone to think he was—just another white-collar crook who made his money cheating the system. The trades in question involved Slaine receiving early warnings about downgrades of stocks announced by a big Wall Street firm.

Slaine was part of a larger circle of friends that profited from the inside tips. The feds had all the information, data points on traders, and more than that, cooperating witnesses to ensure a guilty verdict and a long jail sentence.

Makol was always prepared for the worst, as all FBI agents are when confronting possible cooperators. Some targets pass out, some literally wet their pants (or worse), while others get on their knees and beg for mercy. But Makol had done his homework on Slaine and didn't expect any of that

People who know Slaine said the meeting made him sick, as Makol reduced a career of more than twenty-five years in finance into a life of crime. Even so, Slaine sat stoically as Makol rattled off what the government viewed he had done wrong, the list of witnesses who were prepared to testify to as much, and most of all the amount of jail time he could receive—possibly decades of not seeing his wife or daughter, then just about a teenager, except through a glass partition at a federal prison.

That is unless Slaine became a witness himself and agreed to turn in his circle of friends involved in the same dirty business.

Prosecutors will tell you that insider trading cases are not easy to win, particularly when it involves sleazy witnesses looking to save their own skins, and of course trading records that look bad but are not incontrovertible in proving guilt.

There would be additional meetings between Slaine and his soon-to-be FBI handlers, including one a few days later inside his apartment with his wife present to hear the same gory details. There would also be a fair amount of soul searching with family members.

But in the end, the decision was pretty easy for a man who made his fortune taking calculated risks.

"I'm ready to cooperate," he said.

David Slaine has been described by authorities as not just an important element in what is now regarded as the biggest insider trading case ever, but also as one of the most important informants in the history of white-collar crime. With his help, over the next five years prosecutors snared dozens of arrests (including one of his friends and weight-lifting buddies) and helped establish a perfect record of convictions in the largest insider trading investigation in modern history

Slaine may have started out as a notorious criminal, in the eyes of the feds (friends say an accurate portrait is far more complicated and much less corrupt), but he ended up as a demigod; there was almost nothing he wouldn't do to help with their cause. He wore wires, and entrapped co-workers in corrupt business ventures. According to friends, his success at undercover work came at a severe personal cost; he suffered from depression along the way, and tried on several occasions to convince the FBI that he had done enough. With the constant threat of jail time hanging over him, he spent more than two years of his life as a government insider-trading spy, and he did it with the poise and purpose of a veteran undercover agent. People who knew him during this time say he acted like the same old David Slaine: the self-confident high school football player, basketball star from Malden, Massachusetts, who had made a name for himself on Wall Street for his trading acumen as well as for his toughness, even if inside his head he felt like he was about to explode.

For his assistance in catching other crooks, Slaine didn't spend a day in jail. He now runs a small business, about a half dozen stores that specialize in grooming dogs. He never did reconcile with his wife, but according to one of his FBI handlers he's currently "doing very well," a role model for someone who commits crimes and then does the right thing in the eye of the government. Through his lawyer, Slaine declined several requests to be interviewed for this book.

As *Circle of Friends* will demonstrate, Slaine was important to the success of Perfect Hedge, but he wasn't the only cooperator. Several months after they approached Slaine, another longtime FBI agent schooled in the art of witness flipping, B. J. Kang, secured the cooperation of a woman named Roomy Khan, a former hedge fund trader and Silicon Valley bon vivant, whose circle of friends included various market analysts, technology company officials, and billionaire hedge fund mogul Raj Rajaratnam.

Many more would succumb to the government's deal: cooperate or get ready for jail. And it worked. As this book goes to press, federal criminal authorities have convinced dozens of hedge fund managers and traders to turn against their colleagues. The feds have done this through examining trading records, emails, and documents as well as by gathering direct testimony from cooperators and secretly recorded conversations where dirty information is shared. In the process, the government has racked up more than seventy convictions without a single loss, including nailing Rajaratnam—one of the world's largest hedge fund managers—and later a man named Rajat Gupta, a former CEO of consulting giant McKinsey & Co., who as a board member of Goldman Sachs supplied Rajaratnam with some of his most lucrative inside tips.

Other similarly sized targets are still waiting nervously, including the biggest one of them all: hedge fund impresario Steve Cohen of SAC Capital, the giant hedge fund that has confounded regulators for years with its ability to beat the law of averages in cranking out a steady stream of market-busting returns.

Cohen, known around Wall Street as "Stevie," has proven to be a particularly elusive target, though not for a lack of effort on the part of the government. As of publication of this book, as many as nine former or current SAC traders, analysts, or money managers have been either charged or in some way tied to various insider trading cases; at least one has gone to jail, while others have agreed to cooperate in building a case against higher ups at SAC, including potentially their old boss. Still others, such as SAC star trader and close Cohen associate Michael Steinberg, have chosen to fight. As I write this in April 2013, Steinberg has been indicted on conspiracy to commit securities fraud and four counts of insider trading and faces many of the same decisions faced by people like David Slaine. Unlike Slaine, so far Steinberg has chosen to fight, pleading not guilty, but that could change as it has with others.

Steinberg's arrest came in classic Perfect Hedge fashion—in the early morning hours, and with FBI agents equipped with bulletproof vests and guns at their side providing their targets with a grim introduction to what it's like going up against the federal government's vast white-collar crime fighting apparatus. It is meant as a warning to both Steinberg and anyone else targeted in the inquiry that fighting the government comes at a price, legal experts say.

One thing seems clear: Since 2007, civil and criminal authorities have spared almost no expense trying to snare the man who on paper at least is considered among the world's greatest investors. Steve Cohen and his advisers say SAC's investment record—nearly 30 percent annual returns since the fund began in 1992—is the result of research and skill, flowing from the man at the top of the firm through the best traders, investors, and analysts in the business. Federal investigators, however, appear convinced that same success is the result of having—at least at times—an illegal edge over public investors through the use of inside information gleaned from various confidential sources.

So convinced are they, in fact, that at one point, the FBI even received court approval to wiretap Cohen's home telephone—one of the first times in law enforcement history that wiretaps would be used in a white-collar case. While the wiretaps were unhelpful in making a case against Cohen, the scrutiny continues. SAC recently paid more than $600 million to settle a civil inquiry by the Securities and Exchange Commission without admitting or denying wrongdoing. The inquiry involved a former portfolio manager who allegedly traded on inside information regarding a pair of drug stocks. Just before Christmas of 2012, that former portfolio manager, Mathew Martoma, was himself indicted for allegedly trading on inside information. A key aspect of the indictment was a section where Martoma holds a 20-minute telephone call with Cohen—and then SAC abruptly sells hundreds of millions of dollars of the drug stocks in question.

What exactly was said during that telephone conversation is unclear; what isn't is the fact that the Justice Department has told Martoma that it is willing to trade leniency for his cooperation against Cohen.

Martoma—as he awaits trial—has taken the Steinberg route, both by declaring his innocence of the charges and at least for now refusing to characterize that what he told his old boss was anything but above-board. That might change as well since Martoma is facing a similarly long jail term if he doesn't cooperate. With that, SAC remains on edge; the fund has produced some of the biggest returns in the investing world for more than two decades, but investor cash is starting to drain out amid the scrutiny. Cohen, for his part, has declined repeated attempts to be interviewed for this book. Through a spokesman, he has maintained his innocence, saying he has acted properly at all times. But prosecutors aren't impressed. The indictment of Martoma went to great lengths to point to Cohen as the possible recipient of one of the profitable insider tips that are central to the case. The indictment stopped short of saying Cohen knew the tip was dirty, or mentioning Cohen specifically by name (it referred to him as the hedge fund "owner" and "portfolio-manager A").

But the message was delivered loud and clear.

White-collar law enforcement authorities will tell you that one of the reasons—and maybe the *biggest* reason—that they have approached insider trading with such zeal, particularly since the start of Perfect Hedge in 2007, is to make the investing world safe for the average investor.

They will talk nonstop about the virtues of ridding the investing world of insider trading. To hear it from these folks, getting information that's not available to the public through a high-level connection or by paying for it—the basic definition of insider trading—perverts the very essence of what a market is all about: a level playing field where everyone, regardless of wealth or status, has access to the same information from which they can make educated choices about buying and selling stocks.

And they will tell you that the fundamental purpose of the laws governing the markets is to democratize those markets. They will point out, and rightly so, that the Securities and Exchange Commission, the main law enforcement agency in charge of monitoring Wall Street behavior, was created in the aftermath of the stock market crash of 1929, precisely to level the playing field between the sophisticated investor who buys stocks for a living and has the means to buy information not available to the average person, and that very same average Joe, who has a day job and is investing for retirement.

The two main bodies of law from which most of the rules of investing are derived, the Securities Acts of 1933 and 1934, demand disclosure of information broadly and equally, meaning that the very act of trading on a piece of information that is obtained before it is formally disclosed to the general public is anathema to the notion of fairness that permeates these statutes.

They will also tell you that when someone trades on an inside tip that isn't available to the public, that trade is being made often on stolen or "misappropriated" information, and there are plenty of laws against theft.

These are strong and convincing arguments, which is why insider trading rouses so much anger among average people. The notion that someone has an unfair advantage over someone else seems un-American; after all, our nation is built on fundamental ideas of equality and fairness (indeed, "that all men are created equal").

But step back and consider the following: Are markets *really* supposed to be democratic, and does having better information than the next guy really constitute a fraud that should send someone to jail for almost as long as someone who robs a bank?

In the course of writing *Circle of Friends* it was not difficult to find at least a few academics (Duke law professor James Cox among them) who have concluded that it *doesn't* constitute such a fraud, at least not to the extent that insider trading should be an obsession of federal law enforcement punishable by many years in jail. This obsession, I might add, has diverted resources from real and direct thefts, such as the Bernie Madoff Ponzi scheme, which regulators at the SEC all but ignored for years, until Madoff turned himself in in December 2008.

Madoff's activities cost actual investors real money—nearly $50 billion, depending on how much can be recouped by investigators. Lured by his promises of steady returns, people gave Madoff their life savings; charitable trusts handed him money to fund good causes. They were heartened by the fact that investigators at the SEC had done past inquiries into Madoff and found him to be clear—that is, until reality came calling. And in a flash all the money was gone, since Madoff stole it all right under the noses of investigators, who later conceded they were stretched too thin to conduct a thorough probe.

As you will see in *Circle of Friends*, the SEC or the Justice Department never appears stretched too thin to eradicate insider trading. The question is, why? What is the *real damage* to individuals from David Slaine's having that information, trading on it, and making a profit?

Slaine never forced the person on the other side of the trade to buy or sell his stock. The person on the other side was going to buy or sell the same shares anyway, because the inside information available to Slaine and his circle of friends hadn't been made public.

They were in a sense "victims" of their own lousy investment decisions. The only difference is that David Slaine and his cohorts made money.

Another question to consider: Do average investors really care? Viscerally most would say yes. Anything that gives an unfair advantage to one party over the other should be eradicated from the markets. This gut reaction has been interpreted for decades now by market regulators, and increasingly by federal prosecutors, to mean that the average investor would have less confidence in buying stocks and investing for retirement if they knew the game was rigged by well-connected players making a quick buck based on their exclusive access to market-moving information.

But that doesn't mean the market-confidence argument that regulators embrace holds up. Professor Cox, for one, says there's little in the way of academic research to suggest that insider trading—which has existed as long as there's been a stock market—actually makes people wary of putting their money into the markets.

"There's little in terms of quantitative evidence to prove that investors care" about insider trading when making decisions about whether to buy stocks, Cox says. With that, Cox questions whether insider trading deserves more attention than other white-collar crimes. Higher on his list was mindless risk-taking that brought down the financial system in 2008, causing *trillions of dollars* in losses or the outright market manipulation where traders collude to push prices lower depending on their need, or Ponzi schemes of the Bernie Madoff variety, where people lost altogether tens of billions of dollars.

Regulators would say they focus on these crimes as well, but the facts suggest otherwise. Not a single major financial executive faces jail time for crisis-related crimes. Bernie Madoff was caught, but only after he turned himself in and after regulators were warned of his activities. And yet the news of the day is the dramatic rise in cases of insider trading, a practice deemed by a vast and growing federal regulatory apparatus to be something on the scale of terrorism, when in reality it is not, at least when compared to other more damaging market-based frauds.

Cox explains the difference this way: "When you look around you don't see many bleeding bodies after insider trading takes place. You do see those bleeding bodies with Ponzi schemes and market manipulation in terms of people losing lots of money and never being able to recover that money."

This critical view, as I will show in *Circle of Friends*, isn't widely accepted by the federal law enforcement bureaucracy (or most people in the media). People like David Chaves and his team at the FBI, not to mention the entire enforcement staff at the SEC, believe that trading on insider information is tantamount to robbing a bank because it is stolen information that is being used to help a privileged few to profit.

And nothing good ever comes from stealing.

Or does it? What makes markets function at their best is the free flow of information (related to what financial academics call the "Efficient Markets Theory)." One could argue that when David Slaine obtained information that was not public (and not his) and traded on it, he helped the public know something: The information is being used to price the stock. Most scholars as well as practitioners who study financial markets believe deeply that markets function best when stock prices (or the prices of bonds, commodities, derivatives, options, mortgages, currencies, interest rates, and the whole massive slew of financial instruments we have managed to cook up) reflect *all* the available information. So in that sense, David Slaine helped the markets run more efficiently, not less.

Circle of Friends is not a defense of insider trading—far from it. But it is an attempt to provide some perspective on what our regulators view as the white-collar crime of the century, one that they're now trying to convince the general public would be running rampant were it not for their heroic law enforcement efforts.

And some of these efforts *are* heroic. People like Chaves and his team, as well as agent B. J. Kang, brilliantly turned witnesses like Roomy Khan to convict Rajaratnam. And maybe most of all, the enforcement agents at the Securities and Exchange Commission, led by an understated but determined investigator named Sanjay Wadhwa, are dedicated professionals who believe they are doing the right thing in setting the stage for the most successful insider trading crackdown in history.

During numerous interviews, they've all provided the same defense of their actions: Ridding the markets of insider trading will send a message to the public that government will do all it can to make the markets fair. With ensured fairness comes confidence and with that increased confidence a new investor class will be born (while those who lost faith in the markets following the financial crisis will, perhaps slowly, return).

Yet consider the following, as many academics I have interviewed for this book point out, and a few government officials involved in the crackdown concede:

In the years where people like David Slaine traded on illegal information freely, market confidence, particularly among small investors, was at its height. Boatloads of money flowed into the stock markets from average investors, either directly through the purchase of individual stocks or indirectly as small investors plowed trillions of dollars into equity mutual funds and ETFs (exchange-traded funds, which for the purposes of this discussion function essentially as mutual funds—mechanisms that let small investors buy into much bigger baskets of stocks than they could affordably do otherwise).

So when did confidence begin to dry out? It goes back to 2008, when the financial crisis and persistent worries about the direction of the U.S. economy hit individual investors and small business people hardest. That crisis, caused by greedy bankers who took on too much risk, coupled with weak regulations and poor government oversight, has had more to do with the erosion of investor confidence than anything David Slaine and his cohorts did or are still doing.

The stock markets have recovered their losses from the financial crisis, and yet small investors remain fretful. They've been yanking money out of stock mutual funds since the 2008 crisis, a process that's continued largely unabated even as the Federal Reserve has taken short-term interest rates down to zero, and only recently began purchasing stocks in modest amounts. The Fed's interest rate policy was designed to create what's known as the *wealth effect*. With interest rates so low, the Fed's logic went, investors would flee low-yielding bonds for investments that offered higher returns, like stocks.

But this wealth effect was largely a Wall Street phenomenon. It's interesting to note that this mass migration out of stocks and into bonds, money-market funds, and gold by small investors occurred just as our government launched its crackdown on insider trading. Thus, just as the government was making the investing world safe, investors felt less safe. Small investors have remained in bond funds and gold—but not because they think insider traders are ripping them off. Rather, it's because they believe the markets are vulnerable to a precipitous fall, whether it's because of the burgeoning European banking and economic crisis, the unsustainable deficits that are devaluing the currency (the reason for the gold purchases), the dysfunction in Washington over economic policy (the reason for the purchases of super-safe bonds), a flash crash that sent stocks falling for no other reason than a computer malfunction, or all of the above.

And maybe average investors simply accept the "unfairness" of insider trading as a minor obstacle in their financial lives. It is no secret among average investors that the big players, namely large institutional investors, and Wall Street trading houses have monopolized information flows illegally *and* legally for years. Consider the controversial Facebook initial public offering. In the weeks prior to the stock's IPO, underwriters gave (perfectly legal) private briefings to large investors about Facebook's dimming prospects but gave no such hand-holding to small investors who bought what turned out to be inflated shares through the retail networks of firms like Morgan Stanley. As I write this, months after the IPO, Facebook is still trading below its initial price. Those big investors who got out immediately or didn't play at all are doing much better relative to the legions of small investors who made what in hindsight is a pretty bad bet.

Or maybe they have a better, less idealized understanding of the markets and how they work than our regulators do. Read Friedrich Hayek, or Milton Friedman, or any of the great free-market thinkers and you will come away with one undeniable conclusion: Markets are by their very nature unfair; the smartest traders, those with the *best information*, are *supposed* to pick stocks better and make more money than anyone else.

Now, Americans *hate* cheaters, and they don't like those who have an unfair advantage, which is why when you ask most people about insider trading, they'll usually say that the perpetrators belong in jail.

To that end, the biggest coup of the ongoing insider-trading crackdown at least so far has been the conviction of Galleon Group founder Raj Rajaratnam, who was found guilty of insider trading and securities fraud and sentenced to eleven years in the same federal prison that houses Madoff and mob kingpin Carmine "the Snake" Persico. During the course of his career Rajaratnam made a lot of money trading, accumulating a net worth of nearly $2 billion. Wiretaps, government witnesses, and telephone recordings from informants with inside tips paint a wide pattern of abuse, leading to a well-deserved conviction.

Yet even government prosecutors would concede that most of the money he made for himself and for his clients did *not* come from breaking the law. Largely overlooked by the media was the cost of Raj's illegal dealings. Before his arrest in 2009 (and Galleon's subsequent demise) the fund had accumulated around $7 billion in assets.

To build a fund of that size, Raj and his team conducted many tens of billions of dollars' worth of trades to produce overwhelmingly positive annual returns averaging around 25 percent since 1992 and amounting to *billions of dollars* in winnings for his clients. Yet the feds say he stole only some $70 million by trading on insider information. That figure, even if it is accurate (Raj lawyers claim the amount is closer to $7 million), would mean that the vast majority of his trades, billions upon billions in winnings, were perfectly legal.

It would also mean that the government spent tens of millions of dollars to prosecute a crime that pales in comparison to many other shady practices that have cost the financial markets and American taxpayers untold billions and possibly trillions of dollars in losses. The shadiest of those practices, of course, led to the 2008 financial crisis, one of the world's great economic tragedies.

The financial crisis and its continued lack of identifiable culprits is key to understanding why insider trading is all the rage these days with the federal law enforcement bureaucracy, and why men who run hedge funds, like Raj Rajaratnam and Steve Cohen, have become more recognizable household names than those of our banking titans. Of course, bubbles like the one that caused the risk-taking that led to the 2008 collapse are often more about irrational exuberance than the more rational act of fraud. In other words, they are difficult cases to make, and upon taking office in 2009, and with the after effect of the financial crisis causing massive unemployment, regulatory officials in the Obama administration barely explained those nuances to a skeptical and hurting American public.

What it needed was a white-collar scandal that it could tout as having successfully prosecuted to satisfy the public's demand for Wall Street scalps, even though insider trading had nothing to do with the practices that led to the banking debacle.

At least that's what many of the career prosecutors have told me in their more candid moments while being interviewed for this book. Did they make up the crimes of Raj Rajaratnam, David Slaine, and their circle of friends? Of course not; these cases were based on good detective work, informants, and wiretaps that produced overwhelming evidence that the culprits didn't merely step over the line of what is acceptable behavior—they often drew new boundaries.

But consider the following: The investigations were launched during the waning years of the Bush administration and had been developed by career law enforcement officials from the SEC, the FBI, and the Justice Department. They were developed at a time when Bernie Madoff still roamed free, with some in law enforcement ignoring warnings about his activities, and when risk-taking by the banks grew to enormous heights.

Unlike the minutiae involved in mortgage fraud or Wall Street risk-taking, insider trading cases are, as one prosecutor called them, "sexy," in that they include wiretapped evidence of tipsters getting not just cash but lobsters and real sex in exchange for their services, as *Circle of Friends* will point out. The hedge fund moguls on the other end of the telephone were caught on tape eagerly paying for the information, while bragging about their exploits.

All of this was tailor-made for the Obama administration's white-collar crime point man, Preet Bharara, the U.S. attorney from Manhattan. Bharara is a smart, capable, and ambitious prosecutor. His critics inside the Justice Department and in the legal community have also described him as a Rudy Giuliani on steroids when it comes to using the media to burnish his image and turn the crime of trading on "material nonpublic information" into the Wall Street crime of the century.

Ultimately *Circle of Friends* is less a polemic than a crime story, filled with larger-than-life Wall Street characters and their counterparts in federal law enforcement, and intended to show why each side is motivated to do what they do. This book will also delve into the origins of the crime known as insider trading, which began well before the current hysteria, and should provide some perspective on what actually occurs when someone trades on confidential information, and just how much the markets and society are injured by that act.

But *Circle of Friends* is also about the politics of insider trading—how this sort of Wall Street crimefighting has been used to make headlines and to buff and polish political careers. You may agree that insider trading is as bad as the regulators say it is for market confidence, but the fact remains that countless millions of dollars (the government won't release the exact amount) have been spent to deter crimes that have nothing to do with the cataclysmic events of 2008, which continue to shake the U.S. economy.

CHAPTER 1

PERFECTLY LEGAL

The world's oldest profession is said to be prostitution, but if you're looking for the world's oldest economic crime, insider trading has to be at the top of the list. Historians say people have been looking for an information edge through various means almost from the time people began to buy and sell goods for a profit. When the European *bourses*, or stock exchanges, were created in the 1600s, financiers wasted little time before cultivating sources who could give them access to information not available to the general public.

Such gamesmanship wasn't even considered a crime by the businessmen who in 1792 signed the Buttonwood Agreement—agreeing, under that famous buttonwood tree in lower Manhattan, to a set of rules and standards that would govern how they would trade various commodities, which led to the creation of the New York Stock Exchange.

That doesn't mean average people liked it when rich fat cats used their wealth and privilege to game the market, as one such fat cat, William Duer, discovered. Duer was assistant Treasury secretary to Alexander Hamilton, and the same year the Buttonwood Agreement was signed, he thought he could make a boatload of money by speculating on debt issued by the U.S. Treasury—the first such debt issued by the nascent country.

Duer was looking to make a killing, using his connections with Hamilton and his position in the U.S. Treasury to take advantage of the market for newly issued government bonds. Yet in the end he was the one who was almost killed, and using insider information wasn't his only mistake.

News of his gambit and his use of *leverage,* or heavy borrowing, to finance his bets became the talk of Washington and New York. Leverage is like the financial equivalent of an athlete on steroids. Normally, if you bet $1 on a given stock (or Treasury bond) and it rises to $2, you've doubled your investment. But if you borrowed an additional $9, and invested all $10, the resulting doubling in value would give you $20—*twenty* times your initial $1 stake (or ten times once you've paid back the loan). The leverage magnifies your gains enormously.

The problem with leverage (like steroids) is that the opposite occurs when the trader bets wrong—the leverage turns modest losses into astronomical ones—and that's what ultimately happened to Duer. (It's also what happened to the big banks during the 2008 financial crisis.) When prices of his government bonds began to tank, and the nation fell into a recession, Duer lost everything short of his life. At one point, an angry mob chased him through the streets of lower Manhattan, and according to one account, nearly disemboweled him. He died a little while later in debtor's prison.

The bad example set by Duer didn't do much to persuade financiers that insider trading doesn't pay. Insiders made countless millions gaming railroad bonds during the 1800s by using their connections to key politicians, since the nation's railroad system was heavily subsidized by Congress. The same financiers sold stock in railroads *short* (a trading technique whereby you can profit when stock prices fall) when they knew that certain rail companies would go bust. Bribes were common, and even when the miscreants were caught outright manipulating markets, prosecutions were almost nonexistent.

President Ulysses S. Grant even found himself in the middle of an insider trading scheme, which this time involved his assistant Treasury secretary tipping off business associates about the timing of gold sales. As the tips began to filter through the markets, the price of gold began to fall. After the government sale, gold prices fell even more.

At the time, gold was the nation's reserve currency, and thus the value of the U.S. dollar plummeted. The day in September 1869 was known as "Black Friday," as news spread about how a few fat cats profited while the rest of the country suffered. Even so, it would be decades before the practice was declared a crime.

Indeed, over the next sixty years or so, the courts meandered in and out of the insider trading maze, not really taking a firm stand. The country, of course, had much bigger issues on its hands, including World War I and the growing influence of organized crime, which cornered markets in booze (during Prohibition), broads (prostitution), and buildings (unions). White-collar crime was largely regarded as a fact of life; those who ventured anywhere near a stock exchange, the gold market, or the trading of any security or commodity knew what they were getting into.

Then came the Great Depression.

It takes one to catch one," was what Franklin D. Roosevelt said when he was asked why he would hire a stock speculator to play cop over the stock market.

That stock speculator was, of course, Joseph P. Kennedy—businessman, political insider, rumored bootlegger, and not least, father of a future president—who was tapped by Roosevelt to head his new market watchdog, the Securities and Exchange Commission.

The year was 1933, and the consensus after years of ignoring financial crimes and insider deals was that stock speculation was the root cause of the ongoing economic catastrophe soon to be known as the Great Depression. Stock speculation had been rampant for years leading up to the 1929 market crash among people like Joe Kennedy, a prominent investor who for years earned millions buying and selling on tips that were hoarded among the Wall Street pros.

Not only was insider trading ignored by the courts, but the laws of the day almost *encouraged* it. Companies faced no legal compulsion to provide the public with any information more than advertising that wasn't an outright lie. Financial statements were subject to state laws, which were pretty weak.

In essence there was no legal responsibility on behalf of corporate America to tell the truth to investors, while those who knew better, that is, the corporate insiders, could trade until their hearts were content.

Of course, in such an environment, speculators had a field day, and one of those was Joe Kennedy. He was smart enough to seize on the largely nonexistent regulatory environment, earning a fortune through what we today would consider insider trading and blatant stock manipulation, while keeping his reputation as a "legitimate businessman." Among his favorite practices was said to be one of the oldest scams in the market: the "pump and dump."

Kennedy and his business associates would buy the stock of target companies, spread positive news about them through the press, and dump the shares at a profit. Some seventy years later, the SEC and Justice Department announced a massive crackdown on the practice, which was the business model of a slew of brokerage firms operating on the fringe of the markets and often seeded with money from organized crime. The small firms were known as *boiler rooms* and investors who fell for their schemes lost tens of millions of dollars (as they did in the more modern-day versions). Many of the heads of the boiler rooms went to jail, while their foot soldiers were thrown out of the securities business for good. What the SEC didn't say as it began to roll out such cases was that the scheme had been all but perfected by its own very first chairman.

By the late 1920s, Joe Kennedy was both incredibly rich and ready to be a political kingmaker. Being an Irish Catholic upstart who never forgot his working-class roots (his grandparents left Ireland to escape the potato famine), he was a lifelong Democrat and an early supporter of President Franklin Roosevelt.

Roosevelt, the hyperconfident new president, liked what he saw in Kennedy: Here was a Wall Street moneyman who agreed with him philosophically on the need for an expansive government to deal with the ravages of the Great Depression. More than that, Roosevelt used Kennedy's status as a Wall Street insider to support his broader agenda; in other words, the creation of new laws that would forever reform the way the securities business worked.

Kennedy was soon armed with some of the most powerful new laws in the nation's history pertaining to white-collar crime. Investment schemes, outright manipulation of stocks, distribution of false information—all hadn't merely been tolerated by law enforcement authorities; they had been almost expected because Wall Street was regarded by regulators as "buyer beware" territory.

No longer.

Right after Roosevelt's election in 1932, Congress passed and Roosevelt signed into law the Securities Act of 1933, and later the Securities Exchange Act of 1934. These laws armed the new agency, known as the Securities and Exchange Commission, with broad powers. Shady stock market dealings, by now considered a root cause of the stock market crash and the Great Depression, would become a crime:

> It shall be unlawful for any person, directly or indirectly, by the use of any means or instrumentality of interstate commerce or of the mails, or of any facility of any national securities exchange . . . [t]o use or employ, in connection with the purchase or sale of any security registered on a national securities exchange or any security not so registered, or any securities-based swap agreement any manipulative or deceptive device or contrivance in contravention of such rules and regulations as the Commission may prescribe as necessary or appropriate in the public interest or for the protection of investors.

In plain English, this new agency was seeking unprecedented authority to regulate any market activity it considered "deceitful."

Some crooks were indeed locked up in the post-market-crash era, but not by the SEC under Joe Kennedy. As broad as the laws *sounded*, the commission's powers were actually pretty narrow—it regulated the securities markets but enforced its rules on a civil basis. Companies and individuals could only face fines and censures under the two laws that gave the commission its legal mandate. But the commission had no authority to put people in jail.

Nor did it have much authority to do exactly what today's law enforcers say is the very meaning of the securities laws of 1933 and 1934: to level the playing field for all investors by trying to rid the markets of the scourge known as insider trading. That would have to wait.

> Fiduciary obligations of directors ought not to be made so onerous that men of experience and ability will be deterred from accepting such office. Law in its sanctions is not coextensive with morality. It cannot undertake to put all parties to every contract on equality as to knowledge, experience, skill and shrewdness.
>
> —Arthur Prentice Rugg, chief justice,
> Massachusetts Supreme Judicial Court

The year was 1933. Stock manipulation and the sharing of inside information—the same stuff that the SEC chairman had profited from in another life—was now regarded as among the chief causes of the 1929 stock market crash and the Great Depression that followed. The U.S. Senate launched hearings aimed at holding those culprits responsible. They were known as the "Pecora Hearings," named after Ferdinand Pecora, the chief counsel of the Senate's Banking Committee who led the inquisition.

The Pecora hearings were big news at a time when the American people were reeling from the country's financial collapse and wanted blood, namely banker blood, for the wild risk-taking that had led to the country's economic woes. Pecora forced many of the country's top moneymen to appear before his panel; he was considered a crusader in some quarters, and a publicity hound in others.

Either way his tactics would be copied by prosecutors and congressional investigators for years to come. People who worked for New York State attorney general Eliot Spitzer said his crackdown on Wall Street abuses and flamboyant unveiling of charges in front of rooms packed with reporters was inspired by Pecora.

Decades later, after the 2008 financial crisis, senior executives of the big banks would be taken to task for their sins before modern-day congressional investigative committees, in very Pecora-esque fashion. The son of Sicilian immigrants, Pecora was often photographed with a cigar in his mouth and cultivated the image of a working-class hero going up against the corrupt blue bloods of Wall Street. He didn't just uncover schemes; he badgered his banker targets during his hearings with rapid-fire questions about their various misdeeds. The bankers called it a witch hunt, but Pecora had both the president and the public on his side for the simple fact that he showed how Wall Street insiders benefited unfairly from their privileged status and other conflicts of interest that would easily rank up there with the practices that led to the 2008 banking debacle.

Pecora's hearings also had real teeth. He forced the resignation of the head of National City Bank, one of nation's largest financial institutions and a precursor to mega-bank Citigroup, and his work gave impetus to a series of new banking laws, including the Banking Act of 1933, one of the most sweeping banking reforms in U.S. history.

And yet, even as Pecora railed against Wall Street's chummy circle of friends, insider trading still wasn't viewed as much of a crime, as the case of Cliff Mining and Rodolphe Agassiz demonstrates.

Agassiz, the president of Cliff Mining, had access to what the SEC would label today as "material nonpublic information" that his company was sitting on a potentially huge find of copper. Knowing that this would boost shares of his company, Agassiz then did what today would lead to SEC charges, fines, and possibly time served behind bars—he secretly bought shares of his company on the Boston Stock Exchange.

Shares of Cliff Mining would later soar when news of the copper mine was publicly released. That means someone had to lose money from not knowing the same information.

Enter a businessman named Homer Goodwin, who sold the stock just as Agassiz was buying, and while he probably didn't know it at the time, Goodwin was soon to become an important footnote in the long and convoluted history of insider trading. When he discovered that he had sold his shares before the announcement (and thus missed out on the stock's huge upswing), and that Agassiz had bought shares almost simultaneously, Goodwin sued Agassiz on the basis that the information about the mine was "material" and should have been made public to investors before they sold their shares.

Goodwin's complaints as a company shareholder against Agassiz's actions sound reasonable by today's standards. But not according to the Massachusetts Supreme Judicial Court, or the SEC, Justice Department, or just about any securities regulator back then. Insider trading may have been one of the outrages the Pecora Commission used to generate headlines and class warfare in order to spur implementation of Roosevelt's New Deal legislation, but in 1933 it wasn't even a misdemeanor.

As Judge Prentice Rugg put it, the law "cannot undertake to put all parties to every contract on equality as to knowledge, experience, skill and shrewdness." Agassiz, Rugg opined, didn't put a gun to Goodwin's head. There were no face-to-face meetings and misrepresentations. Both conducted their business on a public stock market. So the trade was perfectly legal.

The logic behind Judge Rugg's defense of the *un*level playing field goes something like this: It is impossible and impractical for laws to guarantee that business transactions provide equal benefits to all parties—particularly in the securities markets, which are by their nature Darwinian, and where you know that your decisions to buy or sell stocks are based on imperfect information.

These days, it's hard to imagine a time when leveling the economic playing field was actually frowned upon by the courts, but even during the New Deal, when the government was redistributing wealth at a pace greater than any other period in U.S. history, the securities markets were considered the last bastion of unfettered capitalism. To be sure, there are vast differences in the markets of then and now. In 1933 individual investors were a tiny sliver of the market participants; these days even blue-collar workers are forced to save and invest for retirement given the erosion of guaranteed retirement plans that corporate America has replaced with 401(k) plans and other investments.

The investor class for much of the sixty years after the 1929 stock market crash was pretty elite: Wall Street executives and wealthy individuals, lawyers, doctors, businessmen. Today average investors open online accounts at E*Trade when they want to buy stocks, and they aren't bashful about looking for quick bucks through frequent trades. The game for the little guy back then was supposed to be long term: Buy stock in a company and watch it grow as the company grows. The overriding philosophy among regulators reflected this perspective—that markets become more perfect in the long run, when all the information, even those trades based on insider tips, get digested by participants and price discovery is created.

And that would be how the SEC under Joe Kennedy and other chairmen would approach insider trading for the next three decades.

In fact, it wasn't until Joe Kennedy's son became president in 1961 that the SEC and white-collar prosecutors began to view insider trading as something that must be eradicated.

When are you gentlemen going to investigate the rigged markets in new issues of over-the-counter stocks?" read a letter addressed to the SEC's New York branch office in May 1961. "There is a lot of funny baloney going on in these issues, with conspiracies up and down the street, one selling to another at higher and phony prices, thereby creating phony markets in new issues, thereby hooking the general public who will eventually hold the bag. Then when the whole thing crashes over the ears of the little guy holding the bag, then you will wonder what happened, when all the time it is going on under your noses."

Another letter delivered just one month later to the SEC headquarters in Washington, D.C., explained how current laws and the SEC's enforcement of them were "wholly ineffective when it comes to preventing insiders, with special knowledge unknown to the public, before the issuance of corporate reports from taking unfair advantage of the public by their purchase or sale of these securities while the public is ignorant of the fact which may exist."

Both letters were part of an increasing pattern of complaints from average investors about the unlevel playing field of the stock market. The country's postwar wealth created many benefits, including a burgeoning investor class of people who for the first time weren't content to sock their money away in an FDIC-insured bank deposit, where it would earn interest at a rate lower than those offered on government bonds. They plowed money into stocks; shares of the Dow Jones Industrial Average were now well above their pre–Great Depression peak, while daily trading volume of shares on the New York Stock Exchange soared to 4 million shares, nearly triple the level immediately following World War II. The markets were booming, contributing to the postwar wealth effect. But many of those new investors who helped push stocks higher believed they were doing so in a vipers' nest. Unscrupulous brokers were selling them stocks to help drive up the price so corporate "insiders" could sell their inflated shares at a profit. Those insiders—the men running America's biggest companies—had access to information well before the public did, and they acted on it by selling and buying shares before major corporate announcements without a peep from the SEC.

William L. Cary, an academic appointed by President John F. Kennedy to run the commission, was somewhat of a renegade among market experts. Yes, people were complaining about an unequal playing field, but the prevailing wisdom among many academics was that insider trading was good—or at the very least produced a societal benefit in the form of more efficient markets (since prices would more quickly reflect all available information, including insider information). If the markets were so rigged, as the complaints suggested, then why were people continuing to snap up stocks more than ever before?

Such were some of the arguments made by a prominent law professor at the time, Henry Manne, now dean emeritus of George Mason University, in his book *Insider Trading and the Stock Market*. In it he stated convincingly (or convincingly enough that regulators used it as a rationale for their lack of enforcement for decades) that without insider trading, asset prices would lag behind true investor sentiment, thus distorting the market.

Cary, however, didn't see the benefits and in fact took great offense at the notion that corporate insiders were using their positions for personal gain. Even more, he argued insider trading violates the fundamental basis of the markets in the aftermath of the 1933 and 1934 securities acts: that information must be disclosed in an equitable manner to *all investors*.

With that Cary took the first giant leap by any federal law enforcement official to make insider trading a crime. He began to expand the SEC, populating its ranks with like-minded legal experts largely from academia who disagreed with Manne's doctrine about the market efficiency of insider trading. He then began to use existing law more broadly, leaning heavily on one part of the SEC's founding mandate, known as Section 10-b of the Securities Exchange Act of 1934.

The securities laws of 1933 and 1934 were revolutionary in their scope in that for the first time the activities of Wall Street were being monitored by a federal agency with the power to sanction fraudsters. As sweeping as the laws were, they stopped short of giving the SEC the authority to put people in jail.

But the law wasn't without its teeth, miscreants could be fined, banned from the securities industry or from serving as an officer or director of a public company. Section 10-b of the act was particularly onerous because it covered just about every activity from outright theft to manipulating stocks, and as Cary would argue, insider trading as well. The rule was broad and open to interpretation, he believed. It allowed the commission to regulate just about anything it considered fraud if it involved "deceit or fraud" in connection with *the sale of a security*.

Three decades went by before the SEC began using 10-b as a weapon to crack down on insider trading, and Cary thought it was way overdue. In doing so, he made history, becoming the first SEC chairman to state openly what is now the accepted wisdom among securities regulators: Insider trading erodes public confidence in the markets, and it's something the commission must do everything in its power to eradicate.

The first case brought by the SEC under Cary's new mandate involved a board member of a public company who inadvertently tipped off a friend and business partner about a market-moving corporate event. What made the case against the brokerage firm Cady, Roberts & Co. so significant involved the SEC's rationale in bringing action: insiders with exclusive access to nonpublic information must either "disclose" that information to the broader market, or "abstain" from trading on it.

The information, in this case, involved a decision by the company, Curtiss-Wright Corp., to cut its dividend, with the likely fallout of lower stock prices in its aftermath. One of the company's board members, a fellow named J. Cheever Cowdin, also moonlighted at a big brokerage firm—underscoring Cary's core belief regarding the incestuous world of corporate America. Cowdin in his role as stockbroker told one of his colleagues at the brokerage firm, Robert Gintel, about the dividend move.

Gintel did what you might expect: He acted on the tip, selling shares before the information became public, and not just his own shares. He also sold shares on behalf of his clients, saving lots of money for investors who benefited from his inside knowledge as prices did eventually fall on the news. Gintel thought he was doing what everyone else was doing, and what the government at least until now had tolerated in the markets—that is, obtain information in any and every way possible, and trade on it even if it was to the detriment of the suckers on the other side of the trade.

Cary, however, saw illegality, based on his interpretation of the securities laws. And his efforts in bringing a securities fraud case would have far-reaching implications for years to come. Gintel had traded on information that was the "property" of the company, Curtiss-Wright, Cary argued. Lowering the dividend was the company's information to dispense as it pleased, and by trading on that information before the rest of the market, Gintel had effectively used stolen information to make a quick buck.

Gintel didn't go to jail and Cowdin wasn't even charged with a crime. For all Cary's efforts, insider trading hadn't risen to criminal status—that would eventually come. Instead, Gintel was charged with a regulatory infraction, a civil charge, and fined $3,000. Nevertheless, an important precedent had been established: The trading of material, nonpublic information was regarded as illegal by the nation's top markets regulator. And this precedent would be repeated and expanded upon for the next fifty years.

"The SEC completely dropped the ball on Dirks."

That was the assessment of the commission's general counsel some thirty years later about one of the most important Supreme Court cases in the history of insider trading law. Ray Dirks was a little-known analyst who would later gain fame for confronting the government's ever-widening definition of what is dirty information.

Just a few years before Ray Dirks appeared before the Supreme Court in 1983, Harvey Pitt had been a thirty-something general counsel of the SEC. In the years that followed, he would go on to have a fairly significant career in white-collar law litigation, representing stock swindler Ivan Boesky during the insider trading scandals later in the decade, and big Wall Street firms for years to come. He built a practice as an attorney who could be tough with regulators and tough with his clients, telling them when and where they stepped over the line and just how far he could push the government in protecting them.

That ability helped land him the job he coveted throughout his career: SEC chief under President George W. Bush. It was Pitt's dream job. He was overwhelmingly confirmed by the Senate in 2001 and he promised to put all his years in government and in private practice to use in doing big things at the agency.

But it was also a short-lived tenure, shorter than most in recent history, as Pitt was pummeled with questions about his ability to crack down on his former clients, the big Wall Street firms, under scrutiny for various misdeeds stemming from the bursting of the Internet bubble and subsequent crash of the Nasdaq index.

Democrats attacked him as a lapdog for his old corporate clients, even as he launched investigations into major post-bubble frauds involving short-lived high-flyers WorldCom and Enron. A memo leaked by a Democratic political operative laid out a damning scenario: Pitt's long years in private practice defending Wall Street bad guys would be used to expose how the Bush administration was soft on corporate crime. But reality was different. Pitt's philosophical stance made him as much of an advocate of tough enforcement as his predecessor Cary had been, particularly in the area of insider trading.

For that, he had a zero-tolerance policy.

Pitt managed to fight back the wave of rumor and innuendo. During his short term as head of the agency, he was actually quite effective at bringing cases against Wall Street firms such as Citigroup, Merrill Lynch, and Morgan Stanley. His knowledge of the securities laws allowed him to start a profitable legal and consulting business after leaving the commission in 2003.

Which brings us to Pitt's curious remark about a stock analyst named Raymond Dirks. In 1977 Dirks caught the attention of the SEC, which had launched an all-out effort to codify insider trading as a market crime. As the commission's general counsel—or its chief lawyer—Pitt reviewed the agency's enforcement actions, including one pending about Dirks. Pitt embraced the post-Cary mandate to test the limits of the securities laws as they apply to trading on nonpublic information. Since there was no insider trading law—just the SEC's evolving definition of what constitutes a dirty trade—commission lawyers were for the most part making it up on a case-by-case basis.

They were making it up big time in their pursuit of Dirks. In effect, the commission's enforcement lawyers were saying that there were no practical limitations to what they considered an illegal trade. In the perfect market world envisioned by the SEC it didn't matter if that trading involved a CEO who sold his stock just before he issued a negative earnings announcement, or if football coach Barry Switzer bought stock after having casually overheard news of a pending merger. (After facing SEC charges, a court said Switzer didn't violate the law.)

That's because the reigning ethos at the commission in the decade that followed Cary's first case was that in order to establish a fair marketplace, the public should know that *all trading* on nonpublic information is illegal.

Pitt would refer to the SEC's enforcement approach regarding insider trading as the "perspiration effect." The SEC couldn't and wouldn't bring every case that came its way, but it would bring enough cases that even average people, not just Wall Street traders, would think twice, or sweat a decision about trading on confidential information. The SEC clearly wanted to make Dirks sweat—and others who followed his lead. Dirks had discovered a fairly significant fraud at an insurance company named Equity Funding. He went to the SEC with the details, but the commission didn't see the merit in the case.

The case it was looking to pursue involved Dirks's own actions. He had alerted his own clients of the fraud before the broader market and he advised them to start trading on the information he had uncovered. His clients were thankful, but the early warning, according to SEC officials, was tantamount to passing on illegal insider information. At least that was the sentiment of the SEC enforcement division at the time.

• • •

Pitt's recollection of his role in the Dirk's case is somewhat hazy. But he does recall being among the few people at the commission who urged caution.

Troubling Pitt was the fact that Dirks didn't exactly hide his findings. Rather he came to the commission with them. To be sure, a profit motive was behind Dirks's attempts to spark an enforcement action that would have crushed shares of Equity Funding that his clients had shorted. But he was far from deceptive, the characteristic securities laws point to as one of the key elements to any fraud charge.

Nevertheless, the prevailing wisdom at the time was pretty clear: There must be one market, not a specialized market for Dirks's customers and another one for everyone else.

In fact, Dirks presented what some SEC staffers thought was the perfect case: He was paid handsomely by his client, a large institutional investor, for exclusive information about a market-moving event, while other investors were left in the dark. The specifics of the case made it even more enticing to the federal agency, who wanted to establish an important precedent to further crack down on insider trading. The information on the fraud came to Dirks from a company insider, so it wasn't already priced into the stock. Dirks either had to make the matter public to *all market participants* or keep his mouth shut.

In the most far-reaching interpretation of insider trading yet, the SEC argued that a man who uncovered a fraud was actually committing fraud simply because he profited from an unlevel playing field.

This was an important development. Insider trading enforcement after Cary left the commission in 1964 revealed just how murky the legal terrain surrounding insider trading cases was. First came a big win for the commission in 1968, when the courts ruled that officials at a company called Texas Gulf Sulphur had illegally traded on information about a major new copper ore find that would boost shares. The upshot of the verdict for the SEC was that it now had a clear definition of just what nonpublic information company insiders can legitimately act upon in the securities markets.

A reasonable standard was established: If a reasonable trader believes the information could move the stock, for example, news of a major find of copper ore or some other corporate event, then company insiders have to keep it private; they can't trade on it until the information is made public.

Keep in mind that the SEC's case brought during the Cary years against Robert Gintel involved a tip that was relayed from a board member to a stockbroker who then traded shares. But in the Texas Gulf Sulphur case, board members didn't relay the information to third parties; they traded on the information themselves. They also issued a press release the commission believed was misleading in trying to downplay the find when rumors began to sweep the market. The victims were the public shareholders of Texas Gulf Sulphur—the people the corporate insiders owed "a duty" to disclose information to if they planned on trading on it.

It was the type of behavior that everyone, from the SEC's insider trading purists to even those who believe there's some broad merit in such dealings, would find particularly repugnant: a group of fat-cat insiders getting rich with no risk while screwing the investing public with bad information.

Next came a setback for the SEC: a case and conviction against a financial printer named Vincent Chiarella, who traded on information he obtained on the job from the companies whose materials he was printing.

It seemed like an open-and-shut case to the SEC, which brought charges in 1977. Chiarella worked at a printing plant that notified all its employees that they were prohibited to trade on any information obtained on the job. One of the biggest lines of business for Chiarella's employer, a New York–based company called Pandick Press, was printing documents used by large investors to make tender offers for other companies. Such tender offers would send shares of the target company soaring, which is why financial printers had often blocked out the names of the target companies in the documents.

Chiarella never went to college nor did he ever come close to a job on Wall Street, but he knew the value of the information he was handling if he could take the next step and try to figure out the names of the target companies whose identities were being concealed.

And he did by observing "the suits," as one observer would later point out, who hung around the printing plant. Over the next fourteen months, Chiarella made more from trading stocks—around $30,000—than he earned as a printer, by piecing together this confidential information and trading on it. It also came at a cost: He was caught by the SEC, which noticed the suspicious trading activity in the targeted stocks. It wasn't long before he was sanctioned by the SEC, forced to give back his trading profits, and charged by New York prosecutors, among the first criminal prosecutions ever for insider trading.

Chiarella was eventually convicted of securities fraud for trading on inside information, and his conviction was upheld on appeal. But the Supreme Court agreed to hear the case, and in a stunning move, reversed course. The court ruled in favor of Chiarella and nullified the SEC's main arguments for bringing the action in the first place: that by handling confidential information Chiarella was actually a corporate insider. That meant, according to the SEC, he owed a "duty" to the investors of the corporate entities involved not to trade on the shares of the target companies before the news was made public.

The Court's decision, announced in 1980, put the SEC on notice that its use of 10-b wasn't a blank check to bring just any case. In fact, the ruling made Swiss cheese out of one of the key arguments that the SEC had used in its war against insider trading: that anyone with access to nonpublic information that can move a stock is a classic insider, owing a duty to shareholders and "victimizing" them by trading on it.

Chiarella was not a company insider in the same way that board members in Texas Gulf Sulphur had been, the court ruled. The government couldn't even call the people on the other side of his trades real victims. Chiarella bought his stock on the market, where people trade all day for different reasons.

In other words, fairness in the markets had its limits.

It would be limited even more three years after the Chiarella decision, and nearly eleven years after the SEC first charged Ray Dirks with insider trading. Once again the commission was before the nation's high court, looking for a bit of redemption, and of course, a further expansion of what the law considers insider trading, even if the agency did pick a pretty lousy example to make its case.

The echo chamber inside the commission failed to come to grips with what Dirks had really done. He had performed a function that was *good* for the markets and for investors. He had uncovered a fraud, and while his clients benefited first, so eventually did other investors as his information became reflected in the price of Equity Funding's stock.

Here's what Pitt meant by the SEC "dropping the ball" on Dirks: After charging the analyst in a civil proceeding, it expected Dirks to take his punishment and walk away. But Dirks wasn't the "sweating" kind of stock analyst. He built a career taking on managements who ran fraud like Equity Funding, and short sellers he believed were wrong about companies they targeted as frauds.

He was also willing to take on the SEC, and he won. The Supreme Court's ruling established a precedent that would define insider trading for years to come, but not in the way the purists in federal law enforcement had wanted. By stretching for the ultimate enforcement tool, the SEC wound up having the law diminished. Keep in mind that nothing in what the commission found Dirks had done resembled the wild quid pro quos of payments and other compensation that would become the modus operandi of the markets decades later, or even the gross abuses found before. He followed up on a tip from a company insider, a former executive from Equity Funding who told him that the outfit was a fraud. He investigated the claim, interviewing executives at the company, and came to his own conclusion about the stock. It was the ultimate in what traders would later call the "mosaic theory"—piecing together various pieces of data and then making a market call.

Common sense may have been missing from the SEC's pursuit of Dirks, but not at the Supreme Court. Neither Dirks nor his initial tippee had stolen the information that Equity Funding was a fraud, because, the court ruled, it's impossible to actually steal information that a company is a fraud. In other words Dirks wasn't a criminal, just a stock analyst who uncovered criminal activity and made his clients a lot of money from it. Case closed.

Well, not quite. The tortured history of what constitutes insider trading had become even more tortured following Chiarella and Dirks. The SEC continued to push for as wide an interpretation as possible, and based much of its efforts going forward on a dissenting opinion of Chief Justice Warren Burger in the Chiarella case.

Burger pointed out that the Court would have been forced to uphold Chiarella's conviction had the SEC not argued that Chiarella was an insider with an absolute duty to either refrain from trading or alert the world of the information. It would have been on stronger ground if it simply said "the defendant had misappropriated confidential information obtained from his employer and wrongfully used it for personal gain," or Chiarella had stolen something, in this case confidential information that didn't belong to him.

With that, the misappropriation theory became the SEC's latest, albeit imperfect, weapon to democratize information and criminalize insider trading.

The 1980s' boom and burst of stock market scandal would later be declared the Decade of Greed by future president Bill Clinton. (No matter that his wife had allegedly earned big sums of money at the time trading in the futures pits, where insider tips and circles of informed friends have been known to run rampant.) The corporate crime wave of the mid to late 1980s would be defined by the illegal activities of a high-level circle of friends, people like the famed arbitrageur Ivan Boesky, white-shoe lawyer/investment banker Martin Siegel, Dennis Levine, the journeyman deal maker who finally found fortune at Drexel Burnham Lambert, or his boss, Drexel's junk-bond king, Michael

Milken—all of whom spent time in jail for their various crimes involving the markets as they related to insider trading.

Milken was never directly convicted of insider trading, although he would spend time in jail for securities fraud involving his role in what prosecutors believed was a string of dubious corporate takeovers at the center of the largest insider trading scandal in recent history. As any judge or mobster will tell you, fraud involving the U.S. postal system or conducted over the telephone, known as "mail and wire fraud," is far easier to prove than demonstrating that information from a confidential source is illegal, and that proved to be Milken's downfall.

The trading of Boesky, Levine, and Siegel was clearer cut, particularly due to the cooperation of all three when confronted with proof of their various misdeeds. (Boesky and Siegel would wear wires to help the feds make cases against their business partners, including Milken.) They faced civil insider trading charges from the SEC, and various criminal charges from the Justice Department that landed each in jail.

The convictions were big news because they showed that insider trading occurred at the highest levels of the Wall Street food chain. And the details were pretty sordid. Siegel, a white-shoe attorney turned investment banker, admitted to handing bags of money to Levine, a mid-level Drexel banker, in exchange for tips about upcoming mergers and acquisitions that Drexel and Milken were financing.

The convictions made the careers of the federal law enforcement officials at the heart of the case, and provided a road map for other politically astute officials looking for ways to leverage crackdowns on white-collar crime to further their careers. U.S. Attorney Rudy Giuliani would become mayor of New York City several years later. The SEC enforcement chief, Gary Lynch, at this time went into private practice, defending big Wall Street firms. Harvey Pitt, the former SEC general counsel, defended Boesky and negotiated his cooperating agreement. Boesky's cooperation became instrumental in the conviction of Michael Milken, the highest-ranking Wall Street executive to be charged in the crackdown.

And yet, insider trading was hardly a settled matter. Milken didn't go to jail for criminal insider trading. The Justice Department in the final indictments relied on more nebulous criminal violations such as mail and wire fraud involving market manipulation. And with good reason: The misappropriation theory was challenged again and again with some success. Foster Winans, a writer for the *Wall Street Journal*, was charged with handing traders prepublication details of his market-moving "Heard on the Street" column. He spent eighteen months in jail for receiving some $30,000 in payments for giving traders an early read on the column, but his appeal reached the Supreme Court, which produced a mixed verdict.

The Court upheld his conviction but was deadlocked on whether Winans, as a newspaper columnist instead of a true corporate insider, had indeed violated the misappropriation theory. The vexing question the Court left unanswered was how someone who didn't work for any of the companies involved in the mergers he reported on, and who didn't pay someone to steal the information, could meet the legal test of insider trading.

Wall Street survived the 1987 stock market crash, and the junk bond market was only temporarily stymied when it lost brainchild Michael Milken to a prison term, but the lessons of the 1980s were short-lived.

Greed was back.

In the early 1990s, Orange County, California, would gamble with complex financial products known as *derivatives* and lose so much money it would be forced to declare bankruptcy. Its Wall Street adviser, Merrill Lynch, would stand by silently counting the millions it had earned from selling these risky products to public officials who had no clue what they were buying. Brokerage firms merged with white-shoe investment banks, meaning firms like Morgan Stanley could now pump up endless IPOs and other stock deals to mom-and-pop investors in its Dean Witter brokerage unit. The 1990s was the decade of the average investor on Wall Street—even if Wall Street didn't miss its chance to screw its most vulnerable customers. A combination of newfound affluence and a need to find investments for retirement made the stock market the place for average investors to save.

As the SEC fretted over how to keep the pressure on inside traders, it failed to grasp how the vast changes on Wall Street, including the creation of mega-banks such as Citigroup, posed potentially bigger problems for the average investor. Stock market research became more suspect; banks themselves were so big that their corporate clients became their best customers, and thus no analyst or researcher would dare slap a "sell" recommendation on a company that was paying his or her salary.

In these new megabanks, the small investor wasn't viewed as a client, but as a conduit used to pump up the value of the bank's real clients—corporate customers such as Enron and WorldCom and countless overhyped technology companies—even if those clients were frauds, as more than a few turned out to be. The small investor had little reason to suspect that analysts were now reduced to little more than touts; such relationships were barely disclosed outside the fine print of research reports.

This compromised research would play a large role in the destruction of small investor wealth following the collapse of the Nasdaq stock market in 2000. What was the SEC doing at this time? Not much when it came to cracking down on Wall Street's research scam or the growing menace of the big banks. In fact the SEC didn't even consider the various conflicts of interest involved in stock research a *real scam* until 2002, when it was prodded by New York State attorney general Eliot Spitzer to investigate the matter.

Through much of this time, the commission's bigger obsession remained insider trading. It's goal: To get the courts to provide a more concrete working definition. A big break came in 1997, when the Supreme Court ruled in *U.S. vs. O'Hagan.*

James Herman O'Hagan was an attorney who in 1988 worked at the firm Dorsey & Whitney in Minneapolis, which was an adviser on a fairly large transaction, Grand Metropolitan PLC's takeover of Pillsbury. O'Hagan didn't work on the deal—he just heard about it inside the firm, which he believed gave him carte blanche (since he wasn't a fiduciary or a classic insider to either company) to buy options and the stock of the target company, Pillsbury, before the takeover was announced. He made millions when, as expected, shares of Pillsbury soared, but he was investigated by the SEC and charged with various levels of fraud, including insider trading. O'Hagan was sentenced to nearly four years in prison.

He appealed the case, and in 1996, an appellate court threw out O'Hagan's conviction, once again calling into question whether the misappropriation theory could be used on nonfiduciaries. In effect, the court ruled that O'Hagan had no duty to the shareholders of Pillsbury to alert them to the sale before he bought the stock.

That would change a year later when the Supreme Court finally codified the definition of misappropriation into modern insider trading law. O'Hagan was being "deceptive," the Court said in its 1997 ruling, since he knew the information about the deal wasn't his, but in fact property of the companies involved in the transaction. By not alerting the entire market to the deal before he traded on it, he had actually stolen or "misappropriated" the information from people who had a duty to keep it quiet, and he did so purely for personal gain. Alas, misappropriation could be expanded to cover just about anyone.

The ruling was about as far reaching as the government could hope for, though it was hardly a perfect tool. All individuals who seek to profit from nonpublic information gleaned through what the Feds consider a "deceitful act" were, according to the courts, now guilty of insider trading.

But proving that deceit could be difficult, as the government would discover. Even with the O'Hagan victory there is still no insider trading statute, just the opinions of federal judges which regulators were forced to interpret. In a business where information is constantly flowing through rumors, speculation, and a hungry business media, proving that someone had stolen confidential information through deceit was no layup.

But O'Hagan was clearly a victory. Depending on their level of intent, people convicted of insider trading could also face years behind bars as sentencing guidelines for white-collar felonies began calling for more jail time. Moreover, the government wasn't about to let some murky court rulings stand in the way of making insider trading the white-collar-crime equivalent of armed robbery, as its increasingly aggressive investigative techniques would demonstrate.

CHAPTER 2

TEN DIFFERENT CAMERAS ON EVERY TRADER

The SEC viewed the O'Hagan victory as a milestone—and it was. Law enforcement had for years relied on the misappropriation theory to combat insider trading despite its gaping hole: It didn't cover the larger universe of potential insider traders, just corporate insiders who traded on nonpublic information about the companies at which they work, or people like Ivan Boesky who pay those insiders to steal company-specific information and then trade on it.

With O'Hagan *anyone* could be successfully targeted for trading on an illegal tip—even strippers who got their stock tips from their Wall Street clientele and a celebrity homemaker who got tipped off to major corporate events before anyone else.

The SEC and the Justice Department wasted little time going after this newly expanded pool of potential criminals and expanding its own ranks. The Justice Department, led by the U.S. attorney for the Southern District of New York, the main criminal agency involved in rooting out white-collar fraud on Wall Street, began hiring attorneys who had a knack for reading balance sheets. The perpetually underfunded SEC, through its politically savvy new chairman, Arthur Levitt, demanded more funds and got them to beef up its own enforcement efforts. The regulatory arms of both major stock markets, the Nasdaq and the New York Stock Exchange, were never much for catching bad guys, but they too were under pressure from Levitt to expand their enforcement staffs, as were the various state attorneys general—epitomized somewhat later by New York's Eliot Spitzer—who were also looking to make a mark in rooting out white-collar crime.

Still, officials knew they needed something more than legal precedent and a few more cops to successfully penetrate the now-criminal and ever-burgeoning circle of friends.

During the seven years that it took the courts to decide what James O'Hagan had done was criminal, the U.S. economy had fallen briefly into recession and then began a long economic expansion. There had been two presidential elections, a bailout of Wall Street over the big firms' investment in the Mexican peso (which collapsed in 1994), and then a roaring stock market that ignited vast changes to the U.S. banking and financial system, in turn making Wall Street bigger and more powerful than ever before.

Wall Street's business model began a substantive shift to more and more risk-taking through trading in far-flung markets to boost profits. Far-flung, that is, both geographically, as the growth of electronic trading united the globe's markets, and in terms of the types of items being traded. No longer were plain-vanilla stocks and corporate and government bonds enough for Wall Street's trading desks, which were under intense pressure to develop new products to sell to investors hungry for outsized returns. Interest rate swaps (where two parties trade their interest flows from loans or bonds), credit default swaps, and even more esoteric financial instruments were being created as rapidly as the market could consume them. Additionally, the firms were turbocharging these profits through the use of leverage, which made their losing trades more catastrophic.

Banks themselves became bigger and more complex. The controversial financier Sandy Weill created the mega-bank Citigroup, which combined investment banking and trading with the traditional commercial banking businesses of consumer lending and deposits.

It didn't matter that Citigroup was technically illegal when Weill merged his firm, the Travelers Group, with banking giant Citicorp in 1998. Even though the Depression-era Glass-Steagall law, which mandated the separation of Wall Street risk-taking from commercial banking, was still in effect, Weill's newly formed Citigroup received a temporary waiver to operate until the law could be changed. For years Glass-Steagall had been a paper tiger. Loopholes allowed banks to slowly encroach on the Wall Street businesses of underwriting and trading.

Weill supplied the final stake through the heart: He hired a slew of lobbyists and persuaded his friends in Washington to kill the law once and for all, and they did without much thought about the future consequences of unbridled risk-taking at commercial banks. Most notably, they failed to consider that consumers' deposits at commercial banks are backstopped by the federal government (meaning, of course, ultimately by taxpayers) via FDIC insurance. And now that these commercial banks were merged with high risk-taking trading operations, taxpayers were essentially insuring the mammoth risk being incurred by the big Wall Street firms. This was all fine and dandy as long as the economy was humming along, but as we all know, matters came to a head with catastrophic consequences in 2008.

With risk being embraced on such a large scale, a powerful new force began to emerge in the financial industry by the mid-1990s. The trader was king on Wall Street. Investment banking deals may have garnered the biggest headlines, but the trading desks at the big firms were the quiet profit centers, and with those profits came a vast expansion of Wall Street's trading culture, including its lust for inside information.

And it was not just at traditional banks and brokerages. Hedge funds—once a little-known investment vehicle for the rich—exploded in size and strength as the market's rapid rise created a new class of people: the superrich, who were not satisfied with steady market returns of mutual funds or dividend-paying stocks.

They turned to a new breed of sophisticated trader, people like Steve Cohen, a former trader at a midsized brokerage firm named Gruntal, who set up his own hedge fund, using the three initials of his full name, S-A-C. Under SEC guidelines, SAC could avoid most disclosure requirements and review while trading with almost no restrictions.

By the end of the 1990s, Steve Cohen's SAC Capital was trading so much that it regularly accounted for 3 percent of the daily volume on the New York Stock Exchange, and about 1 percent of the Nasdaq's daily volume. Cohen amassed enormous wealth during this time—reportedly several billion dollars and growing—but he was far from alone. The hedge fund business soon became the biggest, most active center of trading in the markets, with returns that defied normal market returns, as regulators soon discovered, on a regular basis.

With that, the trader had now replaced the investment banker as the Wall Street superstar, and the hedge funds had replaced the traditional investment bank as the market's power center

They didn't have the swagger of the deal makers—or garner the press attention of the men who put together giant mergers. Most of them kept a low profile even as they were earning salaries in excess of $20 million a year. But they had a never-ending thirst for making more of it and a never-ending thirst for what became known as "actionable" information that couldn't be downloaded off the Internet but did move stocks.

The new Wall Street that emerged in the mid to late 1990s was a business centered on *information*—and getting the best of it to produce those outsized returns to satisfy a new generation of the superrich.

These investors were demanding something better than the stock market averages and they were willing to pay for it.

Enter expert networks: boutique firms that hired consultants specializing in industries like health care and technology that were paid to share their knowledge with Wall Street traders. Heart surgeons suddenly became Wall Street researchers, as did computer programmers.

A well-paid doctor could bring home an income of $500,000 a year, but in helping a trader on a successful market bet he could easily add another $100,000 to his salary. Wall Street "sell side" analysts who worked at banks quit to set up independent research shops that catered to hedge funds. Technology industry consultants worked with the analysts and the expert networks. These circles of friends were growing in size far beyond the networks that existed during the boom years of the 1980s, and as the benefits of this kind of coziness became clear—higher profits, lower losses—the incentive to stretch the limits of legality and share illegal inside information became impossible to resist.

By the end of the 1990s law enforcement was big and increasingly well funded. Even with Levitt crying poverty, the SEC increased its ranks as well. It had O'Hagan on its side to deal with insider trading, and a federal law known as the Racketeer Influenced and Corrupt Organizations Act (RICO). Used to stamp out the mob, under U.S. Attorney Rudy Giuliani the RICO law was extended to include white-collar crimes. Under RICO, the feds could demand longer sentences for actions that were part of a larger organized effort to commit fraud.

RICO seemed tailor-made for crushing the circles of friends, and Giuliani had certainly used it effectively in the 1980s to turn informants like Ivan Boesky on the ultimate target of his probe, former junk-bond king Michael Milken (who by the mid-1990s was just finishing his jail time and returning to society).

The various market regulators had also developed increasingly sophisticated tools to track suspicious trading patterns. And here's what they saw: increased trading of stocks and options before mergers and acquisitions. The volume of the suspicious trading was now far greater than ever before.

It was as if the great wave of insider trading arrests of the 1980s never happened, and Wall Street was back to business as usual: cheating.

It's like you're walking down the street and we've got ten different cameras on you," Cameron "Cam" Funkhouser likes to say when asked about the market surveillance system he created for an agency known as the Financial Industry Regulatory Authority, or FINRA.

FINRA is the new and updated model of Wall Street's attempt at "self-regulation," a modern version of the National Association of Securities Dealers, the regulatory arm of the Nasdaq stock market.

It may seem odd but the nation's securities laws call for the banks and Wall Street investment houses to regulate themselves, before the SEC or the Justice Department gets involved.

These self-regulators—one working on behalf of the Nasdaq stock market, and the other working out of the New York Stock Exchange—were ridiculed a lot over the past three decades for missing various frauds and scandals that involved trading of stocks listed on the exchange. But by the 1990s, and particularly at the Nasdaq, they had become surprisingly good at one thing: spotting people who engaged in insider trading.

And you can thank Cam Funkhouser for that. Funkhouser likes to describe himself as one of those old shoe-leather investigators from the detective movies, and he certainly plays the part. He talks about going "Catholic school" on his targets, the Wall Streeters he suspects to be lying, by barraging them with questions about their alleged crimes before they fold from exhaustion, like a strict old-school Catholic priest with misbehaving students.

When he isn't playing one of the Christian Brothers, Funkhouser falls back on his best imitation of a white-collar Detective Clouseau and plays dumb, which lets him capitalize on the widely held belief among Wall Street crooks that Wall Street cops are stupid.

But, he'll tell you, he ain't that dumb and the crooks aren't that smart. In fact, he says, the guilty ones almost always fall for the act just enough for him to make a case.

A graduate of Georgetown with a degree in business, followed by a law degree at George Mason, Funkhouser began his career at the Nasdaq's regulatory unit in the 1980s right out of school and became an expert in using increasingly sophisticated computer tracking systems to identify and eventually catch insider traders.

It's fair to say that many of the recent big insider trading cases found their roots in Funkhouser's computer tracking system. In its simplest form, the system tracks every trade—and flags instances of unusual trading, namely sales of stocks around major corporate events. Funkhouser didn't invent the program—he just helped perfect it over the years, adding new tracking devices that allow investigators to find nearly any questionable stock sale no matter how seemingly insignificant.

His inspiration, oddly, is Ivan Boesky. Funkhouser wasn't involved in the Boesky case—he was still fetching coffee for his supervisors at the Nasdaq when the scandal hit. But it was the driving force of a career dedicated to eradicating insider trading from the markets through the use of computers. To this day Funkhouser says he hates everything Boesky stood for—he married money for the sake of marrying money; he made a lot of money illegally utilizing a like-mindedly arrogant circle of friends to carry out his scheme, and most of all, Boesky and his cronies all thought they could get away with it. And Funkhouser thinks most insider traders carry the same basic traits.

Most of these guys can't help themselves. And they don't really think they will get caught," is how Funkhouser described the mindset of the typical inside trader. Yes, they are all different in skill sets and intelligence: Some of the people he has nabbed could best be described as "the loser brother-in-law who gets a tip during a family dinner." Others are MBAs from the most prestigious schools "who think no one is watching them." Still others are first-time offenders who get away with it once—"they dip their toe in"—get hooked on the money, and keep coming back for more.

Funkhouser has seen them all and that's why he knows they all carry the same basic trait: arrogance.

Funkhouser's first case came in 1984, about two months after he graduated from law school. The NASD's fairly basic market surveillance methods of the time showed a bunch of unusual trading in shares of the fast-food chain Carl Karcher Enterprises, named after its founder, who parlayed a single hot dog cart in Los Angeles back during the Depression into the Carl's Jr. franchise.

At the time, Karcher was a millionaire many times over—but that didn't stop him from unloading shares of his company right before some bad earnings came out—and on top of that, from alerting friends and family, about the bad news so they could sell their holdings as well.

"I was looking at all these trades and there were all these relatives who sold right before the bad news hit," Funkhouser recalls. The announcement was that profits from the fast-food chain were down significantly from the company's public projections after it had spent gobs of money on advertising for the 1984 Olympics, which were to be held in Los Angeles.

Karcher and six family members were charged by the SEC with insider trading. In the end, they all settled with the SEC for a combined $664,000 in a civil settlement without admitting or denying wrongdoing.

"When I saw all of this my first reaction was 'this can't be happening,'" Funkhouser said. He couldn't get his hands around how rich people would openly break the law to get just a few bucks richer. Karcher's net worth dwarfed the amount of money his family saved on selling their stock—an estimated $300,000 combined.

Yet they all seemed perfectly at ease with flouting the law to save a few bucks.

The techniques Funkhouser used to nail the Karcher clan would be considered pretty rudimentary by today's standards. Suspicious trading patterns were often shown on "blue sheets," or computer records used to spot unusual trading activity before major corporate events. Corporate mergers were a big starting point; Funkhouser noticed almost from the time he joined the Nasdaq that buying of target companies almost always spiked just before deals.

Funkhouser couldn't have picked a better time to get educated on how the circle of friends worked. A raft of insider trading cases reached the highest levels of Wall Street convincing regulators and prosecutors that the dissemination of illegal tips went beyond the Carl Karcher types—that illegality was systemic on Wall Street. Initially, Martin Siegel, Ivan Boesky, Michael Milken, and even Dennis Levine didn't fit the prevailing image among regulators of the typical white-collar criminal who either operated on the fringe of the mainstream investment banks, or, like the Karchers, were corporate executives looking to cut a corner. They were part of the establishment—the places where compliance departments and pedigree were supposed to root out criminality. And what the 1980s crackdown taught people like Funkhouser as well as his counterparts in law enforcement was that the education and pedigree of the establishment Wall Street crook meant that he operated at a higher level through a circle of intermingled professional and personal relationships.

Boesky and Siegel, for instance, met at the Harvard Club in midtown Manhattan. They developed code words when making drops of cash in exchange for insider tips. "Your bunny has a good nose," was the signal Siegel gave to one member of his circle that a corporate takeover was indeed about to go down. Levine, who met Siegel while they both worked at Drexel Burnham Lambert, created a trading account in an offshore bank where he carried out his illegal trades. They exchanged cash through couriers to better hide their illicit payments.

In other words, business and illegality were being commingled easily and effortlessly at the highest levels of Wall Street, which had the money and the means not to get caught.

• • •

The 1980s insider trading crackdown wouldn't be duplicated for at least two decades, even though the practice remained high on regulators' list of crimes. By the late 1990s, Funkhouser had risen through the ranks of the Nasdaq to run its surveillance unit—and perfect its system of catching the bad guys.

The old blue sheets that regulators used to track unusual trading activities were replaced by a vast computer system located at the Nasdaq's offices in Bethesda, Maryland; with the advancement of technology, Funkhouser's investigators were able to pinpoint with even greater accuracy even more trading that had the taint of illegality, leading them on the trail to making some of the most sensational insider trading cases ever.

Such was the case in 1997, when Funkhouser's computers helped SEC investigators charge some traders at J. P. Morgan and Salomon Smith Barney for trading on bank deals just before the mergers were announced, essentially buying the acquisition target and profiting when shares soared.

The traders were throwing down big chunks of money and earning hundreds of thousands of dollars a trade—and their trades were glaring to Funkhouser and his staff, who by this point had a practiced eye for such conduct.

Investigators broke down the data even further and found several small brokerage accounts mirroring those trades. When Funkhouser first started his career, finding suspicious trading in an account of this size was like finding a needle in a haystack. No longer. The system he had helped construct searched for many more variables than a merger or market-moving corporate event, and at infinitely more granular levels.

By 1999 it had become increasingly difficult for insider trading to fly under or through the radar, which accounts for what happened when investigators came across an unusual pattern of trades made by a woman from Miami, an actress best known for her roles in *Babewatch*, *Marylin Does Miami*, and *Marylin Whips Wall Street*.

"I don't know what you are talking about," a somewhat flustered Kathryn Gannon told officials from the SEC when they asked her how she could know how to pick stocks before their prices spiked on merger news.

By the end of the interview Gannon offered up all the implausible explanations SEC officials have heard from the beginning of time: She's so good at trading because she reads the *Wall Street Journal*, talks to people in the business, and is just good at stock picking.

Making the excuse even more implausible was Gannon's occupation, easily confirmed by SEC investigators after a simple Web search: She was an adult film actress who went under the name Marylin Star.

She never went to business school, much less college. According to her online profile, she did, however, plan to have sex with two thousand men for a film to be released on the eve of the millennium called *Gang Bang 2000*.

Investigators believed Gannon's involvement was just the tip of the iceberg and was part of a bigger circle that led to some major player on Wall Street. Their working theory was that Gannon must have some sugar daddy or several sugar daddies at the big banks who supplied their porn-star girlfriend with insider tips, a circle of friends motivated by money and sex—only fitting, perhaps, for an era in which a sitting president had received oral sex from a young intern in the Oval Office.

In order to prove this theory, investigators scanned bank accounts, checked trading records, and conducted many hours of depositions, including the bizarre spectacle of interviewing the porn star herself. A young associate director at the SEC named Lionel Andre hit paydirt in Star's checking account: Star was receiving regular payments from a man named James McDermott, the same James McDermott who ran one of the best-known firms in the bank merger business, Keefe Bruyette & Woods.

This indecent circle of friends would grow wider when in addition to McDermott, investigators found that a businessman in New Jersey, Anthony Pomponio, had also been part of the scheme. His connection to McDermott? Nothing, except that like the Wall Street whiz, he had a "relationship" with Gannon and like just about everyone during the 1990s stock market boom they liked talking about stocks. By the time the SEC got done untangling all the messy details, they boiled down to something like this: Gannon got pillow-talk tips from McDermott and then, when sharing a pillow with Pomponio, passed them along to him.

McDermott was initially shaken by his quick fall from grace. Immediately fired by Keefe, which effectively ended his long and lucrative career on Wall Street, he hired a former SEC enforcement chief named Gary Lynch, by then in private practice, as his attorney to fight the charges.

What made the choice of Lynch ironic was that just a decade earlier Lynch had headed the SEC's investigation into Boesky and Milken, and argued with a missionary's zeal why the crimes of the 1980s deserved such regulatory attention and scorn. Now, on McDermott's behalf, Lynch argued just the opposite, at least initially—namely that McDermott didn't violate the insider trading laws because he didn't use the information himself; he'd merely passed along deal tips to his girlfriend.

But not even the great Gary Lynch could save McDermott with that argument now that the O'Hagan case had widened the pool of people who could be guilty of insider trading by either trading or passing on material nonpublic information. In the end, McDermott pled guilty to misappropriating insider information and spent five months in jail. (Gannon eventually served eight months in a women's prison after initially fleeing to her native Canada.) Perhaps the biggest indignity of all for McDermott wasn't the jail sentence or even being permanently barred from the securities business. It was what he learned from prosecutors as his case became a cause célèbre on Wall Street: He wasn't Gannon's only lover.

As it turns out, he may have been naïve about what motivated Gannon's affections, but he wasn't so naïve when it comes to the ways of

Wall Street—and its use of insider information. Members of his family contend he told them that insider trading occurs all the time—he just got caught. (McDermott said in an interview he made no such statement.)

"Isn't it nice to have brokers who tell you those things," Martha Stewart muttered to her friend Mariana Pasternak as they sat in Stewart's private jet one afternoon, waiting to depart for a planned vacation that would eventually take them to Mexico.

The year was 2001, and Stewart was, of course, the billionaire entrepreneur of homemaking stuff. Pasternak was just a friend. They were going to meet another friend, Sam Waksal, for a little fun and sun south of the border.

That's when Stewart's cell phone rang.

It was her broker's office at Merrill Lynch in midtown Manhattan. Stewart, like most Americans with a few bucks to their names in the 1990s, was caught up in the hoopla of playing the markets. She had a broker at Merrill, Peter Bacanovic, who specialized in celebrity clients, like Stewart, and semi-celebrities like Waksal, a scientist who loved the Manhattan party scene and had long since befriended Stewart; at one point he dated Stewart's daughter.

Waksal was also the CEO of a company named ImClone, which was developing a promising cancer drug named Erbitux. Promising, but not yet approved by the FDA for use. In fact, the company had just received a still-confidential and unfavorable ruling from the Food and Drug Administration on Erbitux. The drug, as it turns out, wasn't the miracle cure for cancer that ImClone and Waksal had marketed it as, at least according to the FDA.

"Sam's trying to sell his shares," was the urgent message that a Merrill Lynch brokerage assistant, Doug Faneuil, said Bacanovic had instructed him to deliver to Stewart as she sat on the runway.

Stewart's reply: "I want to sell all my shares."

Shares tanked the next day when the FDA publicly released its negative findings about the drug's prospect, but not before Stewart, Waksal, and a slew of Waksal's family members, including his elderly father, had sold their stakes and avoided significant losses.

The exact reasons for Stewart's soon-to-be controversial stock sale would be debated during a highly publicized courtroom drama. There was no evidence Stewart knew of the FDA ruling—just that she had an advantage over the general public by receiving early warning that he was selling shares of the company. In fact, Stewart's lawyers argued with some success that she had been looking to sell her shares for months following the advice of her broker, and even had an agreement to sell if they fell below $60, as was the case at the time of her sale.

But in the end, it didn't matter. The trial would last five weeks and eventually land the happy homemaker in jail for a few months not for insider trading but for lying to federal officials who investigated her suspicious stock sale.

Through it all, Stewart would maintain her innocence. Fans said she was made a scapegoat for the public anger that followed the crash of the Nasdaq stock market that would hit average investors particularly hard. Prosecutors at the Manhattan US Attorney's office said the case underscored that no one—not even a rich celebrity—is above the law.

But one thing is certain: the case underscored how the Wall Street caste system works against the small investor. Corporate insiders, of course, sell their stock for many reasons including to pay their taxes. But they also get the first look at all company information—good or bad—before it's released to all market participants.

If Waksal, Imclone's top corporate insider, was selling his stock, he might also know something the rest of the market doesn't. That's why brokerage firms keep such information confidential before it's released to all market participants at some later date. According to Pasternak's somewhat hazy recollection later, Stewart said she liked having a broker who tells you "those things" referring to the early warning she received about Waksal's stock sale.

The Jim McDermott–Marylin Star insider trading imbroglio had been notable for what it said about the times—during the 1990s' bull market, absolutely everyone was making money. The mood of the time was less outrage and more guilty pleasure in watching a Wall Street hotshot implode over his lust for a porn star. And of course, there was a clear violation of the insider trading laws.

The Martha Stewart case had more to do with outrage. Most average people (those with less than $100,000 in investable assets) never get such tips about inside sales. They're often relegated to call centers and websites to get the latest news about their portfolios, and they took some of the biggest hits when the stocks hyped by Wall Street began to crater in the spring of 2000.

They can barely get their broker on the telephone much less a warning that something big was happening to their investment as Bacanovic had given Stewart through his assistant. Stewart held a $228,000 position in Imclone—pretty puny given that her net worth at the time was more than $1 billion. Bacanovic was on standing orders to keep her abreast of any developments he had heard about stock; though there was no evidence that Bacanovic knew about the FDA ruling either, given his relationship as Waksal's broker, he was certainly in the position to know when the company's top corporate insider was unloading his stake.

With that Martha Stewart, the famed homemaker, became a symbol of a market that favored the rich and connected over the average Joe or Jane.

The case also showed something else: Insider trading remained among the most difficult cases to make.

Prosecutors in the New York office of the U.S. attorney's office wanted to bring the toughest charge against Stewart, namely criminal insider trading over selling stock after receiving the confidential information about Waksal's sale.

But they labored mightily over exactly what Stewart had done wrong. "There were problems with the case," one former prosecutor told me. "The money was small compared to her net worth. When it came down to it, she saved so little money (around $50,000) on the trade."

And all they really had as evidence that Stewart committed criminal insider trading was Faneuil's warning that she should dump shares because the Waksals were selling. (Again there was never any evidence that she knew about the FDA ruling.)

Prosecutors would have to prove that Stewart misappropriated or knowingly traded on confidential information that wasn't hers, namely Waksal's own sale, all of which didn't meet the threshold for bringing a criminal case. In fact, she could have just as easily sold her shares only because her broker had advised her to sell, and nothing more.

Again, the only evidence to support an insider trading charge came from the testimony of lowly clerk Faneuil telling her that the *family was selling—not why they were selling*.

Ultimately, the decision rested with the top prosecutor on the case, assistant U.S. Attorney for the Southern District James Comey. Based on the facts at hand, Comey concluded that charging Stewart with criminal insider trading would have been outside even the expanded definition established in O'Hagan.

But there was other evidence that showed Stewart had violated the law—just not the criminal insider trading rules. Stewart, for example, denied having spoken with Faneuil during the day of the sale when she was initially interviewed by prosecutors from Comey's office and SEC officials about the trade. Instead she said she spoke to Bacanovic about the sale and said it was a result of a long-standing stop-loss order hastily exercised by her broker that day. (Ironically, the jury acquitted her of lying about having that stop-loss order.)

With Faneuil's testimony that he was the conduit for the information, Comey decided to pursue a criminal charge of obstruction of justice for lying to investigators.

"What Sam Waksal did was insane . . . if you notice my client isn't even charged with insider trading," Martha Stewart's very able lawyer, the late Bob Morvillo, explained to a skeptical jury in the spring of 2003.

Waksal had just pleaded guilty to insider trading on shares of Imclone—and for passing that illegal insider information about the FDA decision on Erbitux to many of his family members. Shares of the company did in fact tank as Waksal suspected they would, and he saved a bundle selling his stake, but at a huge cost.

Since he was a company insider, he clearly violated the "classic" definition of insider trading as opposed to the expanded version established under the misappropriation theory in O'Hagan. He would spend the next seven years in a federal prison for trading and profiting on insider information, a length of time reflecting his refusal to cooperate and name others who had direct knowledge of the FDA's ruling.

Stewart may have been accused of lying and obstruction of justice, but the government didn't have the goods to hit her with insider trading charges, not even close, Morvillo repeated time and again to the jury. Morvillo's point was obvious: How could Stewart lie about a crime the government says she didn't commit.

The federal insider trading police and ultimately the jury saw the matter differently, particularly with the public's disgust with Wall Street fat cats in the post dot-com era running high. Even more, any case could ultimately advance the government's broader, zero-tolerance policy when it comes to people who trade and profit off of confidential information, even if that information doesn't fit the court's interpretation of criminal insider trading.

During her trial, Stewart's celebrity friends such as actors Brian Dennehy and Bill Cosby made guest appearances as her attorney Morvillo hammered away at what he believed were holes in the government's case and the recollections of the various government witnesses arrayed against her, including Pasternak.

Neither Morvillo's arguments nor the celebrity cameos seemed to sit well with a jury of average working-class New Yorkers. They seemed especially incensed by the notion that anyone, much less a billionaire who baked cookies, should receive preferential treatment, while most average suckers lost big bucks in the stock market.

The evidence that she had an earlier agreement to sell the stock when its price hit a certain level didn't matter much to the jury as prosecutors picked apart the rest of her account on why she sold her shares of Imclone. In the end it took just about a day for the jury to return a guilty verdict.

But Morvillo's arguments did underscore the difficulties investigators faced in pursuing criminal insider trading cases even in the post-O'Hagan environment. The SEC with its lower threshold for culpability would eventually file civil insider trading charges against Stewart, alleging that she *should have known* that Faneuil was misappropriating confidential information about the stock sales of Merrill clients. But Stewart later settled the civil case without admitting or denying wrongdoing. Her fine: A mere $195,000.

Prosecutors took their usual victory lap during a lengthy press conference on the steps of the federal courthouse alerting Wall Street to "beware" because conduct such as Stewart's wouldn't be tolerated. In retrospect, however, they were less sanguine.

They believed the case proved just how difficult insider trading was to prosecute and root out of the markets. Despite all their additional manpower, expanded legal precedent, and computer searches, the best they could do was charge that Martha Stewart lied about something that wasn't a crime.

Proving the crime of insider trading, the government was beginning to realize, would take something else. In fact, FBI agents and prosecutors were now coming to the conclusion that cracking Wall Street's vast inside trading rings was not unlike cracking the mob since they both operated on the pursuit of profit and an ingrained code of silence.

In both cases, there are very few incentives to cooperate with the government.

What eventually made so many mob cases, besides good detective work, were informants who had *incentive* to flip because of incontrovertible evidence that their own misdeeds would put them in jail for far longer than seven years (or for the five months that Martha Stewart served at a federal women's prison known as "Camp Cupcake").

That evidence was usually found on a wiretap.

It would be several years after Martha Stewart was convicted that wiretaps would gain prominence as an effective tool in combating white-collar crime, particularly insider trading. Federal judges at the time were loath to grant such an invasion of privacy for any other potential crime outside of organized crime and terrorism. They established a pretty high barrier to boot: Investigators would have to prove that they couldn't get incriminating evidence any other way.

Meanwhile, Funkhouser continued to scan his computer database for potential miscreants. By the early years of the millennium, an increasing proportion of stock trading was done by sophisticated computerized programs, though old-fashioned stock picking was still very much in vogue by the ever-swelling ranks of hedge funds looking for a performance edge to justify the high fees they charged to investors.

As regulators examined the data, they began to see certain patterns they didn't see in the past, namely performance that didn't just beat the market over the long haul based on long-term bets on companies' performance—which was the mark of great but honest value investors like Warren Buffett. Instead, they were starting to see traders who *consistently* beat the market and had an uncanny ability to buy or sell stocks at precisely the right times.

Another difference from Buffett: This new group of market geniuses comprised people who were far from familiar names on Main Street, even though they were well-known at the big banks for being great customers because they traded so much and demanded banking services. They were hedge fund traders and they also had a knack for buying or selling stocks right before corporate events—mergers, surprise earnings announcements, you name it—at a profit. They had to know something the public didn't know, and given their size and scope they weren't just making a few bucks à la Martha Stewart (Stewart avoided a loss of around $50,000), but millions of dollars on each trade.

If they were trading illegally, that would mean insider trading had now spread like a cancer through the markets. It was no longer confined to a few dumb-ass players like Sam Waksal, Martha Stewart, or Kathryn Gannon, but had now reached large, established players mainly in the hedge fund business.

High on this list of traders whose records seemed too good to be legal was a guy named Raj Rajaratnam, a Sri Lankan–born trader who ran a hedge firm called the Galleon Group. And another trader drew the fed's attention: a man from Stamford, Connecticut, who ran a firm called SAC Capital and was known simply as "Stevie."

Walking through the SAC parking lot in Stamford is a lot like walking through a Ferrari, Lamborghini, or Bentley dealership.

Inside the firm's headquarters, some traders toil for thirteen-hour shifts each day. The most successful earn millions; those who aren't successful are almost immediately shown the door. But those who make it can be set for life after just one good year, earning millions for a single profitable idea.

So aggressive are the traders at SAC that they monitor every change in a stock's performance, however infinitesimal to most investors. "I deal with big funds and they call you when shares move a buck or two away from their trade," said one analyst who regularly deals with big fund accounts, including the traders at SAC. "But at SAC if a stock goes three cents in the opposite direction of his trade the trader is immediately on the telephone freaking out."

The reason for the freak-out is the man whose name was on the door, Steve "Stevie" Cohen. Funkhouser barely knew who Stevie Cohen was when trades from his firm, SAC Capital, a massively successful hedge fund, began to appear on his surveillance screens. Cohen rarely appeared in the media, and he kept a low social profile. And yet, right around the time that Martha Stewart was going to jail over lying about her suspicious trades, this little-known trader from Stamford was starting to make investigators jumpy.

Cohen was basically invisible to the public but on Wall Street he was considered a rising rock star. "He's everyone's first call," then Bear Stearns chief executive Jimmy Cayne would say when Cohen's name came up. Word spread that he was charging his customers almost double the fees of most hedge funds. Whereas the vast majority of hedge funds charge investors 2 percent of their assets under management, and another 20 percent of their returns, SAC charges 3 percent of assets and 50 percent of its returns, and even after subtracting expenses, Cohen had been handing his clients an average of 30 percent in profits since he opened shop.

It was pretty obvious that Cohen's customers were more than happy to pay all those fees and expenses because Cohen and his traders reciprocated with returns far exceeding anything else on Wall Street.

Steve Cohen is known on Wall Street as "a trader's trader" because he might be—at least on paper—the best that ever lived. He began reading the *Wall Street Journal* when he was eleven, trading stocks in high school, hanging out at a local brokerage office in his hometown of Great Neck, New York, and further perfecting his market skills while in college.

He had already made a name—and a small fortune—for himself at the age of thirty at the Wall Street firm Gruntal & Co., albeit quietly. At Gruntal, he was a star trader without a name, known for "reading the tape," a Wall Street term for traders who look at stocks and their trading patterns, factor in the market chatter, and make money by guessing the stock's next move up or down.

Gruntal was the perfect place for Cohen; it was a no-frills firm for a no-frills guy known for wearing polo shirts instead of tailored suits. More than that, people who know Cohen say it was a replica of what he wanted to start on his own: a firm dedicated to making money trading, and little else.

He stayed at Gruntal for nearly a decade, and launched SAC Capital (his initials) in 1992.

His style of trading was hyperaggressive; the reason for his traders freaking out was that they were on standing orders to make money on small increments of stocks, so-called teenies, which when multiplied with volume could produce big results. He demanded market knowledge that wasn't available on the Internet; he traded so much, he wanted the Wall Street desks that got his commissions to reciprocate in kind, through more and better market intelligence.

As evolving legend would have it, he did it through a trading style that resembled that of a day-trader, rapidly buying and selling stocks. Or as Cohen put it in a speech: "We trade a lot, over twenty million shares a day. A broker's dream come true. We trade fast . . . it's not growth investing. It's not value investing. It's short-term catalyst investing."

At SAC Cohen soon doubled and tripled the $25 million initial investment he had to work with (half of it his own cash) in just a couple of years. By the end of the decade, he was a billionaire and his fund one of the most successful in the hedge fund business. At the same time, Funkhouser's computers and those now running at the SEC and the Justice Department were picking up disturbing patterns that the profitable trades were often made before corporate events.

How Cohen managed to achieve such consistent, over-the-top success became a matter of fierce debate on Wall Street, in the media, and increasingly among regulators. His friends, mainly at the big banks—those "brokers" he referred to on Wall Street who get paid fees for executing the massive volume of trades from SAC—simply consider him a genius. Larry Fink, the head of the big money management firm BlackRock, described him as an "information junkie," someone who knows more about stocks than just about anyone else alive.

With that power comes privilege; even people who admire Cohen and his firm say he and his team will use SAC's leverage as a major supplier of trading order flow to get first dibs on research, or market intelligence that's only handed out by Wall Street to its best customers.

All of which is perfectly legal.

What isn't legal—if you believe criticism from competitors and even some former employees—were allegations that SAC used confidential tips as part of their trading strategies. These detractors describe

SAC as something close to a sweat shop. Cohen sits in the middle of SAC's massive trading floor listening to investing ideas from traders and portfolio managers and occasionally barking out orders. Traders and portfolio managers need to hit certain yearly performance benchmarks or else face termination. "If you're up fifteen percent one month and down two percent the next you can get fired," one former trader said. At SAC it's called hitting your "down-and-outs." Cohen even hired a psychiatrist as a coach for his traders so they can better handle the stress of his daily grind and reach their peak performance.

Those who hit their marks are rewarded handsomely, and when they leave SAC on their own accord to set up their own hedge fund, they can expect to receive an investment from Cohen himself.

It's this pressure to produce, according to people who have worked for Cohen and those who know about his activities, that at the very least creates the environment for traders to push the envelope. As SAC grew through much of the 1990s into the next decade, those whispers began making their way back to investigators, including a growing number of SEC officials, FBI agents, and more than a few prosecutors who began taking a deeper dive into SAC's trading activity and the secrets to Steve Cohen's success.

CHAPTER 3

DO WHATEVER IT TAKES

Pathmark was once the largest grocery chain in the New York City area. It was so successful it remained open twenty-four hours a day, seven days a week, featuring football-field-sized stores that stocked just about everything in the world.

But by the 1990s the chain was falling apart; *Forbes* magazine called its stores "unkempt, dirty, and outmoded" while continuing "to stock scores of the dreary no-frills offerings customers have shunned for years." Pathmark filed for bankruptcy reorganization in 2000. It secured bank financing and began to rebuild some of its most dreadful outlets. The company would soon emerge somewhat healthier and regain its listing on the New York Stock Exchange.

But Pathmark would never return to its glory days. Not even close. Underscoring its downmarket status, a grungy Pathmark in Long Island, New York, was featured in the Michael Moore documentary *Sicko*, about the healthcare crisis and the poor souls at dead-end jobs with no health insurance coverage.

As bad as things were, Pathmark still had a brand that was recognizable in Middle America. And that brand caught the attention of a white knight, billionaire grocery store magnate Ron Burkle, who in 2005 took a 40 percent controlling interest in the food chain through his investment company Yucaipa Companies.

From the moment Burkle announced his investment, the speculation on Wall Street was that he would do his best to unload the stake when the timing was right. But first he needed to repair a company that suffered from years of neglect, by cleaning up the 140 stores now under his control and replacing the old management with a new one.

It doesn't appear that Wall Street paid much attention to Pathmark's transformation. Shares hovered around $11, and Pathmark continued to lose money. But rival chains did, making offers to buy Pathmark to expand their reach. Burkle, wasting little time, agreed to the first serious offer he received, unloading Pathmark to A&P in a deal that was announced in early 2007. According to media reports, Burkle pocketed around $150 million on the Pathmark sale. He celebrated it in style with a "swanky dinner with Bill Clinton, Jay-Z and Bono," raved the *New York Post*.

But Burkle wasn't the only one making a fast buck on Pathmark; in fact, someone on Wall Street may have made an even faster one.

"How the fuck did Steve Cohen know about the deal?" raged a Pathmark board member to one of the company's corporate attorneys. "Someone has got to tell the SEC!"

The news of SAC's investment in Pathmark slid across the wires on December 21, 2006—a couple of months before the chain's publicly announced sale to A&P. SAC had bought 2.6 million shares, a 5 percent stake, in a money-losing company. Sure, there had been plenty of talk and at least one trade-publication report speculating about a possible Pathmark sale, given Burkle's propensity to wheel and deal. In early December 2006, during Pathmark's third-quarter earnings conference call with Wall Street analysts, Pathmark CEO John Standley was asked by a Wall Street analyst "whether or not you guys may be looking to possibly merge with one of your competitors . . . for instance, A&P. . . . Are you guys looking to possibly do that?"

"We're not making any comments about rumors about anything," Standley shot back. "We're not going to do that."

But based on the filing, Cohen's hedge fund appeared to be betting big that Pathmark was on the verge of completing something significant. SAC's timing was possibly too good, one former Pathmark board member recalled in an interview years later.

That's because SAC's December 2006 filing disclosed that it was accumulating shares just as both sides were finally drawing up official merger documents, the board member said. The deal was on schedule to be announced in late February 2007, nearly two months to the day *after* Cohen's fund placed its bet. When the deal was announced as planned in February 2007, shares of Pathmark soared, of course, handing a nice profit to those who saw the deal coming.

"SAC made a fortune," the board member who worked on the deal said. Initially, this executive reckoned that a leak came from inside Pathmark, given its precise timing and Cohen's growing reputation for having a circle of friends unmatched in the investment business. "We all thought it had to be a leak from the board."

Or maybe there was no leak and SAC's trade shows how much of a legitimate edge professional traders have over average investors and just how futile it is for regulators to be obsessed with leveling the market for everyone. Indeed an SAC insider remembers the trade differently. SAC officials had been following the company closely, and weighed the public comments by the analyst community about a Pathmark-A&P deal before buying shares.

And these insiders say it's unclear how much money SAC made from the trade. Around the time the Pathmark deal was announced, some SAC traders were shorting shares (a trade where money is made when stock prices fall, or money is lost if shares rise) believing that the stock would fall at some point. It didn't and as a result, SAC lost some money.

Either way, the Pathmark official said the firm alerted the SEC to

Cohen's well-timed trades, and that's where it ended, at least as far as this person knew (the SEC never filed charges on the matter). The Pathmark official would later remark that giving a tip to the SEC was like sending information down a "black hole."

To be fair, while the SEC has had its problems (Madoff, the financial crisis, etc.), tracking possible insider trading, with Funkhouser's computers and its own databases, isn't one of them. When it came to looking at suspicious trades at SAC Capital or anywhere, the problem had less to do with incompetence, or lack of effort, and more to do with not having the *right kind of evidence* to make a case.

In 2003, Cohen's firm already had escaped a possible fraud charge when the SEC looked into whether one of its traders had placed market bets ahead of research reports published by the trader's fiancée who worked on Wall Street. The SEC at another point considered fraud charges against SAC for possible front-running, buying or selling stocks ahead of the orders of some of its customers. Again nothing happened.

And Funkhouser, over at Nasdaq's market surveillance unit—soon to be relabeled the Financial Industry Regulatory Authority—was amassing a laundry list of suspicious trades from SAC's headquarters in Stamford and handing them to the SEC for a closer look.

The closer look, however, led to dead ends. Cohen and his traders always seemed to have the right answers involving the suspicious trading.

As for the front-running charges, Cohen and SAC traded so much that the trading ahead of other people in the market could be just coincidence. Then take the individual stocks Funkhouser was examining, or even SAC's Pathmark trade. SAC traders were known to have the best circle of friends in the investment business, so it could have come from anywhere: a banker, a trader, someone on A&P's board, or one of those "industry" experts that regulators were only beginning to hear about from their contacts in the hedge fund business. Finding any possible leak would be like finding that needle in a haystack, only worse, because Wall Street and the hedge fund business were by now far bigger than any barn.

Indeed, one of the major enforcement hurdles faced by regulators was the growing complexity of Wall Street's circle of friends. The expert networks had yet to make it on the government's radar screen by 2007, but they were making their mark with hedge funds. The biggest of these outfits, including Primary Global Research and Gerson Lehrman Group, were private companies, so the exact size of their operations was largely unknown, but their importance to the hedge fund business can't be overstated. By the mid-2000s, every major hedge fund looking for a competitive edge (and that meant all of them) had a relationship with the industry expert networks, for the simple reason that the thirst for information—particularly the stuff that could move stocks—was immense.

"Hedge funds are on the phone with these experts all the time and if they are not giving them the right info, they're going back to supervisors and asking for more and someone else," a former industry expert explained as he reflected on the growth of the industry and the pressures faced by experts for "actionable information"—often a code word for information that violates the law.

Also breaking into the circle of friends (and going largely unnoticed by regulators) was the old "sell-side" analyst, now reinvented as an "independent researcher" for the hedge fund business. Since around 2003, analysts who worked at the big banks were being demoted and downsized as regulatory pressure prevented them from aiding and abetting deal making. They would find a second life in the booming information business that centered on trading, even if many of them would succumb to the same sleazy behavior in their new incarnation as "independent" analysts.

Wall Street or "sell-side" research began as a tool to gain market intelligence for traders and investors, but that changed in the late 1970s when Congress deregulated commissions on stock trades. Before then, investors would pay analysts for information; analysts who did their homework and recommended winning trades got reimbursed with a hefty share of these trading commissions.

Now analysts faced extinction unless they joined their firm's investment banking business and began touting stocks—using their research to promote stocks of companies that were the corporate clients of the big Wall Street firms.

This conflict would lead to one of the great Wall Street crimes in recent memory, when, during the Internet bubble, investors lost countless billions of dollars buying overvalued and sometimes worthless stocks at least in part based on stock ratings later found to be fraudulent.

Insider trading may be a fraud on the market, and a deceptive act, as the courts have ruled, but the federal government's decades-long obsession with stamping it out came at a price: Bigger frauds with more identifiable victims went unaddressed or received far less attention.

None were bigger and with more identifiable victims than Wall Street's peddling of advertisements for their investment banking clients under the guise of research. The exposure of this crime—and the crime of the government's inattention to it—can be traced to the waning days of the Internet bubble, when firms were placing buy recommendations on just about any technology company they could find, though not because they were making money and were good long-term investments. In fact many of these companies were start-ups that barely had revenues, much less profits.

Nevertheless, Wall Street had convinced enough investors through their incessantly hyped research that these companies would be successful, and they spared no hyperbole to entice investors. The scam lasted through the great technology bubble that began roughly in 1995, with the IPO of a browser technology company called Netscape, through March 2000, when technology stocks began their painful correction, and for years later.

During this time, of course, the SEC and other regulators made great strides in their pursuit of insider trading even as they ignored complaints about Wall Street fraudulent research. With the boom in technology stocks growing through the 1990s, a "virtuous circle" was created: Analysts wrote glowing reports, companies sent their investment banking business to the firms those analysts were employed at, and then everyone repeated the process all over again. The SEC, meanwhile, sat by and watched.

That would eventually change, and not because of anything the SEC or other regulators did but thanks to the actions of a pediatrician and part-time investor from Queens, New York. In 1999, Debasis Kanjilal went to his Merrill Lynch broker and asked for some information about how to make some quick money on Internet stocks. He had about $600,000 in the market—a sweet spot for any broker looking for hefty fees and commissions that well-off retail or individual investors often generate for brokerage firms.

Kanjilal was handed the research of an analyst named Henry Blodget, a former journalist turned Wall Street analyst, who made the transition to Wall Street like a lot of smart Ivy League grads did during the 1990s Internet and technology bubble. And presto, Blodget had become a star.

His gift, at least superficially, was in understanding the new-economy companies at the heart of the Internet craze and translating their business model in a way that was clear to the non–Wall Street professional. This research was then distributed to clients, including increasingly wealthy individuals like Kanjilal who watched business television and read the *Wall Street Journal*.

As technology exploded in the 1990s, Blodget was in the right place at the right time. He was a good writer so his reports were widely read in the media, and he soon found a home at Merrill Lynch, after a short but hypersuccessful stint at Oppenheimer, where he famously predicted in 1998 that shares of Amazon.com, the online bookseller, would rise to $400. They did shortly thereafter. With that, Blodget's star was born. Merrill Lynch, the nation's then-largest brokerage firm, came calling and hired Blodget to run its technology research team. Blodget became one of the most recognizable figures for the millions of small investors who bought stocks through Merrill's brokerage arm during the great bull market for technology stocks.

Henry Blodget went from being viewed as a visionary to what many considered a tout—an analyst who seemed to have nothing but nice things to say about the companies he covered. Debasis Kanjilal knew none of this, of course, when his Merrill Lynch broker handed him a Blodget research report and he handed his broker $600,000 to follow Blodget's advice and begin snapping up shares of tech companies.

Over the years, Merrill had vehemently denied conflicts of interest whenever the business press occasionally raised the matter of whether it skewed its reports to suit the needs of its investment-banking customers. But after tech stocks began to crater and Kanjilal lost most of the $600,000 he invested using Blodget's research as his guide, the good doctor went to an attorney for answers.

That attorney, Jake Zamansky, knew the research game better than the guys in the Manhattan U.S. attorney's office or the people in Washington at the SEC. He had once defended so-called bucket shops, small brokerage firms that operated on the fringes of Wall Street but used the Wall Street research business model as their guide. At the bucket shops, the only difference was that some analysts were bankers as well; Zamansky thought it was more honest than what he saw at the big firms, where analysts like Blodget posed as independent thinkers when in reality they were trying to win deals.

Zamansky would eventually file a lawsuit against Blodget and Merrill—the first of its kind against an analyst, especially one of Blodget's stature—and win a $400,000 settlement on behalf of Kanjilal. Merrill's decision to settle stemmed not just from the controversy surrounding the case—which earned lots of press coverage in the aftermath of the bursting of the Internet bubble—but from what Merrill's management knew about the process of disseminating market information to its small investor clients.

That process largely guaranteed that small investors received what were essentially sales pitches in the form of research reports.

Investors just like Kanjilal were now sitting on huge losses as Internet and telecommunications stocks began to reflect their true value, which in many cases was nothing. Zamansky's lawsuit was largely ignored by the SEC and the Nasdaq's stock market investigators but not by the recently elected attorney general of New York State, Eliot Spitzer, and one of his deputies, Eric Dinallo, who spotted a story in the *Wall Street Journal* about Blodget issuing a rare downgrade of a stock—but only after Merrill was denied an investment banking deal.

Blodget's deposition and Dinallo's investigation in which he subpoenaed Blodget's emails showed that the analyst's glowing stock recommendations to small investors varied markedly from his private emails, where he described those selfsame stocks as "pieces of crap," "dogs," or occasionally "POS," for "piece of shit."

For some reason, those very candid phrases never made it into Blodget's research read by small inverstors. In the weeks after Blodget gave his deposition to Spitzer's investigators, he resigned from Merrill with several millions of dollars in salary, bonuses, and severance. Merrill, meanwhile, kept the Spitzer investigation quiet while its research machine continued to churn out reports as if nothing were happening.

Across town, the Nasdaq kept falling—from a peak of 5,000 at the top of the bubble in March 2000 to just under 1200 in early 2002. Somewhere close to $5 trillion of investor wealth had disappeared.

Can you blame it *all* on the faulty research of Blodget or his fellow analysts? *No*, but nearly every investor will tell you that they perked up when Blodget's research hit the wires.

In the coming months, the public would see just how well oiled that sales machine had become, all under the noses of the SEC. Jack Grubman, a technology analyst at Citigroup's Salomon Smith Barney unit, had even more latitude than Blodget to promote those companies that rewarded his firm with investment banking business (and indirectly, rewarded him, via a remarkably generous pay package).

Much of Grubman's research wasn't just conflicted—it was conflicted and thoroughly horrible. He called on investors to "back up the truck" and invest all that they had in a company called WorldCom, a telecom outfit he claimed would revolutionize the wireless business. He kept a high rating on the company nearly to the day it declared bankruptcy. An accounting fraud would later send senior management to jail.

It was that insight that helped Grubman earn as much as $25 million in one year and millions more before he was forced to resign. Soon regulators at the SEC and the Nasdaq would finally force him out of the business for good in a settlement that called on the big firms to radically change the way they handled research. Some of those structural changes fell flat. The ratio of buy recommendations remained virtually where it had been before the entire investigation began.

But analysts could no longer pose as investment bankers—and get paid like bankers. A bigger "Chinese wall" was erected to separate research from investment banking so analyst bonuses could no longer be based solely on how many deals they helped the bankers win.

Spitzer and the SEC (finally) made certain that the era of the banking analyst moonlighting as a banker was over. But that gave rise to another type of compromised research: the business of "independent research analysts" catering to the whims and pressures for inside information from the big hedge funds.

One of those analysts was a man named John Kinnucan.

Being independent didn't mean John Kinnucan was on the side of the angels—far from it. Yes, information, as opposed to hyping stocks, mattered again to investors, and they were ready to pay for it as an increasingly competitive industry of information seekers (hedge fund traders) demanding an edge from the new and burgeoning business of information providers (analysts and expert networks).

Steve Cohen was clearly one of those edge seekers as his fund grew in size and importance. His marketing brochure even boasted of SAC's "edge" over the competition, which everyone inside the hedge fund business and an increasing number of regulators understood to be its uncanny ability to beat the markets by demanding the best research and information.

With market-busting returns (72 percent in one year) money kept flowing into SAC. In just five years, SAC had more than tripled in size; it was now heading toward $14 billion in assets under management and competing against other funds with a similar thirst for fresh information—much of it, regulators were starting to believe, based on the increasing frequency of suspicious trades from illegal sources.

The researchers and experts were possibly the biggest source of information for the hedge fund business. But these researchers couldn't distinguish themselves from one another simply by passing on earnings projections based on orders for the components that went into building a computer. They needed more. They needed something others didn't know.

Increasingly, the trading community wanted the actual earnings number itself—or something close to it. For that, the independents went out and hired their own experts to cough up any tidbit from inside their companies. As for the experts, no one cared if he or she had attended MIT and understood how a microprocessor worked.

To satisfy the gamblers on Wall Street they would have to do what was necessary—which often meant dishing out company secrets—or they wouldn't be able to count on a paycheck from their hedge fund masters.

"It was all about the money," a former expert explained about the pressures in the job to step over the line and provide clients with anything that could move the stock, "even if it was illegal."

Those on the information side of the business quickly understood the new definition of "independent research." The growth of hedge funds didn't necessarily mean more business for the experts and the analysts or more autonomy for the information providers. With the Dow rising to around 14,000 in late 2007, and the eventual financial crisis yet to take its toll on stocks, just about anyone could make money buying a mutual fund that tracked the broader markets. Hedge funds needed to show results that are better than that to justify those huge fees, the highest being charged by the most successful shops in the business.

So a certain breed of information provider was in demand, one who was ready to push the envelope and at times break the rules.

It didn't begin that way, at least for John Kinnucan. "There was a need for real research; that's why I left Wall Street," he explained as he looked back on his decision to leave Wall Street. Kinnucan set up his own shop as an independent researcher, out of his home, right around the time Spitzer was making the Wall Street research business nearly untenable.

Real research, however, was exactly what made Kinnucan such a valuable commodity for the hedge fund looking to score big. Kinnucan knew his way around the industry; he was more than familiar with the business models of Apple, Cisco, and a slew of smaller tech companies. But his niche was in knowing where to find the right kind of actionable information that the big hedge funds were looking for.

And it didn't take long for him to hit paydirt, even if his old Wall Street colleagues thought he was taking a big risk by creating a company called Broadband Research and working out of his home producing market research and charging for it.

The thirst and demand for information from hedge funds, and as it turned out, Kinnucan's malleable ethics, had in a short time produced a business that earned about $1 million a year. What's more, he didn't even have to leave his house too often, since his long years covering technology provided him with a network of sources—a separate circle of friends—who were more than willing to dish out insider tips for the right amount of money over the phone or by email.

Kinnucan, of course, had seen the rise of the hedge fund business for years. The best of them, like Steve Cohen's SAC Capital, Ken Griffin's Citadel Investment Group, and the Galleon Group, run by Raj Rajaratnam, offered returns far better than what the market was offering even in those good times.

How did they do it? Conventional wisdom was that since hedge funds were lightly regulated (in contrast, SEC rules curtailed risk at mutual funds sold to "average investors" by preventing certain investment strategies), they had a freer hand to trade using derivatives and other esoteric securities that allowed them to amp up returns relative to more highly regulated entities. The other part of the conventional wisdom was that Cohen and his ilk were simply brilliant. Because people like Cohen and Griffin were such savvy investors, they knew just how much risk to take and not blow up.

Cohen and those of his caliber, so the thinking went, gathered data points from the expert networks and the researchers like Kinnucan along the way, assembling these disparate small bits of data into a "mosaic" that would tell the trader whether to buy or sell a stock. It was all highly scientific—small pieces of information that meant almost nothing on their own but could fit together as part of a mosaic that painted for the trader a compelling picture of whether to buy or sell a stock.

The mosaic theory was all the rage in the hedge fund world through most of the late 1990s and into the next decade. Its beauty: Each piece of information collected might be derived from a nonpublic source but would not in and of itself move the market, so it fell within acceptable standards.

But the highly competitive nature of the hedge fund business would soon make the theory obsolete, as Kinnucan would later explain, recalling the words of one of his clients: "If you can call me tomorrow, and tell me here is what Oracle sales will look like this quarter, and I can buy the stock at the end of the day and it goes up ten percent tomorrow. Then I will buy your research all day long. . . . But if you are going to give me analysis on Oracle, everyone has that."

Kinnucan understood the dynamic at work. His clients wouldn't actually ask for him to divulge secrets, or get others to do so, but they didn't have to. He knew that an early read on a company's quarterly earnings was much more valuable than some guess on how many semiconductors Apple was using. The trick was getting *inside* companies—gaining exposure to midlevel executives who either knew sales numbers or even the latest earnings report or had a good indication about their direction.

Kinnucan had sources all over the tech industry whom he would schmooze with fancy meals, vacations, and outright payments to get what he needed. Walter Shimoon, then an executive at a company called Flextronics, was one of a handful of technology executives on Kinnucan's payroll, providing not just industry insight but cold, hard nonpublic data about stocks that were passed on to Kinnucan's clients.

Kinnucan's client list grew to include big hedge funds like SAC Capital and Citadel, and major mutual funds as well. It was all so easy if you were someone like Kinnucan, who had the right sources: No more laboring over reports, which had been standard fare on Wall Street, demanded by the analysts' supervisors so company brokers would have something official to peddle to small investors as a reason to buy a stock.

"We didn't write up many reports," one independent analyst told me. "Instead we were on the telephone all day, sending IMs [instant messages] and talking to our sources to get whatever data we could feed to our clients."

Did the clients ask *where or how* they were getting this information or whether it was legal?

Rarely, at least according to the researcher's account. "You would go into a trader's office and say 'You want to buy Google.' The first question he asks is 'Why?' By listing a bunch of general reasons, you lose that business because he wants to know something he doesn't know, not what is already out there.

"So you call your friend in Google's finance department and get something. It's a culture of justifying trades via information no matter how you get it. The Feds can't prove anything because no one wrote anything down."

For such circles of friends (and circles of friends-of-friends), the "proving" part of that scenario was about to change.

CHAPTER 4

A REGULAR GUY

It's unclear exactly when Steve Cohen and his hedge fund first appeared on regulators' radar screens, but by the time the Pathmark trade went down, Cohen and SAC were under scrutiny by the SEC, FINRA, and increasingly the FBI and Justice Department. His trades were regularly flagged by the increasingly sophisticated computer networks that tracked suspicious market activity. Government officials believed producing returns that beat the market every year is suspicious enough. Doing it year after year by snapping up stocks right before major events was thought to be nearly impossible by the government snoops, unless, of course, you were cheating the system.

Cohen had many defenders—though most of them either worked at the firm or at firms that benefited from its trading order flow, or were investors who benefited from his market-beating returns and kept shoveling money into SAC. Cohen was lauded by the *Wall Street Journal* as the "Hedge Fund King." *Time* did the *Journal* one better, naming him to its list of most influential people. *Forbes* made his star status official, ranking him as the "Top Billionaire Art Collector" in 2005, based on his love of expensive art and his salary, which hit $1 billion that year.

"The guy's just very good at understanding money flows, the way money flows into and out of the market," Jonathan Ludwig, a money manager who worked at SAC in the mid-1990s, told the *New York Times*.

Ludwig told *Times* reporters Alex Berenson and Geraldine Fabrikant that it was Cohen's "mind" rather than his connections to an informed circle of friends that accounted for his extraordinary performance—nearly always beating the market averages, and by wide margins.

All of which may have been a great selling point with investors as Cohen's funds soared in value, but not with regulators, who increasingly questioned the SAC narrative put forth by his cultish Wall Street followers and some reporters. What wasn't myth was his success, which he was increasingly willing to flaunt, much to the chagrin of regulators. As Cohen's net worth soared into the many billions, he purchased multiple homes, further expanded his fancy art collection, and found a new wife. He was known to remain extremely private, though friends say the vast security apparatus he set up around his 35,000-square-foot mansion in Greenwich, Connecticut—everything from armed guards to a multitude of cameras surveilling a fourteen-acre estate—is aimed less at protecting him than it is his family. Cohen himself was now making the rounds in Manhattan and Greenwich as an affable dinner partner to a coterie of friends, some of whom worked on Wall Street and a few who didn't.

Even with these indulgences, there was something surprisingly down-to-earth about "Stevie," as all his friends called him. He continued to dress the way he had when he was a mere multimillionaire, in casual clothes; sweaters, and khakis, almost never in a suit. Cohen's "regular guy" attitude with friends became legendary. No gold watches, no bodyguards, and no arm candy when he's around town.

However, none of this earned him any points with the feds. There were just too many inconsistencies in the story that Cohen was achieving these results through sheer brain power and hard work. First, markets don't really work that way—they never have. Even Buffett has big losing years.

Yet as investigators perused Cohen's investing record, they could barely find a losing one (it finally came in 2008, during the financial meltdown). The too-good-to-be-true market performance on its face might not mean all that much if it weren't for the buzz coming from inside SAC. Insider trading wasn't outwardly encouraged, certainly not by Cohen himself or anyone in management. But the general consensus from former workers and people now cooperating with the feds as they began to ramp up their examination of insider trading—interviewing and deposing various witnesses and turning the occasional cooperator—was that SAC looked past this kind of illegality when it occurred.

Not only was SAC hypercompetitive, but traders described the atmosphere as a hedge fund version of "don't ask, don't tell." There were lots of lawyers and compliance people, for sure. The firm's compliance manual basically likens insider trading to mortal sin. But as cooperators described the situation, in the ruthlessly competitive environment of working at SAC, such behavior was tolerated as long as it produced results and no one was getting caught.

Investigators noticed something else, too: Sometime around 2002 SAC began decentralizing the information flow among the various specialized groups at the fund, moving Cohen, who would directly manage just a portion of SAC's money, away from the center of the information flow. Still he would be briefed on performance, and seemed to know the performance of his company's big trading positions. Traders and analysts would recommend stocks and strategies, and he would use that information in the trading of the portfolio under his specific care while prodding them on their "conviction" levels, usually on a 1–10 scale, people who worked with him say, with 10 being the highest conviction or 100 percent certitude of a trade's success.

Cohen's remake transformed SAC from one large freewheeling enterprise fund into several different ones, which was jarring for investigators who were now monitoring SAC on a regular basis. But not Cohen, who could trade dozens of stocks at the same time, and had rapid recall on the price of his buys and sells.

Indeed, the structural change didn't affect his performance—it was still amazing. The pool of data showing that SAC had a knack for snapping up shares and selling them just before news broke continued. Again, was it enough to bring charges? The consensus among the government's Cohen watchers was they didn't have the goods to charge either Cohen or his firm, at least not yet.

There is growing evidence that today's unregulated hedge funds have advanced and refined the practice of manipulating and cheating other market participants. The potential harm hedge funds can inflict on other market participants has no real limits. The (trillions of dollars) under hedge fund management are on steroids."

That statement, made in 2006 before the Senate Judiciary Committee by a former SEC enforcement attorney named Gary Aguirre, wasn't exactly news to securities regulators who were growing increasingly frustrated by their inability to bring cases against big hedge funds and Wall Street traders they believed were cheating the system. SEC officials often complained that the standard tools for investigating insider trading—witnesses, emails, and trading documents—had their limits in showing intent to commit a crime as difficult to prove as insider trading.

Aguirre, for his part, believed something more sinister was at work. He had been fired from the SEC, he claimed, because he dared to accuse a big hedge fund manager, Art Samberg, the chief of Pequot Capital, of insider trading and then attempted to depose the person he believed was the possible source of a leak of confidential information to Samberg, Morgan Stanley chief executive John Mack. Aguirre said he was told that the SEC didn't want to bring cases against major Wall

Street players, a source of political contributions to whatever party was in the White House.

Aguirre's proof that politics, rather than a lack of evidence, had stalled the Samberg probe is a matter of debate. He had been studying suspicious trading patterns among big hedge funds for nearly a year. His investigation began with an alert from the government's market surveillance system that significant hedge fund trading just before market-moving events was nearly a daily occurrence.

He opened an official investigation into these trades, particularly as they related to Pequot. Aguirre said he couldn't get his supervisors on board, particularly in deposing Mack, one of Samberg's closest friends and former business partner. Aguirre believed Mack was a key player in the alleged scam since he ran the firm advising on one of the deals in question. But Mack had powerful friends in the Bush White House and was a big fundraiser for the president.

The case was closed in November 2006, after Aguirre said his direct supervisor warned him of Mack's political connections. Aguirre was then fired from the SEC over alleged performance-related issues. Aguirre said it was politically motivated to protect a Wall Street crony of the president, and he sued the commission for wrongful dismissal.

His firing and his allegations against Mack and Samberg made its way into the *New York Times*, and it became a hotly debated topic on Wall Street and in Washington. Yes, Samberg traded stocks before market-moving events, but Aguirre's claim that Mack had leaked deal information to Samberg lacked solid proof. In off-the-record interviews, Aguirre's former colleagues at the SEC questioned his investigative skills and what they said was his erratic style of deposing targets. They considered him a zealot who in the course of his work drew connections where they didn't exist.

Thinking someone committed insider trading is very different than proving a crime notoriously difficult to pin down. As for deposing Mack, commission officials initially said they blocked it because it would have been a waste of time. There was just no evidence that Mack had even spoken to Samberg about the trades in question. After Aguirre's accusations were made public, the SEC eventually took Mack's deposition only to put the matter to rest. No charges have been filed against Mack over the matter.

Still, Aguirre was clearly on to something about Samberg. One of the trades Aguirre was investigating involved Pequot's purchase of shares of a company named Heller Financial, just before its 2005 purchase by General Electric. Morgan Stanley worked as an adviser on the deal, and Pequot snapped up shares of Heller just before the GE purchase when shares spiked.

Again, there was no evidence linking Mack to Samberg's decision to buy Heller stock, even if Samberg earned $18 million on the Heller stock purchase. There was also suspicious trading in shares of Microsoft in 2001, with the hedge fund placing big bucks on trades just before a market-moving event. Traders, particularly good ones like Art Samberg, don't risk millions on bets based solely on hunches, Aguirre argued.

The SEC may have ignored Aguirre's investigation, but not Senator Charles Grassley of the Senate Judiciary Committee. During subsequent hearings, and with Aguirre as its main witness, the SEC was portrayed as a patsy for Wall Street. Meanwhile, Aguirre's own view about how Wall Street's circle of friends operated was remarkably accurate.

The Heller case went nowhere, but Aguirre's Microsoft investigation found new life after the committee disclosed emails between Samberg and a former Microsoft employee he had hired to work at Pequot. The employee was contacting former colleagues at Microsoft for confidential information about company earnings. The emails also suggested that the former Microsoft employee shared that information with Samberg, who traded on it.

Why the SEC didn't act on that evidence when it dropped the case in 2006 is unclear. SEC officials maintain they just didn't have the goods to proceed even as Aguirre continued to argue the evidence was strong. More obvious is what the Commission did about a year later: It reopened the probe into Samberg's trading of Microsoft.

In 2007, Samberg settled insider trading charges with the commission, and was barred from the securities business. Unfortunately for the SEC, it couldn't even take credit for nailing one of the hedge fund world's most prominent players. In addition to what Aguirre pointed out, the scheme was also publicly disclosed in the former Microsoft employee's divorce proceedings.

The bungling of the Pequot/Samberg case only ratcheted up pressure on the SEC to nail a significant player in the hedge fund business, and by 2007 the rumor mill surrounding SAC's uncanny ability to beat the markets every year by wide margins was running full blast. Examples of what regulators believed were suspicious trades before market events made their way to the SEC, the FBI, and the U.S. attorney's office in Manhattan almost nonstop.

Understanding the SAC information machine became part of the job requirements for regulators looking at insider trading. It wasn't just that firms gave Cohen their best tips on the market direction because he was such a big customer. SAC was said to *demand* preferential treatment from it's friends on Wall Street. These weren't even illegal confidential tips, but stuff the average investor can't get at home, such as market chatter about large trades and other bits of trading desk intelligence available only to the big Wall Street firms and shared with only their best customers.

The "demands," of course, weren't made by Cohen himself. By now Steve Cohen was an established member of the Wall Street glitterati. He had been invited to join a posh country club in Rye, New York. His fancy art collection, now among the biggest in the world, became the envy of the super-wealthy, as did his enormous wealth itself—around $6 billion and growing.

But his traders weren't above playing hardball. Again, none of this is necessarily illegal but it does underscore how much the markets are stacked against average investors in a *perfectly legal way*. According to people on the Wall Street trading desks that did business with SAC,

Cohen's traders would exert tremendous leverage on their counterparts at the hypercompetitive big banks, who had no problem handing over premium market intelligence in exchange for the lucrative commissions generated by handling SAC trades. Did this market intelligence at times step over the line into inside information of the illegal variety? It is impossible to know for sure, though regulators and white-collar-crime investigators certainly believed it did. At FBI headquarters in lower Manhattan, preventing another 9/11 terrorist attack was clearly top priority, but snaring SAC started to become a priority, too, particularly for one veteran agent, a white-collar investigator named B. J. Kang.

Kang had been investigating white-collar crime since around 2004. He goes by his initials, B. J., people at the FBI say, because his real, Korean name is difficult to pronounce. A fellow colleague referred to him as a "relentless, aggressive" investigator, though one lawyer who dealt with him distinctly recalls that for a man who made a living investigating financial crimes, initially Kang didn't have a firm handle on how Wall Street, particularly how the hedge fund trading business, really worked.

What he lacked in knowledge he made up for in tenacity, particularly when it came to developing witnesses. His specialty was turning targets into cooperators, in a direct, intimidating manner. No yelling or raising the specter of prison rape, as was often the case when agents looked to flip a bad guy into an informant.

Kang would simply lay out the cold, hard facts: Long prison sentences and a productive life interrupted unless complete and total cooperation was given.

He also was known as a guy who could smell a rat from a mile away, and Kang was starting to believe that Cohen's hedge fund smelled pretty bad. Kang was first introduced to the inner workings of SAC and Steve Cohen when attorneys for a company called Biovail briefed him on their lawsuit (now dismissed) against the big hedge fund.

One of the attorneys, Michael Bowe, explained the allegations made in the case: SAC, he said, manipulated shares of Biovail by hiring a research firm to publish negative reports about the company to help drive down shares and support SAC's short position on the stock.

Bowe then explained how he believed SAC worked—which jibed with much of what Kang had already heard about the fund's modus operandi. It was a "kill or be killed" trading shop, where people were paid to make money, and how they made it, at least to the outside observer, didn't seem to matter even if SAC boasted it had the most sophisticated compliance system in the hedge fund world.

Biovail's claims against SAC didn't involve insider trading allegations per se, but as Bowe claimed in his conversation with Kang, SAC was a place that tolerated almost any activity as long as no one got caught.

All of which only increased Kang's interest in SAC as details of the fund's operations began to make their way into the business press. Regulators took note of a bizarre sexual harassment lawsuit involving two SAC employees, a senior trader named Ping Jiang, who made $100 million in 2006 trading for Cohen, and his assistant, a lower-paid junior trader named Andrew Tong. When investigators peeled back the tabloid fodder—the junior trader filed a same-sex harassment lawsuit accusing Jiang of forcing him to take female hormones, which were supposed to make him a better trader—court documents offered up some juicy allegations about Cohen's operations. The lawsuit discussed SAC's obsession with secrecy and included an allegation that his boss, Jiang, manipulated stocks.

SAC and Jiang vigorously denied the entire matter including the sexual harassment, and the case was later dismissed, but the notion that SAC played dirty wasn't isolated. Kang spent some time investigating another case involving a lawsuit filed by an insurance company, Fairfax Financial, also a Bowe client, which lodged similar charges against Cohen and his traders. That case was also dismissed.

Kang and the FBI couldn't make cases on either claim, but the feds now had what they considered a pretty stark account of the type of firm Cohen ran: an aggressive trading shop, Darwinian in nature, where traders are paid by performance, fired for lack of it, which seemed to perpetuate a win-at-all-costs environment.

SAC's incredible returns (32 percent in 2006 and 14 percent in 2007, while the S&P 500 notched gains of 16 percent and 5 percent, respectively) kept adding up to support this theory that now stretched from the SEC to the U.S. attorney's office for the Southern District of New York, to the FBI and just about every other place that investigated insider trading. There was too much smoke surrounding SAC. And the smoke kept getting thicker with each and every winning trade that seemed to defy odds. Funkhouser's computers showed, for instance, that the fund bought shares of Genentech just days before a positive announcement concerning one of its cancer-fighting drugs spiked shares 45 percent. SAC also had a knack of selling shares before negative announcements, particularly in the biotech sector.

The firm would explain the good timing as nothing more than the result of hard work and good research—all of which also undoubtedly occurred inside Cohen's shop. Yes, it had hired expert networks, and independent researchers like Kinnucan, to share their knowledge and insights into the various industry sectors that its funds were based on, including technology and health care. But no one piece of information would cause an SAC trader to buy shares of Genentech. Rather, the fund's traders and analysts were experts in creating the "mosaic" that led to the successful trade by assembling many pieces of information, much of it from publicly available sources.

This explanation didn't wash with a different circle of friends, one that involved the nation's top Wall Street regulators. The suspicion was that SAC was at the very least bending the rules, and bending them badly because they could. The influence of big banks might be powerful in the market but SAC's influence somehow loomed larger. Its massive size, combined with its trading frequency, already made SAC an A-list client. Add to that Cohen's own growing stature in financial circles and the fund could exert tremendous leverage on bank trading desks for market intelligence or just about anything else.

Case in point: Other hedge funds would pay Wall Street market makers with so-called soft dollars. As a substitute for cash, they would add a Bloomberg terminal, a *Wall Street Journal* subscription, or even pay for the bar mitzvah of a fund manager's son. SAC was known as a "full commission" firm, meaning it paid for those trades not in soft dollars but in real dollars—all cash. It was yet another controversial, though completely legal incentive for Wall Street firms to hand SAC its best tips, and market knowledge that gave the fund its vaunted "edge."

"I told Cohen to stop his managers from approaching my traders with their offer to give commission in exchange for information if we execute SAC trades," said then hedge fund manager and future convicted swindler Bernie Madoff about SAC's business practices.

Madoff, of course, isn't a reliable witness (Cohen through a spokesman, denies the conversation took place), but some of what he said did corroborate what federal investigators had received from other more reliable sources. By 2007, Funkhouser's team had sent nearly two dozen referrals to the SEC to look into suspicious trading at SAC, but even more scary, at least according to Funkhouser's data, is that SAC wasn't the only possible bad guy in the business. Far from it. The technology developed by people like Funkhouser, as well as the commission's own surveillance systems, underscored the severity of the problem: Insider trading had become a crime wave. And it was done in the open as shares of companies "secretly" involved in mergers would inexplicably begin to rise.

The worst part for the regulators was that the Wall Street bad guys didn't seem to think twice about breaking the law. The *Financial Times* examined the suspicious patterns in an article titled "Boom Times for Suspicious Trades." The mergers-and-acquisitions business was booming through 2006 and into early 2007, showering billions of dollars of profits on investment banks. But the M&A boom also touched off a rash of what appeared to be illegal insider trading in the form of profitable trading just before the corporate event was publicly announced, with a spike in trading volume before deals became public.

Nearly two-thirds of all deals over the past year fell into this category, the *Financial Times* concluded, including one of the year's most high-profile buyouts: News Corporation's $5.6 billion purchase of Dow Jones & Co. (owner of the prestigious *Wall Street Journal*).

The Dow Jones deal would eventually lead to SEC civil charges against a Dow Jones director for allegedly tipping off a prominent Hong Kong couple about the transaction. The director, David Li, paid $8 million fine, roughly the amount of profit the couple made by trading on his illegal tip. Under terms of the settlement, Li didn't admit or deny wrongdoing.

The Li case was hardly the deterrent that the feds were looking for, however. The chatter inside the hedge fund business was that the top cops weren't up to the job of catching the really bad guys, who were smart and well protected by amounts of money the hedge funds were doling out for the best inside tip. Informants like John Kinnucan were paid as much as $1 million a year for their work, and $1 million is a lot of hush money.

Meanwhile, the big traders had their handy excuse for knowing what was happening before it happened: the mosaic theory. "We would bring someone in suspected of insider trading and they would give us a million ways they traded legally, by creating a mosaic of information—not from hearing from any one source," said one former prosecutor. "It was pretty effective because just showing that someone traded before an event is never really enough. You need more because most people on Wall Street will fight before they settle."

For all the obstacles faced by regulators and prosecutors, the groundwork was being laid for the most successful assault on insider trading in modern history. The SEC was now regularly sharing this detailed information about suspicious trading activity at SAC and elsewhere with its counterparts in the Justice Department and the FBI—a change from the previous practice of each agency working on its own and sharing information just before a case was made and competing for the biggest headlines. A regulatory circle of friends was developing to combat the one on Wall Street. The new law enforcement triumvirate passed on tips, briefed each other on depositions, and took the first tentative steps to jointly investigate cases that would pay huge dividends in the not-so-distant future.

Why the change of heart? At the SEC, enforcement agents realized that the threat of the same relatively small fine it levied against Martha Stewart meant almost nothing to a hedge fund trader, who could make that in a single transaction. What they needed was the threat of jail time that only criminal cases could bring. Meanwhile, the Justice Department finally came to the conclusion that though the SEC might have missed some big frauds, its agents were fairly good at unearthing insider trading cases from mountains of trading data.

Overall, the realization among *all* the regulators was that for all their laws and court precedents and expertise, they were up against a foe better financed than they had ever seen. The hedge fund business grew astronomically in size. It attracted more than $100 billion in new cash in 2006 with double digit returns that beat prior the year's stellar performance. Profits like that buy a lot of loyalty and a nearly impenetrable circle of friends.

The teamwork wasn't paying dividends just yet, of course; as much as Kang tried, he had no luck bringing a case against Cohen. The same was true for the SEC, and the Justice Department's Southern District office concluded that nothing they had seen so far would merit a criminal indictment against any major hedge fund player. But it would shortly, and the payoff would be enormous, thanks in large part to a midlevel SEC enforcement attorney toiling long hours in New York.

CHAPTER 5

WHAT FRIENDS ARE FOR

I'd rather kill myself than go to jail," was how hedge fund trader Erik Franklin described his decision to cooperate with federal officials investigating what the government billed as the largest insider-trading bust since the days of Ivan Boesky.

That was probably an overstatement since the ill-gotten gains from Boesky's fraud were tremendous (he ended up paying a $100 million fine) and the Franklin scheme netted its participants around $15 million. But untangling Franklin's circle of friends—a close-knit group of drinking buddies and Wall Street acquaintances—set the stage for what would rank among the largest inside trading busts ever.

Franklin didn't kill himself and he didn't go to jail, primarily because he helped the feds uncover the entire five-year scheme, which began in 2001 when he worked at Bear Stearns as a money manager for an internal hedge fund named Lyford Cay. The illegal trading, government investigators discovered, ran almost nonstop through 2006 as an initial circle of friends expanded its ranks to include individuals working at firms such as UBS and Morgan Stanley and the growing hedge fund business.

The Bear Stearns connection was important, investigators discovered. The Lyford Cay fund was named after an exclusive resort in the Bahamas where the fund's lead broker, Kurt Butenhoff, had vacationed. Butenhoff was a veteran of the firm who made his fortune (he earned as much as $10 million a year) by handling the trades of Bear's billionaire CEO James "Jimmy" Cayne and some high-net-worth clients, including an ultrarich commodities broker named Joe Lewis.

Lewis, who would eventually become Bear's largest shareholder just before the firm's implosion in 2008, lived on Lyford Cay himself, in a mansion outfitted with trading screens in just about every room showing the performance of the markets and his various investments. He was said not to be an investor in the Lyford hedge fund, but Butenhoff's boss Cayne was, which made its performance a top priority at Bear.

Also making it a top priority was what the Lyford hedge fund meant for Bear itself; the firm's clients increasingly wanted from their Wall Street financial advisers what they could get from the most successful hedge funds like the Galleon Group: investments that beat the market.

Bear, like most big banks, had responded by creating its own hedge funds. What regulators also found out was that the hedge funds at the Wall Street firms may have been copying the same sleazy trading techniques rampant in the broader industry.

In Franklin's case, the specific scheme he engaged in found its roots at a meeting in 2001, where he hooked up with a friend named Mitchel Guttenberg at the famous Oyster Bar restaurant in Grand Central Terminal, just blocks from his office at Bear headquarters in midtown Manhattan.

Guttenberg owed Franklin $25,000 from a personal loan. Among the up-and-coming Wall Street thirty-something set, loaning a friend $25,000 is akin to a $25 loan made by one friend to another in Middle America. But this isn't the Midwest. In midtown, Franklin broached a way for Guttenberg to repay the favor. Guttenberg worked in the research department at the bank UBS and was privy to pre-market information about analyst research and market calls.

The scheme proposed by Franklin went something like this: To pay off his debt Guttenberg would tell Franklin what the UBS analysts were saying about a particular stock before the call was announced to the broader market. Franklin would, in turn, arrange his trades accordingly, shorting before downgrades, for example, and going long or buying shares that would benefit from positive analyst calls.

Guttenberg agreed, on one condition: After he paid off his loan, they would begin sharing the profits. The arrangement lasted for years. As it matured, so did the methods used to pass on information. They initially passed money inside Doritos bags, but later used personal banking accounts. They started using disposable cell phones and codes to signal upgrades and downgrades in order to hide their tracks more effectively.

They traded in what they thought were barely discernible blocks of stock—10,000 here; 7,500 here; and the occasional 70,000 share block over there—on the assumption that the computers like those at the SEC or run out of Funkhouser's unit were too busy looking elsewhere for big frauds.

Over the years, their circle of friends widened. Franklin left Bear in 2002 for a hedge fund named Chelsey Capital, where he crossed paths with traders like David Slaine. But he kept his personal accounts at the firm, which traded on the same insider tips. His broker Rob Babcock now worked on the Lyford Cay fund and would piggyback Franklin's personal trades both for the fund and for himself.

A couple of other traders at Bear with access to Franklin's trading activity joined in, copying his trades with the pre-market knowledge of the UBS analyst recommendations.

Even as Lyford Cay was closed down in 2004 (Lewis remained a trading client of Bear and Butenhoff), much of the scheme continued. A husband-and-wife team of lawyers, Christopher and Randi Collotta, made their way into the circle of friends, by providing confidential tips on upcoming mergers and acquisitions in which Morgan Stanley was an adviser. Randi Collotta worked in Morgan Stanley's global compliance department, where she was supposed to be safeguarding such secrets at least until they were made public; she and her husband began trading on the confidential merger information, and tipping off others. They included a Wall Street trader, the feds discovered, who turned out to be a high school friend of her husband, who then tipped off Babcock who in turn tipped off Franklin.

But what are friends for?

That's a truism on Wall Street when it comes to sharing inside information; friends share information mostly because friends trust each other, whether it's because of shared life experiences or because committing illegality creates bonds of its own. Shared guilt nurtures the shared responsibility to keep quiet.

But that shared responsibility only extends to the point when someone like David Makol or B. J. Kang shows up at your door and offers you a deal, as was the case with Erik Franklin. Now five years into his little network of trading on inside tips, Franklin had been feasting off his illegal gains at yet another hedge fund, this one set up with his own money, called Q Capital.

Franklin's practice of keeping this circle of friends out of the sights of the feds by trading in barely noticeable amounts had proven to be a very good trick. But by extending the scheme into the arena of mergers and acquisitions, they had opened themselves up to one of the key variables checked by people like Funkhouser and his ever more sophisticated tracking system. The trade in question here involved a stock called Catellus Development. In 2005 it was being taken over by a company called ProLogis in a deal where Morgan was the adviser. That was the whisper that made its way from Randi Collotta to Babcock to Franklin and to the others, all of whom quickly began snapping up shares, even through accounts held by family members. The circle's big mistake was using Franklin's father-in-law's trading account in their activities. That relatively small brokerage account somehow touched off alarm bells inside the commission and connected the dots to the wider circle, much the same way the porn star's bank trades led to Jim McDermott.

It wasn't long before the SEC questioned Franklin on the trade. Flustered, he made up a false account of how it occurred. That was dumb since he had just added perjury charges to his potential criminal resume. But then he did something smart, and reached out to attorney Michael Bachner who told Franklin he was in serious trouble. Based on what the SEC was asking, it wouldn't be long before the Justice Department and the FBI added criminal insider trading charges to the mix.

If Franklin fought the charges and lost, he faced years in jail. If he turned himself in and cooperated, he probably could work out a deal that would reduce or possibly eliminate jail time.

Franklin decided to cooperate. Makol, who would loom large as the insider trading probe progressed, gave Franklin his standard pitch: If you want to stay out of jail, you have to tell us everything. Franklin has told people the experience was jarring, and he was "near suicidal" at the prospect of jail time. With that, he turned over detailed records of his dirty trades to the government, including the names of people he did them with, and like Ivan Boesky and Marty Siegel, he agreed to wear a wire so investigators could snag the others.

Franklin began by fingering Guttenberg and then his friend Babcock, who made for an especially juicy target because he was still at Bear Stearns. As part of his deal for leniency, Franklin eventually pointed to others involved in insider trading, including David Slaine, then a Wall Street heavyweight who went to work at Chelsey Capital. Slaine wasn't named in the eventual charging documents; the feds, as we shall see, had bigger plans for him.

Meanwhile, investigators believed the deterrent value of nailing a Wall Street trader was huge. Indeed, Babcock fancied himself as a tough jock, particularly in the macho atmosphere of the Wall Street trading desks where he worked. But rather than go to jail, the former college lacrosse player agreed to cooperate as well, wearing a wire and helping the feds nail down others involved in both the UBS trades and in passing along Morgan Stanley's pre-merger deal information.

Like Franklin, Babcock was rewarded for his cooperation and pleaded guilty to a felony but no jail time. Guttenberg wasn't so lucky; he was sentenced to seventy-eight months in a federal prison.

Babcock has told friends that while working as an informant at one point he tried to get his boss Butenhoff to concede to knowledge of the illegal activities, but without any luck. "He kept asking me weird questions," was how Butenhoff later described Babcock's efforts. To date, Butenhoff hasn't been charged, much less questioned by federal authorities about being part of the ring.

Babcock, for his part, has also told friends that he recently touched base with Franklin to patch things up. "Rob basically told Erik that he harbors no hard feelings because Rob helped catch others," said one mutual acquaintance. "It was kind of like an Alcoholics Anonymous meeting with everyone 'fessing up to their sins."

"Greed is at work," Manhattan U.S. attorney Michael Garcia announced as the feds unveiled the case in March 2007, calling it the biggest insider trading bust since the infamous Ivan Boesky case back in the 1980s. To illustrate the sweep of the investigation—including the sheer number of people involved and the number of stocks that were traded illegally—Garcia stood in front of the large board of names and photos with lots of arrows diagramming the various schemes at work by this particular circle of friends. The illegality was breathtaking in its scope; it occurred at major Wall Street firms (Morgan Stanley and Bear Stearns, even though the firms weren't directly charged) and at hedge funds. Lawyers and traders were involved. Taken together, it appeared that insider trading was rampant across the financial business—not just inside hedge funds, which were only now facing heightened supervision from the SEC through new inspection laws, but also in places that the SEC and a host of regulators had been watching for years: the big investment banks.

As the feds were announcing the breaking of the Franklin-Babcock ring in March 2007, the first rumblings of the financial crisis had begun, and ironically at Bear Stearns, which was holding mountains of debt tied to the increasingly fragile housing market.

Still during the first quarter of 2007, Wall Street firms posted record profits sustained by taking massive risks in the trading of complex securities. Working anywhere in the financial business meant a huge pay day, from the trader to the chief executive. Steve Cohen earned roughly $1 billion in 2006. Jimmy Cayne, who ran the smallest of the big banks, Bear Stearns, earned a salary and bonus of $34 million for 2006, in a check that was delivered and announced in early 2007.

The difference between SAC Capital and Bear was of course in how they each managed risk. Cohen would take the necessary precautions to protect SAC and its investors from the worst that the looming financial crisis would offer. "You're all idiots!" Cohen screamed one morning to his portfolio managers as he implored them to begin selling out of their positions and start hoarding cash in the face of the coming financial storm.

Cayne, meanwhile, did almost nothing until it was too late. Mortgage bonds on the balance sheet of Bear and the rest of the big banks were falling in value, and their implosion set in motion a chain of events that in about a year's time would lead to the demise of Bear itself. The rest of the banking industry's largest players would have also collapsed were it not for a historic bailout financed by the American taxpayer.

Likewise, the first glimmers of the financial crisis had barely made an impression on government regulators as insider trading had now emerged officially as public enemy number one for the white-collar cops. That was the warning made by the prestigious law firm Skadden, Arps, Slate, Meagher & Flom to its clients, many of them Wall Street traders and hedge fund traders, around this time. It didn't matter that the then SEC chairman, Chris Cox, a former congressman from Orange County, California, and an appointee of President Bush, was known as a libertarian on most matters involving the economy, meaning he favored low taxes and less government regulation, except in the matter of insider trading. According to the firm, Cox adopted the SEC's long-held position that trading on material nonpublic information was a threat to the "integrity of the markets." As such he created a "working group" inside the commission dedicated specifically to tracking down insider trading cases, and particularly among hedge funds, where the feds believed for good reason that problems continued to fester.

Still, the length of time it took to crack the Franklin-Babcock-Guttenberg circle of friends only underscored just how difficult breaking the code of insider trading had become. It had taken five years for the most sophisticated surveillance systems in the world—now employed not just by Funkhouser's crew but also at the SEC and the Justice Department—to snare a bunch of Wall Street frat kids who traded high-level insider information hidden in bags of Doritos.

Hell hath no fury like a women scorned," agent B. J. Kang must have thought as he listened intently to the story of Patricia Cohen, the ex-wife of Steve Cohen, and the allegations she made about her ex-husband.

Patricia Cohen had many axes to grind against her ex-hubby, including the fact that when they divorced in 1992 and she received her share of Steve Cohen's wealth, he wasn't a billionaire—indeed, far from it. He had just launched SAC Capital, a firm devoted, as he would later say, to "information arbitrage," a fancy way to describe the practice of finding out the best information available, and trading on it all day and every day to extract the maximum amount of profit.

When he started with the chunk of money he made while at Gruntal, no one outside the Wall Street trading community really knew who Steve Cohen was. His claim to fame in the popular culture: a 1992 appearance on a tabloid show called *Christina*, where he discussed how he was sleeping with his soon-to-be-ex-wife, Patricia, while he was dating his soon-to-be-new-wife, Alexandra.

Cohen, then with a full head of hair (an odd sight to those who've only seen him since he made his fortune), described his philandering this way: "A lot of these things occurred in the first year when I still wasn't committed to Alex and maybe I used the ex as a wedge. . . . I had gone through a pretty messy divorce and wasn't ready. . . . It wasn't a clean separation. . . . We went back and forth for a while," he said, before adding that he and his first wife had "some financial difficulties."

Times had changed, obviously. Some fifteen years later, Steve Cohen never appeared on television (unless clandestinely filmed) and gone were the financial difficulties. He had built one of the world's largest hedge funds and made a lot of money. He lived with wife number two and seven children in a mansion in Greenwich, Connecticut.

And Patricia Cohen merited only a few sentences in the Wikipedia bio of her now famous and famously rich ex-husband. Patricia and Steve Cohen had been married for ten tumultuous years. The couple were married during the stock-market boom of the 1980s and divorced in 1990. They had two children together. Like all married couples, they fought, though at least once, according to Patricia, it was violently. When they divorced, Patricia got custody of the children, their apartment, and $1 million on top of child support, which Cohen believed was more than a fair deal.

Patricia Cohen never thought it was all that fair, particularly after her millionaire ex-husband became a billionaire ex-husband. Cohen, meanwhile, moved on with his new and relatively happy life. Patricia never quite moved on, remaining single, and according to Cohen's friends, envious of the life Steve had created.

That's one side of this messy story. The other side, outlined in a *New York* magazine account, went something like this: Patricia was watching a *60 Minutes* profile of Steve Cohen, which alleged, among other things, that he manipulated shares of a company called Biovail. After some digging through old records, she had what she believed was proof that Steve hid assets from her during their divorce. She decided to file a lawsuit to recover $8 million she said was rightfully hers.

The case would have been just another footnote in Steve Cohen's Wikipedia page were it not for what else made it into the court documents: Not only had he shortchanged her, but, she said, during their ten-year marriage Cohen engaged in insider trading and money laundering.

The case would be thrown out of court and then successfully appealed by Patricia's lawyer. The charges were denied by Steve Cohen; his press handlers privately described Patricia as a loose cannon looking to cash in on her ex-husband's fame and fortune. But the insider trading charges were big news, even bigger for the various law enforcement groups investigating what they considered suspicious trading at SAC.

Keep in mind that for all the noise surrounding SAC, Steve Cohen's record was remarkably scandal free. He was sanctioned once by the New York Stock Exchange in 1995 for a trade deemed manipulative that he had made back during his last days at Gruntal, in 1991. It would be Cohen's first regulatory infraction and, as I write this in the spring of 2013, the only one. But Kang and others inside the SEC were convinced he and people at his fund weren't playing by the rules, and it wasn't long after Patricia went public with her lawsuit that the FBI sat down to hear her story, people with knowledge of the conversation say.

Patricia Cohen spoke with Kang, sources say, on at least two occasions, elaborating on many of the facts she had laid out in her lawsuit. Those facts were pretty embarrassing. Cohen had been deposed back in 1986 by the SEC, which was investigating suspicious trading while he was working at Gruntal. The commission focused on General Electric's acquisition of RCA.

According to Patricia Cohen's lawsuit and the account she gave to the FBI, Cohen snapped up shares of RCA before the deal was announced in 1985—and shares soared. He was tipped off by a college buddy who worked at the infamous Drexel Burnham Lambert—one of the firms working on the transaction, and which employed both Marty Siegel and Dennis Levine, two of the principal figures in the 1980s insider trading crackdown. In fact, according to Patricia Cohen, the RCA deal tip that made its way to her ex-husband had originated with Levine himself.

Just to underscore her point, she said Cohen asserted his Fifth Amendment right against self-incrimination several times during an SEC deposition about the trade, something SAC's press handlers still won't deny.

After the deposition, she told FBI officials that Cohen was petrified that he had been caught and was about to be charged. "His ex-wife told the FBI that in private he's far different than his public persona as a master of the universe. She said he was basically crying," according to a person with direct knowledge of the matter. "He was afraid he was about to get locked up, at least that's what she said."

Cohen was never charged. The SEC dropped the case even after Cohen's refusal to answer questions. And for all the juicy details Patricia Cohen spewed about her ex, she was essentially a witness with a huge axe to grind, and she had no real proof, just her own word, of his misdeeds.

Kang knew he needed more. Given all the money Cohen paid out to consultants and expert networks, getting one of those guys to flip might prove impossible—at least until this point it had. Investigators toyed with the idea of putting someone inside SAC, a Wall Street version of Donnie Brasco—the FBI agent who implicated the mob. They quickly dropped the idea for the simple fact that they believed it was easier to get inside the mob than the close-knit financial community, where experience in the business trumps bonds of ethnicity.

By now government investigators were coming to the conclusion that a more effective weapon was needed, such as an informant with long years in the business who could pass the smell test with Cohen, or a court order to tap Cohen's phone. All of that would have to wait as federal investigators turned their full attention in this increasingly target-rich area to nailing a suspect they thought might go down if not bigger, then at least faster.

Sanjay Wadhwa developed a little trick when taking depositions from Wall Street master-of-the-universe types accustomed to having and getting their way. Not long after joining the SEC, he noticed that targets became more compliant, more willing to 'fess up to bad behavior, when they were ushered into one of the group of large conference rooms at the SEC's headquarters in lower Manhattan and forced to face the windows.

What they were confronted with was an imposing site: a phalanx of government interrogators dressed in dark suits with the lower Manhattan skyline in the background. The message Wadhwa wanted to deliver was pretty straightforward: You have done something wrong, and you're up against a foe with unlimited resources, so think twice before lying under oath.

That was the position Raj Rajaratnam, the biggest target in the government's insider trading crackdown, found himself in one afternoon in June 2007.

It was an odd technique coming from Wadhwa, who was at the time a midlevel SEC enforcement agent known for his quiet, albeit steady, determination. Most SEC investigators come to the agency to get experience before moving on to lucrative jobs at the big banks. The revolving door between Wall Street and Washington is a source of constant criticism. It is no wonder regulators ignored credible evidence that Bernie Madoff, a longtime fixture of the Wall Street trading establishment, had been conducting a massive Ponzi scheme. Many wanted to work for Bernie and triple their salaries.

Sanjay Wadhwa made the reverse commute, which was only fitting now that he was on the verge of cracking possibly the biggest insider trading case ever. In 2003, Wadhwa left a boring but lucrative profession as a tax attorney to work at the SEC. It was a bold move, but one that made sense to him at the time: He was still single and he was bored with corporate tax work. The idea of investigating Wall Street crimes intrigued him. It was around this time that the New York State attorney general, Eliot Spitzer, uncovered mountains of Wall Street abuse, and the SEC, the federal government's traditional enforcement agency in the world of white-collar crime, took a backseat to Spitzer's efforts.

What made Spitzer so powerful (and such a dangerous competitor for the SEC) was that he combined prosecutorial skills with a real working knowledge of Wall Street. He was the scion of a mega-wealthy real estate developer and as a result knew Wall Street and its key players from private schools. Wadhwa wasn't in Spitzer's league as far as contacts were concerned, but as a tax attorney he had the skills to read financial statements and investigate complex corporate crimes.

And he was willing to work cheap, a requisite for any SEC employee. Wadhwa's first case involved whether specialists on the floor of the New York Stock Exchange were overbilling clients, effectively charging greater commissions than the "best price" called for under existing laws. The result was a string of high-profile enforcement actions against some of the biggest floor brokers in the country, and a broad settlement with the big firms that transacted business at the NYSE, which led to hundreds of millions of dollars in fines and penalties.

But it wasn't enough. The SEC had been exposed by Spitzer as a slow-footed bureaucracy, unable to see big scandals staring them right in the face—such as the research analyst investigation Spitzer had spearheaded earlier in the decade.

But Wadhwa discovered something else. The entire analyst investigation—which involved untold billions in potential losses—or the $50 billion Madoff scheme would each be treated as a *single case* by the SEC's bean counters, who were forever trying to show that the commission was doing all it could to combat corporate crime.

As such, investigators like Wadhwa were discouraged from taking on complex, time-consuming investigations and were prodded by management in Washington to keep the wheels churning by going after low-hanging fruit. Ironically, the management of the SEC wanted the same thing from its investigators that the hedge fund managers wanted from their traders: lots of wins.

The only difference was that the hedge fund guys also demanded huge payoffs for their wins, whereas the goals at the SEC were pretty puny. The SEC's administrators seemed to care more about making their numbers than about cracking big scandals.

This mind-set irked Wadhwa, who saw it as a professional stumbling block, unless, of course, he could find a case that could set him apart. He thought he had one in 2005: a brokerage account held under the name of a Croatian seamstress, Sonja Anticevic. She displayed an amazing knack for buying shares of companies before corporate events, including buying Reebok just before it was purchased by Adidas in 2005. Instead of giving in to the pressure from his bosses and moving on to a case with greater numbers potential, Wadhwa dug deeper. This was one savvy seamstress, or so it seemed. She bought Reebok call options through a New York broker, which earned her more than $2 million, and she wasn't alone in the scam.

Big bucks were being wired in and out of her accounts from banks in Austria. Wadhwa quickly got an injunction to freeze the brokerage account and filed charges against Anticevic, even though she was living in Croatia at the time. The case sparked a media storm in the Balkan nation. Reporters swarmed her house. Anticevic said the account wasn't hers and that she had little if any real understanding of Wall Street. In one interview she said the closest she ever got to high finance was through a nephew, a former Goldman Sachs broker named David Pajcin.

It didn't take long for Wadhwa and his supervisors to make the obvious connections. When Pajcin and another Goldman broker, Eugene Plotkin, became privy to corporate secrets, they traded on them through a network of accounts, including one held by Pajcin's aunt in Croatia. Anticevic's name may have been used in the plot—perhaps she even received a few bucks for her help—but the scheme had Wall Street, with its questionable mores, written all over it.

Wadhwa was now working closely with the federal criminal authorities, a blueprint he would employ on a much bigger case just a few months later. The FBI agent assigned to the case was David Makol, known, much like Kang was, for his ability to turn witnesses. The assistant U.S. attorney was Benjamin Lawsky, a lawyer with a bipartisan résumé (he clerked for Republican judges, but was a committed Democrat) and a penchant for big cases in prosecuting terrorists, drug dealers, and now insider trading.

Makol and Lawsky offered Pajcin a deal: Cooperate or go to jail. His cooperation brought more light to the scheme, which was later described in the *New York Times* this way: "Mr. Plotkin's arrest in April 2006 was the first of a number of insider-trading cases brought by federal prosecutors and the Securities and Exchange Commission that year and 2007. But none matched the scheme involving Mr. Plotkin, a fixed-income associate at Goldman, and a former co-worker, David Pajcin. Their plans involved a former Merrill Lynch analyst, a New Jersey postal worker who served on a grand jury, two workers at a magazine printing press and an exotic dancer."

Plotkin was later found guilty and sentenced to almost five years in jail. Pajcin pled guilty and avoided jail time. Anticevic, the retired seamstress, was charged by the SEC, fined, and then later acquitted, but Wadhwa had taught his supervisors a valuable lesson: It takes time to produce cases that matter.

He was about to show them something else: It pays to have a diverse workforce. Wadhwa was born in New Delhi and came to the United States when he was nineteen to embark on his career in finance. His South Asian heritage gave him immediate access to a growing and close-knit community of other finance types of similar descent.

Wall Street, it should be noted, has always displayed a clannish behavior involving ethnicity. WASPs dominated the banking business through the nineteenth century, but with immigration from various parts of Europe came Wall Street's broader integration. J. P. Morgan, the original WASP bank, remained a super power, but upstarts reflecting the country's new entrants were everywhere: German Jews created the mighty Goldman Sachs; Jews from Eastern Europe created Bear Stearns; and Irish-American brokers ran Merrill Lynch.

Those divisions have been blurred considerably. Hank Paulson, a Christian Science farm boy from Illinois, ran Goldman in the 1990s. Stan O'Neal, an African-American whose grandfather was a slave, became CEO of Merrill Lynch in 2004, replacing David Komansky, the Jewish son of a Bronx postal worker.

By 2007, another wave of immigration from Asia had begun to transform Wall Street again. Fueled by the same grit and determination as prior entrants, Asians were now holding senior positions across Wall

Street and running major hedge funds, including one of the world's largest and most successful, the Galleon Group, founded by Raj Rajaratnam.

Sanjay Wadhwa knew a lot about finance. He earned a specialized degree in tax law and an MBA to go along with his law license. He could read a balance sheet upside down, and what his supervisors at the SEC liked about him was that he could make sense of it all for them.

His knowledge of the South Asian community was about to serve him well, when he stumbled across what he thought was a modest scam: A hedge fund name Sedna Capital was engaging in what Wadhwa thought was *cherry picking*—a practice in which hedge fund managers allocate winning trades to certain privileged customers, and the losers to others.

The fund was run by a trader named Rengan Rajaratnam, who didn't ring any bells as far as Wadhwa was concerned, until he dug a bit deeper and noticed that among those in the privileged class was Raj Rajaratnam.

Raj Rajaratnam was something of a wunderkind on Wall Street, particularly among South Asians. He was born in Sri Lanka, the son of a wealthy businessman, educated in England and at the University of Pennsylvania's Wharton School of Business. He began his career at Chase Manhattan Bank, and later the investment bank Needham & Co. He showed an immediate understanding of technology companies and it wasn't long before he was running a technology hedge fund for Needham. Soon he took a controlling interest in the fund and changed the name to Galleon Group, after the ships in the Spanish Armada that carried gold and yet were able to sail through turbulent seas.

Galleon started with just $250 million in assets. Its objective was to match rapid-fire trading—the same stuff done by SAC Capital—with intense research. Rajaratnam, the founding partner, was a former analyst and the operation's big thinker, while Gary Rosenbach, who had been his head trader at Needham, ran the desk.

Rajaratnam boasted that he and his people visited three hundred companies per month; unlike SAC, where the scorecard is looked at every day and even every minute of the day, Rajaratnam said his traders weren't rewarded simply by making money. "They are there to limit losses," he was quoted as saying. "I don't want them to hit home runs."

One competitor marveled that Rajaratnam "sucked the air out of the room" when raising money from investors. He targeted the top players at major technology outfits, the same places he researched at Needham. They would be valuable to Galleon not just as clients but also as sources of information for Rajaratnam's trading.

The strategy seemed to work. By 2007, Galleon had $7 billion under management, about half that of SAC Capital, but more than matching SAC's returns, or for that matter Bernie Madoff's no-lose recipe for success. People inside Galleon say the fund's returns were extremely volatile on a monthly basis, and Rajaratnam's trading was particularly volatile, with the Galleon boss having a huge year in 1999, and getting killed in other years.

But in the end, the fund's freewheeling culture where traders bet against each other seemed to work. In 2007, as the financial crisis began, Galleon earned its investors more than 12 percent returns; it lost just 3 percent in 2008 when the financial world collapsed. Its best year since its inception was 1999, when it cranked out returns that surpassed 90 percent amid the technology stock bubble. Like SAC and Madoff, it never lost money even during down years in the markets (except of course, 2008). On average Galleon returned 25 percent since its inception in 1997.

Rajaratnam became incredibly wealthy. He was now, according to Forbes, among the three hundred richest Americans, worth around $1.7 billion, though he wasn't your typical Wall Street fat cat. He was described by former employees as a family man who, when he wasn't working, spent time with his wife and children. He was also extremely generous, particularly when it came to giving to charity. "This country has been good to me," he remarked, according to one former employee, as he wrote out a check for $500,000 to the New York City fire department after the 9/11 terrorist attacks.

He had also briefly caught the attention of the FBI for contributing money to an organization thought to be associated with the Tamil Tigers, the now-defeated guerrilla group that was then fighting for an independent Tamil state within Sri Lanka. (Rajaratnam, through his lawyers, has said he never directly financed the Tamil Tigers, though he hasn't been bashful about his support for Sri Lankan independence.)

Galleon also was well-known both to Wadhwa and the SEC. Over the years the firm's trading patterns had been flagged, raising the same suspicions that SAC had—namely, that Galleon had managed to pick precisely the right time to buy or sell stocks. And, like SAC, nothing seemed to stick to Galleon, at least so far.

Sedna was displaying the same knack for picking winners as Galleon did, Wadhwa concluded after a preliminary look through its trading accounts. But his gut told him it had less to do with Rengan's market intelligence than that of Raj. "If anyone is giving him insider tips, it's his older, more successful brother," Wadhwa thought as he considered his next move. Wadhwa's hunch was that whatever Sedna was doing, what he had come across was bigger than simply cherry-picking stock trades for its best clients.

He was right. As he studied Raj's trading records, a similar pattern appeared. They both were trading in the same stocks (though Raj was wagering far bigger bets) and their trades were extremely well timed around market-moving events.

You guys are on a fishing expedition," snapped Galleon attorney Jerry Isenberg as SEC officials camped out in the fund's offices searching trading records, allegedly as part of a routine examination, but in reality, part of something far more serious.

Wadhwa explained that his staff was just doing its job, and nothing more.

Which was true, but what he didn't say was that the "job" was no longer focused on Rengan Rajaratnam, or the lower level fraud of cherry-picking, but on whether his brother Raj Rajaratnam was engaging in insider trading at a very high level.

Sometime earlier, the examinations staff paid a visit to the offices of Sedna. Wadhwa had a good reason to send the SEC's examinations unit as opposed to the enforcement staff. The SEC conducts routine examinations all the time. Enforcement officials with their subpoenas and threats of filing fraud charges raise too much suspicion, and at times, may lead to the risk of the destruction of evidence.

Under the guise of simply kicking the tires, the inspectors were actually looking for trading records, emails, and IMs—instant messages that are commonly used to communicate between *tippers,* or the people who supply the inside information, and the end users of it, known in legal circles as *tippees.* The results of the examination confirmed what Wadhwa's more cursory inquiry had suggested: Sedna's trades were large and well timed to market-moving events, and as Wadhwa would say, "in the right direction." If the announcement was bad, Sedna would short stocks; if the announcement was good, it would buy them up. Wadhwa would later describe them as "highly suspicious" because the search of emails and instant messages, or IMs, and telephone logs showed regular correspondence between Sedna and Galleon, and that they were trading the same stocks.

"Bingo," Wadhwa thought after hearing the results of the examination now taking place at Galleon. Jokes about fishing expeditions aside, the examiners went about their business at Galleon's New York City offices largely unfettered, and with that came success: The team was able to identify evidence that both Sedna and Galleon had been trading a number of stocks, many of them in the technology business, and successfully just before corporate announcements. One stock seemed to catch Wadhwa's eye, AMD. Rajaratnam's trading of the chipmaker's stock would loom large as the investigation continued.

As far as Wadhwa was concerned, the trades were just too good to be legal. He also believed he had enough to bring to the criminal authorities to launch a broader case. It was something he learned quickly while at the SEC. Acting alone the SEC can only do so much; it can't put people in jail, and when confronted with a lengthy jail term, people often cooperate. For that, he'd need to call in the feds.

The cooperator they hoped to turn was Rengan, who was brought into the SEC offices to describe the trades and to explain why he spoke to his brother so much during the trading day when both of them had such high-pressure jobs. Wadhwa described him as "cocky, brash, and at times nervous." Wadhwa noticed that Rengan was shifting around in his seat a lot while being asked about questionable trades and his conversations with Raj, and that he refused to make eye contact.

At one point during the deposition, Wadhwa looked at Andrew Michaelson, one of his deputies. Both had come to the same conclusion: The case against Rengan was only the tip of the iceberg, and their primary target should be his older brother.

None of this seemed to impress a couple of assistant U.S. attorneys and FBI agent Kang as they listened to Wadhwa lay out his facts: The suspicious trades were more than just coincidence and the product of hard work, as Rengan described them during his deposition. Both funds had been trading in highly suspicious patterns, and if Wadhwa's hunch turned out to be right, Galleon, one of the biggest hedge funds in the business, was playing dirty.

Raj Rajaratnam was well-known inside the Justice Department, and not just because of his associations back home (which were unknown to Wadhwa at the time). Informants had been whispering his name for years for alleged insider trading. He had been targeted years earlier by a felon and FBI informant named Roomy Khan, but the matter was dropped.

For all the noise involving Galleon, there was never enough to make a case, and at the meeting, Wadhwa heard the same thing. There wasn't enough in what he was saying for them to drop everything and launch a full-scale investigation. Criminal insider trading cases need more than just a few odd coincidences. Who was Raj getting his insider tips from? Certainly not Rengan, who was probably piggybacking on his brother's trades.

Their advice to Wadhwa: Come back when you get more.

By now, the SEC's presence inside the Galleon offices wasn't so welcomed. Galleon's attorneys were becoming increasingly suspicious of their demands for more records, more IMs from Rajaratnam, and more phone records. The examination team was effectively thrown out of Galleon's offices, a completely legal move since it was operating without a subpoena.

But Wadhwa was undeterred—either by the FBI's brush-off or by Galleon's roadblock. "These guys are either brilliant or they know something more," Wadhwa told his boss, David Markowitz, one of the senior enforcement officials in New York.

Markowitz didn't hesitate: "Call him in."

CHAPTER 6

BIGGER FISH

About an hour into Raj Rajaratnam's deposition in June 2007, Wadhwa realized that none of his usual tricks were working—but not for a lack of trying. The testimony was given at SEC headquarters in the World Financial Center in lower Manhattan. Rajaratnam was accompanied by two attorneys from Shearman & Sterling, which specialized in SEC cases.

Wadhwa had seated Rajaratnam facing the window, in front of three SEC enforcement officials, including Markowitz and Andrew Michaelson, who like Wadhwa, had left private practice to join the commission.

Michaelson had been with the commission less than a year, but Wadhwa decided Michaelson would ask most of the questions. This freed him up to monitor the questions and to keep in contact with his examiners who were still poring over the Galleon documents.

All three SEC officials were dressed in dark suits and maintained a look of seriousness. A court reporter sat at the end of the rectangular table, typing every word from the star witness. The entire arrangement is designed to rattle even the most confident white-collar crooks.

It didn't work. Wadhwa and the SEC team later said they never quite saw someone as confident as Rajaratnam was that day. He explained in compelling detail how he was able to time his trades so perfectly, figuring out to buy a stock named Polycom just before a positive earnings release. At one point he denied outright that he traded on inside information. The way Rajaratnam described it, his fund made money because he was smart, he hired smart people, and he paid them very well. Because of his experience in the business, he worked the mosaic like no one else on Wall Street.

Though he certainly didn't have the physique of a fighter—he was a large, overweight man—friends would say that Rajaratnam viewed himself as a warrior, along the lines of his countrymen in Sri Lanka, forever fighting a valiant struggle for freedom. Rajaratnam's enemy was the market, and he had fought as an immigrant-outsider on Wall Street to create one of the biggest hedge funds ever.

But in this particular skirmish, Rajaratnam chose a different defense. He turned on the charm. During his deposition, he was funny, gregarious, and imposing, not just because of his broad shoulders and girth. He simply "controlled the room," Wadhwa would later say as he weighed Rajaratnam's various explanations for stock trades utilizing the mosaic theory, and his side comments about the markets or his description of how he runs one of the world's largest hedge funds.

Still, the command performance was utterly unconvincing to the SEC agents in the room. His answers didn't contain any smoking guns, but he didn't help himself, either. Can anyone be this good? Not as far as the SEC is concerned. If the mosaic theory could be honed to such perfection, wouldn't other very smart people start hedge funds that beat the markets year in and year out?

As far as Wadhwa was concerned, Rajaratnam lied to the SEC for about eight hours, giving implausible explanations for buying shares of AMD just before a positive earnings announcement, and repeating every so often, "I love what you guys do to protect the integrity of the securities markets."

During one of the breaks, Wadhwa received a message on his BlackBerry from an SEC staffer assigned to plow through the Galleon documents. The investigator had found IMs between Rajaratnam and someone named "Rumi," who professed to have something "really interesting" to share with the Galleon founder.

It wasn't the only red-flagged IM or email the staffer came across from this Rumi person. There were dozens of others. The two were chatting on a regular basis about the markets and specific stocks. The language was coded at times, it appeared, but sometimes it wasn't.

Rumi must be supplying Rajaratnam with valuable information. Wadhwa called Michaelson and Markowitz aside. "This looks pretty interesting," he said.

"Let's just nonchalantly bring it up and see what he says," Markowitz whispered. Wadhwa nodded and emailed the staffer: "Get me more."

Wadhwa kept a straight face through the rest of the deposition. Still he couldn't help thinking that Rajaratnam was everything brother Rengan wasn't: funny, smart, and charming, and most of all, a world-class bullshit artist, which is why he probably went so far on Wall Street.

Rajaratnam waxed poetic about how the mosaic theory had made Galleon one of the world's most successful hedge funds. The mosaic theory had been invented by famed investor Philip A. Fisher, laid out in his seminal book, *Common Stocks and Uncommon Profits*, first published in 1958. Fisher had actually called the investing process "the scuttlebutt method," underscoring its process of gathering together various pieces of information—scuttlebutt, so to speak—and then determining whether to buy or sell based on the resulting "mosaic" of information.

The mosaic theory may have made sense on Wall Street, but to the investigators at the SEC, including Wadhwa, it was an invitation to fraud. By culling various pieces of information from many sources, it almost forced investors to seek out information that might not be available to the public, to identify the most profitable trades. What's more, with everyone doing this, the pressure was ever greater to find that piece of information no one else had—the deep inside dope.

The questioning during the deposition also showed just how far the SEC had veered from its original focus, of tying Rajaratnam with Sedna and his brother Rengan in a probe of cherry-picking, to one focused almost exclusively on Galleon and its founder and insider trading. "Are you familiar with the term *insider trading*?" Michaelson asked Rajaratnam. "Do you believe it's wrong? . . . Do you recall any instance where you've come into contact with information that you believed was material and nonpublic in any respect? . . . Has Galleon ever made a trade on the basis of nonpublic information? . . . Have you ever suspected that anyone at Galleon ever engaged in insider trading?"

Rajaratnam stayed on his game, denying the use of insider information and falling back on the mosaic theory as the explanation for his success.

At one point, though, Rajaratnam was asked to give more detail on where he got all the pieces to fill in the mosaic. The SEC had learned from mishaps in the past; during its research analyst investigation, the commission was embarrassed when Attorney General Spitzer uncovered emails that showed analysts privately deriding stocks they rated highly. The SEC didn't subpoena emails back then; it did now.

That's when Michaelson brought up the mysterious "Rumi," whose name the SEC staffer had initially gotten wrong, mistaking Rumi for Roomy. "Who is this handle, Roomy81@aol.com?" Michaelson asked, adding: "Did you ever talk to her about AMD?"

Rajaratnam explained that Rumi was actually Roomy Kahn, a former Galleon trader, Intel executive, and friend who lived in Silicon Valley. As far as why he bought shares of AMD when he did, it had less to do with any insight Khan provided and more to do with Galleon's extensive research process. Until now she was also unknown to the SEC, even if she had been a confidential FBI informant against Rajaratnam years earlier. She was part of Rajaratnam's circle, and the FBI's as well, willing to do whatever it took to make money and stay out of jail.

But it is here in answering the AMD questions that the smooth operator slipped, though it's unclear if he knew he had done so. Rajaratnam explained away his IMs with Khan as having little consequence; they were little more than idle chatter about the market, and he actually had a "source" at AMD—although he claimed the source merely crunched numbers for him.

Well, thought Wadhwa and the team, what would an executive at AMD be doing crunching numbers for Raj? And if Khan knew so little about stocks, including AMD, why would the head of one of the nation's biggest hedge funds be having so many conversations with her?

Markowitz and Wadhwa briefly exchanged glances and moved on to other matters with the confidence that they finally had their man.

These guys make monkeys out of individual investors, the SEC's insider trading regulations and the attorney general's office," read an anonymous letter addressed to the SEC's New York enforcement staff in March 2007. The letter arrived just months before Rajaratnam's deposition. Galleon was founded as a hedge fund that focused on technology and health care; its investors were major technology company executives, which aided the firm in researching the industry.

The letter said the information passed on to Galleon from those executives, however, wasn't so innocent. It involved insider information, not mere industry trends and nuggets of data. It claimed that Galleon traded insider information for prostitution and "other forms of illegal entertainment," which Wadhwa later learned involved lavish dinners and expensive trips such as an African safari.

Wadhwa had never been able to find the source of the letter, and the prostitution allegations never materialized, but whoever it came from was clearly on to something. If anything, the Rajaratnam deposition only reinforced the investigators' opinion that the Galleon hedge fund was run by someone who had too many coincidences going for him at the same time to be clean.

Rajaratnam's explanations about his top-notch research staff and strict adherence to the mosaic theory couldn't explain all those winning trades before key events. Moreover, good research often produces not just great *long-term* performance, but also *short-term* losing streaks. Warren Buffett's Berkshire Hathaway is a prime example. But how does one trade in and out of stocks constantly and with such precision?

The bottom line, the investigators concluded, was that Rajaratnam couldn't—at least not without a little help from friends such as this mysterious Roomy, who they believed figured prominently in Rajaratnam's circle. Over the next two and a half months, Wadhwa and his team continued to dig, uncovering additional IMs showing Khan tipping off Raj about a Polycom trade and other stocks. She wasn't his only source.

"Sanjay, you gotta see this," said Jason Friedman, one of Wadhwa's top investigators. Friedman handed Wadhwa a set of trading documents discovered during one of many late nights the Wadhwa team had spent during the investigation, which now entered the "stealth" phase, meaning there was no additional contact with Galleon or Rajaratnam, as the SEC worked quietly to build its case.

What Friedman found was that Rajaratnam was so plugged in that he frequently communicated with an executive at Intel, one of the handful of tech stocks Galleon liked to trade. The executive, Rajiv Goel, had been a classmate of Rajaratnam at Wharton, so it made sense that they had some contact. But Friedman discovered that Goel had a Charles Schwab brokerage account that was accessed from an IP address located in Galleon's office, suggesting it was used to funnel payoffs to Goel for inside information he supplied Rajaratnam. A little more digging and the SEC discovered that Rajaratnam had dealings with Wharton alum Anil Kumar, who worked at the prestigious consulting firm McKinsey & Co.

Access to a McKinsey partner was a key get for anyone interested in insider trading, since the big consulting firm does business with just about every major corporation, advising them on activities that have a direct impact on share price, such as mergers and acquisitions. Even better, as investigators discovered, Rajaratnam had forged ties to a former McKinsey chief executive, Rajat Gupta, now in retirement but still a presence in corporate America.

Many of Rajaratnam's circle of friends shared common ethnic bounds, college ties, and most astonishing of all, an absolute desire to make money by cheating the system. When Wadhwa heard the news about Kumar, for example, he could barely contain himself. "Why don't we just charge the entire fucking Wharton class of 1983," he snapped.

That was the case Wadhwa was making once again to the Justice Department lawyers at their headquarters in lower Manhattan. They should join in the fight, he argued, and take the case to the next level. Wadhwa had given them more evidence to build their case: He had Raj's confirmation under oath that he had a "source" inside AMD and that he regularly chatted with Roomy Khan about the markets. Wadhwa believed Khan was paid by Rajaratnam to supply him with inside tips. He couldn't find the direct money trail, at least not yet, but he had found lots of indirect payments made by Rajaratnam to Khan in the form of information.

Even better was what Wadhwa and his team found out *after* Rajaratnam's deposition. In July, just weeks after being grilled by the SEC, investigators found evidence that Rajaratnam traded on inside information concerning the pending takeover of Hilton Hotels by private equity firm Blackstone Group—a $26 billion leveraged buyout that shocked the markets, but apparently did not come as a surprise to Rajaratnam's circle of friends.

Trading records showed that both Rajaratnam brothers and Khan snapped up shares just before the deal was announced, earning millions of dollars, particularly in the case of Raj Rajaratnam (who bought 400,000 shares of Hilton). Most fascinating was how they bought the stock on July 3, during an abbreviated market session just before the

Fourth of July holiday. They crammed all their trades in the last half hour that the market was open, which set off massive alarm bells on the SEC's stock-trading surveillance system.

What wouldn't be known, at least for a while, was precisely why the Rajaratnams had bought the shares with such gusto, and why Rajaratnam kept in such close contact with Khan. As investigators later learned, Khan had passed the Hilton tip to Rajaratnam through a source at the ratings agency, Moody's Investors Service, which was analyzing the deal.

It didn't end there. Trading records showed that two weeks later Galleon had suddenly bought 25,000 shares of Google just before it announced strong quarterly earnings. Another smallish fund, Whitman Capital, also bought shares of Google before the announcement, as did Khan. The reason was discovered as the investigation progressed: Khan had a source inside Google's investor relations department who had provided her with the numbers before they were made public. Khan, in turn, gave them to Rajaratnam, and a Silicon Valley money manager, Doug Whitman, who was also on her friends list.

The Justice Department assembled what it considered its insider trading A-team for the meeting at which Wadhwa made his case: Assistant U.S. Attorneys Lauren Goldberg and Joshua Klein, widely regarded as experts in the prosecution of white-collar crime, and the FBI's B. J. Kang, now one of two go-to agents (Makol being the other) in the prosecution of insider trading.

The feds listened to Wadhwa's presentation and made a few admissions of their own. Roomy Khan wasn't quite the mystery woman that she had appeared to be. She worked for Rajaratnam in the 1990s as a trader and she had long been suspected of providing insider information to Rajaratnam when she was an employee of Intel, the big chipmaker, in 1998.

There had been lots of suspicious trading just before key events such as earnings announcements. Intel set up an internal sting operation, placing a camera near a fax machine. Khan was caught in the surveillance video dialing Rajaratnam's telephone and sending him an early copy of a press release about earnings. By 2001, the FBI had assembled enough evidence to offer her a deal: Plead guilty to securities fraud for supplying Rajaratnam with insider trading, and avoid jail by cooperating with them to build a case against Rajaratnam.

It was a lucky break for Khan for several reasons. Khan avoided serious jail time, and before long, the Justice Department's investigation into Rajaratnam would be dropped. Some people inside the government say the case became a low priority as the FBI began diverting its resources to investigating terrorism following the 9/11 attacks. Others say those FBI agents still assigned to the matter couldn't develop any of Khan's leads.

In any event, her activities as a government snitch and a felon would remain under seal, and her friendship with Rajaratnam would continue as if nothing had ever happened.

Goldberg and her colleagues then discussed the suspicions they had about Rajaratnam's involvement with the Tamil Tigers—they appeared to receive money from the Galleon chief, albeit indirectly.

But it was the Justice Department's past investigation of Rajaratnam and Khan for conspiring to trade on insider information that had Wadhwa's head spinning. Wadhwa knew Galleon had appeared on the insider trading watch list in the past. Still, details of the Justice Department's earlier probe were remarkable. The FBI had wanted to put Rajaratnam in jail six years earlier, using Khan as its primary witness. She had agreed to cooperate, under one condition: complete and total immunity. In exchange, she would disclose "how Rajaratnam did it and who he gets his information from" and stay clean herself.

The feds lived up to their end of the bargain, but Khan didn't live up to hers.

Still, that was yesterday's news. Today's story was how to finally nab Rajaratnam, given the new evidence that Wadhwa brought to the table, and was it worth doing a second dance with Roomy Khan. Just about everyone in the room that afternoon knew that Roomy Khan by herself was largely damaged goods. She was already a crook with a sealed case that would nonetheless be opened for the entire world to see. Rajaratnam's lawyer would have a field day with her credibility—or lack of it. On top of her rap sheet, she had led the FBI down so many dead ends when she was a witness in the early Rajaratnam probe that no jury would convict Rajaratnam on her word alone.

Yet they also came to the conclusion that Khan, not Rengan with his blood loyalty to his other brother, was their best hope to break the Rajaratnam circle. Kang could try to flip other members of Rajaratnam's circle of friends whom Wadhwa had come across, but based on the nature of the conversations, Khan appeared to be Rajaratnam's best source of dirty information and, more than that, someone Rajaratnam obviously believed he could trust, given the pair's long relationship. When Kang discussed all of this with his supervisor, Rich Jacobs, in a small conference room in the FBI's lower Manhattan headquarters, they quickly came to the same conclusion: In order to make a case against Rajaratnam they needed more than trading records and some IMs. They needed Roomy Khan—and probably something else.

After long hours reviewing Raj's IMs, trading records, and other documents Wadhwa had provided them, Kang and his supervisors had developed what they thought was a pretty good character study of the Galleon chief. He would be an amazingly valuable witness himself because he had assembled a large circle of friends—employees at technology companies, other traders, and of course Roomy Khan, as part of his conspiracy to cheat the markets.

But he had gotten away with insider trading for far too long, which only stoked his massive ego. In Rajaratnam's mind he was smarter than the teams of government investigators who had been searching his trash for so long. And even if they did actually catch him, the betting among the government investigators was that a guy who could lie through his teeth for eight hours during an SEC deposition would also believe he could beat the rap, and beat any Roomy Khan–like witness they threw at him.

And he probably would unless they could get him on tape.

It's unclear exactly how the decision was made to give the FBI that perfect hedge in nailing one of the market's biggest players using telephone wiretaps. But based on conversations with various people in law enforcement, the decision began with a request from Kang's supervisors in the FBI.

They brought their plan to Reed Brodsky, the assistant U.S. attorney who had been specializing in insider trading cases. Brodsky understood the sensitivity of the matter (the federal wiretapping law was supposed to focus on terrorists and mobsters) but also how difficult it is to win insider trading cases, unless they have the culprits in their own words committing the crime. Brodsky made that case to his immediate boss, Michael Garcia, the Manhattan U.S. Attorney, who ultimately agreed.

And there was no better target to use wiretaps on than Raj Rajaratnam. Federal prosecutors, like their counterparts at the SEC, had come to the conclusion that Rajaratnam symbolized all that was wrong with the markets. He had created a trading firm based primarily on breaking the law as it applied to the use of material nonpublic information.

Moreover, they believed they were on to something big in the history of the government's crackdown on insider trading. Galleon traded so frequently and so widely that Rajaratnam's connections stretched all across Wall Street.

A top Merrill Lynch broker, investigators discovered, had accompanied Rajaratnam on a vacation to Jamaica. Another Rajaratnam associate on Wall Street was Lloyd Blankfein, CEO of Goldman Sachs, one of the firms that served as Galleon's prime brokers. Galleon traders were among the hedge-fund world's best paid and best connected, with friends all across Wall Street and at major hedge funds, including SAC.

In other words, by breaking Galleon and Rajaratnam, the government believed they could finally crack into a much larger circle of friends.

Investigators weighed whether they could get the needed corroborating evidence against Rajaratnam to convict him *without* a wiretap. Roomy Khan in and of herself was a terrible witness, and even if she didn't come with baggage, it would be a challenging case. There were so few major criminal insider trading convictions in the past because the quality of the evidence was often circumstantial or weak. He-said-she-said trials are risky. Targets often claim they didn't know they were trading on illegal information, and intent is a key ingredient of any fraud case.

That's why getting Rajaratnam on tape was crucial, and not just the taping that occurs when a witness like Khan decides to flip, and she records their conversations either with a wire or with a recording device on *her* telephone.

Officials in the Justice Department were now weighing was a wiretap on Rajaratnam's *own* cell phone, which would completely unlock his circle of friends.

To get wiretapping permission, investigators would need to convince a federal judge that they had probable cause to believe Rajaratnam committed securities fraud. They would also have to prove that they couldn't get the necessary evidence to convict Rajaratnam in any other way. Government officials determined neither would be difficult to meet given all the resources now being assembled against Galleon and its founder, which produced lots of good evidence with more to come particularly if they could convince Roomy Khan to go undercover.

For all her baggage, Roomy Khan was exactly the type of mole they were looking for: She had the trust of Rajaratnam, and she knew Wall Street and Silicon Valley, so she could snare others who were part of the bigger ring they believed existed.

And she would have no choice but to cooperate once Kang had his patented chat with her and laid out choices: Either help put her benefactor and good friend in prison, or be prepared to serve a long term behind bars herself.

Convincing a target, even one as guilty as Roomy Khan, to cooperate with the government is never an easy task. It is a cat-and-mouse game. As an agent you can't give up too much information because you need to keep the target guessing. It's the fear of the unknown that causes many of these targets to start crying the moment the FBI explains their dire situation.

And you usually only have one shot to make an impression, which is why agents like Kang and Makol are so valuable. The Galleon investigation had now become a top priority not just at the SEC but also at the Justice Department, and its intensity and focus were largely a secret outside of the circle of law enforcement officials toiling twelve to eighteen hours to develop evidence. The risk in trying to flip someone like Khan is her loyalty to her circle of friends, whom she might alert and thus damage the case.

Kang's skill was in breaking that loyalty. Kang spent days preparing how to make his approach, or as one colleague put it "B. J. made night and day into one." He had seen all the reactions from white-collar criminals. Some just sit there and sweat as the reality of being caught sets in. Some faint; others lose control over their bowels and beg for mercy (in that order, FBI agents tell me), while still others calmly assess their options. One thing *most* of them have in common is an absolute willingness to do anything necessary to keep themselves out of jail.

But the decision to cooperate almost never comes easily with white-collar criminals. Mob suspects accept being caught as the price of their business. With the death of the conspiracy of silence known as *omertà*, they calmly accept proffers and witness protection. Being a mob rat doesn't quite carry the same stigma as it did years ago, particularly when everyone is doing it.

Not so in the white-collar world. Here government investigators discovered a certain lack of self-awareness about the nature of their illegal acts, and their consequences. Most consider themselves good people—no matter how much they lie, cheat, and steal. Others think that they're merely rubbing up against the line between what's legal and illegal, while others know they've crossed over and into the dark side but think they're too smart to get caught.

It's arrogance that lands them in jail—that and misplaced trust in the equally untrustworthy people with whom they're committing illegal acts. And when they're caught, the objective is to show how their world has fallen apart—particularly when a B. J. Kang explains how they might be spending some significant time in prison with some of the more undesirable people in the world.

Kang decided that the direct approach with Khan would work best: He would just lay out the evidence at hand, namely all those IMs with Rajaratnam that looked pretty sleazy, and the money she was making from her secret dealings. And scare the hell out of her with threats of jail time since she was a second-time offender.

Repeat offenders can spend more than a decade in prison—particularly those who make a lot of money breaking the law, which is the category Khan would find herself in. Galleon made millions off the Hilton Trade but Khan didn't do so badly herself, making a quick $600,000 by purchasing shares of the company just prior to the Blackstone takeover. And that was just the beginning.

Roomy Khan lived in a $13 million mansion in an exclusive Silicon Valley gated enclave known as Atherton. Kang would later describe the home as a "sprawling palace," with large walls surrounding it. So this is what you get for making six hundred thousand dollars on a single trade, Kang thought, as he approached the residence with another FBI agent, Kathleen Queally. If you combined both agents' government salaries, they wouldn't earn half as much as Khan and her circle did with just that one piece of insider information on the Hilton trade. It's hard to believe that the inequality of their situation was lost on either of them as they approached her front door.

But there was more to Khan's story than her expensive home, as Kang and his partner's research had discovered. True, she and her husband lived richly (her husband, Sakhawat Khan, was an engineer who had thirty patents under his name for chip designs), but they seemed to have run through much of their wealth.

In other words, Rajaratnam, the billionaire, might have the will and the financial means to fight, but odds were that Roomy Khan, knowing her financial situation and how much jail time she would face, would have compelling reasons for becoming the most important witness in the Galleon probe and perhaps the most important witness in the government's long crackdown on insider trading.

At least that was their bet as they rang Khan's doorbell and a woman with dark hair and brooding eyes answered.

"Roomy Khan?" Kang asked.

"Yes, that's me," she answered.

"I'm Agent Kang and this is Agent Queally of the FBI. . . . We need to talk."

Khan's response only added to the suspense. "What took you so long?" she said before letting both agents into her spacious home.

CHAPTER 7

THE FLIP

Any government hopes that Roomy Khan could immediately be flipped from conspirator to cooperating witness were quickly dashed. Khan, of course, had seen this drill before. It had been six years ago that she had secretly agreed to cooperate against Rajaratnam in return for her own freedom. So she knew that in order to score a no-jail deal this time around she would have to provide the feds with much more than just dirt on the Galleon boss.

As Kang entered her home he immediately got down to work. He told Khan she had been caught trading on inside information. They had plenty of evidence and if she went to trial she would be going as a two-time loser, given her past record. If she wanted to avoid serious jail time, she needed to cooperate.

As Khan listened, Kang further explained the crimes they were certain Khan had committed: passing insider tips to Rajaratnam on various stocks including companies like Polycom, Hilton Hotels, Google, and probably a lot more through her well-maintained source network in the Silicon Valley tech community.

Kang described to her the intercepted instant messages and how they provided enough evidence to arrest her almost on the spot. Then he emphasized that since she was a two-time offender, what she faced if she went to trial and lost—which is what happens, they explained, to more than 90 percent of those indicted for various white-collar crimes—was years in jail.

"I'm a consultant," she initially and almost defiantly explained in response. She never mentioned her business relationship with Rajaratnam, just that they were friends. Her communications with the billionaire about stocks were merely Rajaratnam's attempt at being "nice" to her, she said.

Khan explained that she had worked for Galleon in the past, tried unsuccessfully to get rehired a few years back, but a mutual friendship built over a love of trading stocks and a common ancestry continued. And she wasn't that rich, she told Kang. Despite her big home, cars, and swimming pool she and her husband had hit a rough patch financially (the full embarrassing details would come out later, including underpaying her maid and possibly violating state labor laws). Khan pointed to the five computers and six telephone lines in her home. She explained how she went to conferences and company road shows in order to do her job as a consultant and a trader for a company called Trivium Capital Management.

The information she passed along to Rajaratnam and others was not stolen from companies, as is insider information of the illegal type. Rather, she maintained, she was merely doing what a good reporter does: talking to a lot of people at these public events and passing along what she heard. Mainly what she had been passing along to Rajaratnam was "broker chatter."

Her explanation hardly impressed Kang, who knew full well that insider tips are often passed around at such venues, and was convinced that Khan was someone who feasted from this underworld of sleaze (as her lifestyle, including the $13 million, 9,000-square-foot mansion he was sitting in, made evident).

The FBI's experience with cooperating witnesses is good but not perfect. No real statistics exist on recidivism among bad guys who turn stool pigeon and provide information, but the general consensus is that when most people are given a second chance to start a new life after a life of crime they go on the straight and narrow.

But there are always a few who don't. Sammy "the Bull" Gravano infamously became a drug dealer after cutting a deal in order to put away for life someone the feds considered a bigger criminal: John Gotti. In return, Gravano avoided a long jail sentence for murder and racketeering. Gravano, friends would say, yearned for the gangster life.

Likewise, it seemed like Roomy Khan had never gotten insider trading out of her blood. She was well sourced inside Silicon Valley, particularly among the burgeoning South Asian community, which, government officials believed, acted no differently than past immigrant groups—that is, being insular and chatty with people they consider their own.

It didn't hurt that Khan had the intellectual aptitude to game the system as long as she had. She was well educated, having graduated with a degree in physics and a master's degree in engineering from Columbia University. Combining that with her contacts in the hedge fund world, she was able to move effortlessly between the high-tech world of Silicon Valley and the trading desks of Wall Street, where knowledge of companies and their inner workings often translates into big money.

Put it all together and Kang, along with the rest of the federal investigators assigned to the Galleon case, believed that Kahn had, like Gravano, returned to a life of crime. One key difference, of course, was that Roomy Khan didn't commit murder or sell drugs. So giving her another chance to set things right seemed appropriate.

Not that Kang emphasized just how palatable the government found the prospect of letting her go once again. In fact, he did just the opposite, reiterating to Khan in no uncertain terms how ready he, the FBI, and the U.S. Justice Department were prepared to put her in jail for a long time.

To emphasize his point, as the meeting continued, he showed Khan what he considered one of the more incriminating IMs, dated January 9, 2006, where she appears to have told Rajaratnam that she needed to get back to her sources inside the company for guidance about when he should trade Polycom, a technology company that manufactures videoconferencing equipment and trades under the symbol PLCM.

"donot buy plcm till i (get) guidance; want to make sure guidance OK," the IM stated.

Of course, the notion of "guidance" could mean a lot. For example, she could be doing her "channel checks," a key component of the mosaic theory where analysts check with various sources of legal information—other analysts and market participants, not necessarily those with insider information—to confirm their mosaic investment thesis.

Or she could be utilizing her network of friends inside the Silicon Valley tech community to find out confidential information about the company, as Kang and the Justice Department believed. Khan said that wasn't the case. She told Kang she was no longer speaking to corporate insiders "because of the trouble she got into with the FBI several years ago."

Kang wasn't buying it and kept pressing. He asked about the IMs regarding her trading of shares of Hilton before its purchase by Blackstone. She responded that she bought the shares of Hilton not because of any insider tip but because the publicity surrounding Paris Hilton going to jail for violating the terms of her probation was somehow good for the stock. It had nothing to do with advance knowledge of Blackstone's purchase.

As the interview entered its second hour, Kang's relentless questioning was taking a toll. Khan was growing increasingly nervous and agitated with each and every question that Kang just kept hammering away with, sprinkled with more than an occasional reminder about how much time she could be spending in prison if he were forced to charge her.

He later recounted to associates that the interview was a "rollercoaster ride" that lasted two hours and that Khan must have lied to him "a thousand and one times" during the meeting, before the wear and tear of having stern-faced FBI agents in her living room calling her a crook finally hit her in full.

That was when Roomy Khan began to cry.

"I know, I know, I'm going to jail if I don't cooperate," she said in a state of panic.

"So what will it be?" Kang asked. "Jail or cooperation?"

"I have to cooperate," she said, sobbing at the prospect of going to jail and giving up her lifestyle and all the accoutrements that her circle of friends had provided.

"She's in the right place," was the word Kang relayed to Wadhwa just minutes after he had finished with the first of what would turn out to be many interviews with Roomy Khan during the next six months, as a precursor to her full cooperation against the government's primary target: Raj Rajaratnam.

Wadhwa deserved the first of many calls since the case was his as much as anyone's on the government's payroll. The former tax attorney had now earned a coveted status among the top investigators at the SEC. He was the guy the FBI called to describe the progress of high-level cases, not the other way around. Khan's initial lies during the interview were, as far as Kang was concerned, enough to put her away. (Remember, Martha Stewart went to jail for lying to investigators looking into suspicious trading, not because she was caught in the act.) But that would have to wait. Kang needed to touch base with his supervisors and come up with an official cooperation agreement to exchange evidence and testimony for leniency that Khan's attorneys would sign off on, thus leading to the final step: a wiretap that would snare Raj Rajaratnam once and for all.

The late fall of 2007 was a momentous month on Wall Street, though it had nothing to do with Kang's progress in making Raj Rajaratnam the white-collar version of public enemy number one. That's when three of the biggest chief executives on Wall Street, Stan O'Neal of the big brokerage firm Merrill Lynch, Chuck Prince of mega-bank Citigroup, and Martin Sullivan of insurance giant American International Group (AIG), resigned from their posts as it was revealed that they were part of a very different frenzy from the one that had transfixed the regulatory community at this time.

Each had played a role in the mania of risk-taking that in less than a year would upend the financial system, causing Wall Street firms Lehman Brothers and Bear Stearns to go broke. Those that remained managed to survive thanks to government bailouts.

The ousting of the big three CEOs were the initial shock waves of that cataclysmic event known as the Great Financial Crisis of 2008. Merrill and Citigroup were once supercharged companies that had feasted on risk for years, basically by underwriting and holding countless billions in faulty real estate investments that were worth just pennies on the dollar as the economy sank and the valuation of formerly overpriced housing began to reflect the economic climate. AIG's sin was that it had insured all that risk (primarily through writing financial instruments known as *credit default swaps*) despite not having enough money to cover these pending bills.

All firms would require some degree of government assistance to survive the eventual tumult along with the rest of the big banks, transforming what was initially a mild recession into a financial cataclysm that in many respects hasn't fully ended. Indeed, as I write this, the Treasury Department is finishing up its sale of the AIG stock it took in return for the bailout (at an eventual profit to the government), the Federal Reserve is debating whether to continue propping up the economy through what economists term *quantitative easing,* and the newly reelected President Obama and Republicans in Congress debate what to do about the government's sad fiscal state, which is due in large part to the enormous amount of spending undertaken in attempts to ameliorate the economic pain of the recession.

But more than the countless billions of dollars of taxpayer money used to bail out the banks (plus the billions more in higher taxes to come) is the human cost of their recklessness. Millions of people out of work; banks not extending credit to small businesses or to home buyers; new and costly regulations put in place to prevent another banking collapse; regulations that have sapped the industry of much of its growth and job creation. If you think Wall Street bankers in five-thousand-dollar suits are the only ones squeezed by these new rules, consider the impact outsourcing and layoffs have had on back-office personnel and other jobs held by average, hardworking people at the big banks.

The great risk-taking of Wall Street and the banks went unnoticed for years. In fact, it went unnoticed largely even after the system was showing its first signs of a collapse in November 2007. One of the great truisms of regulation is that the regulators rarely catch the scams and the overindulgence until it is too late to do anything about it. The reasons for this ineptitude vary, though many Wall Street experts pin it on the experience of the typical SEC enforcement agent, who is long on legal theory (most have gone to law school) but short on financial knowledge.

But that rationale is an overstatement. Sanjay Wadhwa and his team of investigators were well-schooled in the ways of Wall Street and could read a balance sheet as well as many a Wall Street analyst. There was just one problem: While the excessive risk-taking that led to the 2008 financial crisis was taking place, Wadhwa and his team were busy cracking down on insider trading, as were their counterparts in the various white-collar crime units at the FBI and the Justice Department.

It's ironic that Kang himself made only a slight detour as one of the arresting officers of Ponzi schemer Bernard Madoff, though it was hardly a highlight of his career. The person who should be credited is Madoff himself. He had called the feds in December 2008 (just about a year after Kang made his initial introduction to Roomy Khan) to turn himself in as his scheme fell apart. That's because big investors began pulling money out of his fund while Madoff was unable to find new investors amid the unfolding financial crisis.

Madoff, of course, operated illegally for twenty years while government investigators, concluded on several occasions that he ran a clean operation—this despite numerous clues and complaints that he was running a scam. One of the ironies of the government's Madoff fumble is that investigators failed to use their own logic when confronted with insider trading. Steady returns that beat the market over extended stretches of time are strong signals that cheating is taking place.

In retrospect, some people in the Justice Department and the Securities and Exchange Commission say it was a manpower problem—they didn't have enough people to look at *everything* and catch Madoff. Yet, through 2007 and 2008, there was no vast shifting of manpower and resources from the Rajaratnam case either at the SEC or the FBI to crack down on any of the major financial crisis frauds.

The reason? "The insider trading case just looked way too sexy for us to change course," was how one regulatory official put it.

Yes, it was "sexy" (to regulators, at least) but was trying to catch Raj Rajaratnam trading a stock with insider tips worth ignoring some of the biggest financial catastrophes in a generation?

Neither the FBI nor the SEC seemed to care as they began assigning additional resources to what they considered the crime of the century.

Most people think of the FBI as a well-oiled machine, run with an iron fist by an all-knowing director in the tradition of the agency's founder, the legendary J. Edgar Hoover. The reality is that the FBI is like any other government bureaucracy. Activities aren't always coordinated; fiefdoms develop and interoffice rivalries over resources and credit for cracking the big cases are common.

By late 2007, two of the most senior supervisors in the FBI's white-collar division were engaged in just such a rivalry inside the FBI's New York headquarters, at Foley Square.

One of the teams was run by a supervising agent named Richard Jacobs, an aggressive man with a Marine crew cut who talked with the rapid-fire cadence of a drill sergeant. Jacobs was familiar with the workings of Wall Street. He had been a banker for six years before joining the FBI in 1999. According to a profile by Reuters, in his role as a special agent, Jacobs had even posed undercover as a stockbroker to break up an investment scam.

The Jacobs team, known as C-1 inside the FBI's office, included B. J. Kang. Its main objective starting in mid-2007 was nailing Galleon chief Raj Rajaratnam by completing a deal with Roomy Khan.

The other was led by David Chaves, who ran a team known as C-35. Chaves's experience was more diverse than Jacobs's. Chaves began his FBI career busting drug cartels and learning the fine points about wiretapping targets. Wiretaps are commonly used in drug and mob-related investigations, which prepared him for the next step in his career as he focused on criminal rings in the white-collar world.

His group broke up the Babcock-Guttenberg-Franklin circle—the insider trading ring that will go down in history for passing along payoffs in Doritos bags, and exposing just how entrenched the practice had become at major Wall Street firms as well as in the blossoming hedge fund business.

Its counterweight to B. J. Kang was special agent David Makol, also a specialist in the art of getting bad guys in the white-collar world to flip and provide evidence against bigger bad guys.

Any rivalry between the two teams was tempered by a shared vision that Wall Street had become a cesspool of illegality where the passing of insider tips was commonplace. They also shared something else, even as they worked on different cases: a desire to nail the biggest case out there.

Both Chaves and Jacobs developed their approach to insider trading from long years in the trenches of white-collar crime. In addition to bringing down the Doritos gang, Chaves had led the team that worked on the Martha Stewart case and understood how inside information eventually makes its way from within the corporation to a trading desk and quick profits.

Wall Street had certainly come a long way since the days of Martha Stewart. In just five short years, investigators discovered, the number of hedge funds had exploded, as did their trading profits. Chaves researched the returns of some of the biggest. Both SAC and Galleon were on his list and he saw something that defied common sense: They both made money nearly each and every year and had been doing that for years. The 2007 Babcock-Franklin-Guttenberg circle of friends—Chaves liked to call them *clusters*—confirmed his worst fears about Wall Street and the hedge fund business and their use of illegal information for profits. The clusters were more like a hydra-headed monster with its tentacles spread from Wall Street to hedge funds to law firms, any place where nonpublic information can be found and illegally acted upon.

Yet when these players were caught and the fear of long jail sentences hit home, they fell like dominoes, or to be more precise, they reminded him of the famous scene at the end of Quentin Tarantino's movie *Reservoir Dogs*, when all the bad guys pull guns on each other and shoot one another dead. His goal was to get more dominoes.

Indeed, to break up the bigger rings that he knew existed, Chaves needed someone else, someone higher up the Wall Street food chain who would give him access to the bigger world of Wall Street's version of organized crime—the insider trading conspiracy that he was convinced was much larger than anything law enforcement had seen in a very long time.

Chaves is known inside the FBI as the "velvet fist," for his ability to squeeze a lot of information from witnesses in the nicest possible way. He was fond of saying that "if people want to change their life, we're here to help."

He was also known for his devotion to the broad ideological approach of the federal law enforcement bureaucracy toward investigating the white-collar crime of insider trading. To Chaves insider trading was a pox on the free market system, and if not prosecuted and held in check, it will destroy the public's confidence in the markets.

For most investigators looking into the activity, the *pure evil* of insider trading is a given. There isn't much debate assessing how much time should be devoted to ridding the world of the practice or whether the agency's resources could be deployed to fight more dangerous crimes, where the victims are more tangible than the "market" or "market confidence."

All of which might be heartening news for the Ponzi schemers like Bernie Madoff, who ripped off investors and charities for nearly two decades, but bad for those who appeared on the FBI insider-trading watch list.

Chaves and Makol applied one of the FBI's best good cop, bad cop acts in the business, converting hardened insider traders into true believers in their cause—none more devout and successful at breaking up illegal trading clusters than a veteran Wall Street trader named David Slaine.

By 2007 David Slaine was one of those Wall Street legends who barely made it into the press. He was quoted every so often about market gyrations, particularly when he ran the Nasdaq trading desk for Morgan Stanley during the mid to late 1990s.

He made a short item on the news wires when in 1998 he left Morgan and joined Galleon Group as a founding partner. Similarly he made wire service news when he was suspended for ninety days from the securities industry along with a handful of other traders for manipulating stocks in the Nasdaq index through the trading of options while he was still at Morgan, which in the world of Wall Street is like getting a traffic ticket for speeding through a red light. It wasn't acceptable behavior, but it wasn't career killing, either.

As with many traders on Wall Street, to Slaine the burgeoning and lightly regulated hedge fund business represented the endless potential to make money. While at Morgan, Slaine had told friends he wanted to get on the "buy side," Wall Street slang for working at a hedge fund (the term applies to the primary objective of funds to "buy" securities and invest. Conversely, working at the big Wall Street banks is known as the "sell side" since their primary function is to sell those securities).

The reason was quite obvious to anyone who knew him: He wanted to make the really big bucks that hedge funds were shelling out, particularly to people like himself who had the connections to make the right trades.

The big Wall Street banks, with their large compliance staffs, made risk-taking more difficult, while hedge funds were all about taking risk and keeping lots of the profits on successful trades. Hedge funds also rewarded traders with friends who could provide expert guidance on the next merger opportunity or earnings call. The traders and the firm they worked at regarded these confidential tips as nothing more than business as usual.

Slaine's connection to Galleon wasn't its charismatic founder, Raj Rajaratnam, but Gary Rosenbach, Rajaratnam's right-hand man, and who, like Slaine, was a veteran trader. Slaine left Galleon in 2001 after what was later described as a somewhat tumultuous three-year stint. At the time no reason was given, and considering the amount of movement around the hedge fund business it was totally acceptable for traders to leave one shop, including an established place like Galleon, to venture out to an even smaller place where they could keep a bigger percentage of their earnings. People who know Slaine said he and Rajaratnam had remained friendly even after he left the firm. His real falling out was with Rosenbach, his friend and immediate boss. Some of the details are in dispute, but later Slaine would say he was uncomfortable with the firm's business practices, including its use of inside information

Not so uncomfortable that Slaine wouldn't eventually dabble in it himself. He left Galleon to start his own hedge fund with two traders who had left SAC Capital. The fund dissolved for performance reasons, and then after bouncing around a bit Slaine landed at a hedge fund known as Chelsey Capital, the same Chelsey Capital where Erik Franklin had worked when he was busted for insider trading in 2007.

Slaine was there for only a short stint, less than a year beginning in February 2002, before ultimately setting out on his own, using his connections to both hedge funds and the Wall Street banking business to manage money. And he had largely dropped out of sight except for several honorable mentions in a book about the Wall Street trading culture, *The Other Side of Wall Street*, written by Todd Harrison, a former trader turned financial website entrepreneur. Slaine was described as a tough but fair trader who loved the action of "the desk" as much as he loved working out. Harrison also described Slaine as someone who understood at least some of Wall Street's dark side; it's a place where many of your friends exist as long as you help make them money.

With his muscular physique and blue-collar Boston accent, David Slaine was an intimidating presence even on Wall Street trading floors. People who know him say he came from fairly humble beginnings on the Wall Street scale where many of its highest paid people attend private academies and Ivy League colleges.

Those close to Slaine describe him as a product of a broken home, in middle class Malden, a suburb of Boston (voted in 2009 as the "Best place to raise your kids," by *Bloomberg Businessweek*). He was a standout high school athlete, and later attended Clark University in Worcester not far from where he grew up. He was known to his many friends as "Slaineo," for reasons that no one seemed to recall, but it sounded cool and didn't annoy Slaine. In fact, for a legendary hothead, Slaine had many friends. He earned his way to the big investment bank Morgan Stanley because he was a gifted trader; he would eventually run the firm's trading desk that specialized in technology stocks, just in time for the tech bubble of the mid to late 1990s.

Morgan Stanley, thanks to its star Internet analyst Mary Meeker, had cranked out huge profits underwriting and trading technology stocks, and Slaine was in the middle of the action. When Slaine first got to Wall Street in the early 1990s he barely had enough money to make rent. One person who knows him said he "slept on a mattress in his living room" because he couldn't afford the entire bed.

That soon changed. He was now rich, earning millions of dollars a year, becoming a legend at the firm all while developing a deep network of contacts across Wall Street given his position at one of the financial world's power centers.

For Slaine, however, it wasn't all about making money. These same people say he took young traders under his wing and aided them in their careers. One of those was Harrison, as the two bonded over stocks and lifting weights.

Another one was a fellow weight lifter named Craig Drimal, whom Slaine brought with him as a trading assistant when he moved from Morgan Stanley to Galleon Group in 1998, his first foray into the lucrative but high-pressure hedge fund business. Unlike Harrison, Drimal would figure prominently in Slaine's new career as an FBI informant.

By the time Harrison released his book in 2011, David Slaine had been a key witness in the government's ever-growing insider trading crackdown for about five years. Ironically, Slaine's involvement in the probe had little to do with his time at Galleon and much to do with his purported reason for leaving the fund.

Slaine's name surfaced with the FBI with its piercing of the Babcock-Franklin-Guttenberg insider trading ring in 2007. Slaine had left Chelsey a few years earlier but Franklin had a pretty good recollection of what he had done in the past, namely trade on insider tips.

Franklin and another cooperating witness told Chaves and Makol that Slaine dabbled in the same inside information received from Guttenberg's UBS pipeline of analyst recommendations as they had done, trading profitably on the upgrades and the downgrades before they were made public. His trades were relatively small, and not as frequent as the others. But he was far from innocent, they said. Slaine even used the tips to trade on his personal account.

The scheme, of course, was pretty simple, and to Chaves it underscored just how much easy money could be made through insider trading, Wall Street's version of a crystal ball. Guttenberg would tell Franklin when UBS was ready to upgrade a stock, so he could start buying shares before the public announcement. Just before the downgrades were about to hit the tape they "shorted" those shares, and profited from the decline that occurred once the ratings were publicly announced. It was such easy money, anyone with a computer and a lack of morals could do it.

They pointed Chaves to Slaine's trading in a technology company called Nvidia in November 2002. Slaine, who ran Morgan Stanley's Nasdaq trading desk, was familiar with the company since it traded on the tech-heavy exchange. A good "tape reader" might be able to figure out when to buy and sell for a profit.

But that's not how Slaine was doing it. Instead, he followed Guttenberg's tip: A UBS downgrade was coming the next day. Slaine and Franklin quickly shorted the stock. After the downgrade, they covered their position for quick profits on a 200,000 share position.

Franklin helped refer the government to more than twenty trades Slaine made using the UBS insider tips. A little arithmetic showed that Slaine made as much as $500,000 from this circle of friends alone.

In Chaves's opinion, they had probably only scratched the surface—though the more thorough investigation seemed to suggest that Slaine wasn't a serial insider trader, particularly compared to others now being targeted in the probe. Still, his résumé suggested he knew *a lot* about Wall Street's dark side. Based on all the places Slaine worked, it reeked of the type of information-sharing clusters that Chaves now believed existed at every major hedge fund.

Slaine had worked on Wall Street for about twenty years and he traded at major firms like Morgan Stanley and at Galleon—so he covered the highest levels of Wall Street and hedge funds. He brushed shoulders with traders who worked everywhere, including Cohen's SAC Capital.

Government agents began digging into Slaine's background. While his record wasn't exactly spotless, he had stayed off the regulators' radar grid, which was a plus since he couldn't be fingered as a possible cooperator. By early 2007 Slaine's net worth was estimated at tens of millions of dollars, though he didn't live lavishly by the standards of a very above-average trader. He did charity work for poor people in the Bronx, and playing off his affinity for dogs, he even started a charity to find homes for retired police dogs. He had an Upper East Side Manhattan residence, and a summer home in the Hamptons.

He continued to lift weights and trade and was a devoted father.

Unlike many other rich Manhattanites, he wasn't very politically active; campaign contribution records show he gave money to Connecticut Senator Joe Lieberman, "probably because someone asked him," said one friend.

Government investigators, meanwhile, did a little more research and found that Slaine had formerly worked briefly at a hedge fund called CJS Partners, which he had opened with former SAC traders. The feds had long concluded that most of the roads in the insider trading road map involved some connections to SAC even if investigators still couldn't come up with the evidence to bring charges.

In other words, they believed Slaine was the prototype of the modern insider trader with an extensive network of contacts, both on Wall Street and at major hedge funds (thanks to being at Galleon, he had the taint of working for what the feds considered the ultimate dirty shop). If the witnesses could be believed, he had a massive circle of friends who feasted on insider tips.

Slaine appeared smart enough to disguise his trades, for sure, never getting too greedy by placing such a large bet that it would stand out on the regulators' computer screens. He only dealt with people he trusted—or thought could be trusted.

He was, to Chaves's mind, the perfect cooperating witness.

Knowing what he knew about Slaine, however, Chaves couldn't discount the possibility that upon approach the trader might have an urge to fight—literally. Slaine seemed like the type of guy who might take a swing when told he was a crook. That is, of course, unless he were confronted by an agent of equal size, strength, and seriousness, which is exactly what Chaves had in mind.

David Makol had been with the FBI for ten years. He came from the SEC, where he worked in the examinations unit, and made use of his background in forensic accounting. He ultimately moved to the FBI, where he immediately began to work on white-collar crime, specializing in insider trading.

Makol had been on Chaves's squad since at least 2002, working on the Martha Stewart case as well as one involving former Goldman Sachs and Merrill Lynch brokers who enticed a forklift driver to get them advance copies of a market-moving column from *BusinessWeek* magazine.

Despite his pedigree, Makol, at just over six feet in height, can be an intimidating presence, particularly with his FBI badge in his hand, which according to people who have been subject to some of his methods, can make him seem three inches taller. He can be blunt in explaining to targets what they face if they don't cooperate: lots of jail time that will change their lives forever and damage the people they love.

According to people with firsthand knowledge of his tactics, Makol has been known to squeeze every last piece of information from cooperators and to use every mental trick at his disposal. At times, he plays good cop to his colleagues' bad cop. Or depending on the situation, Makol simply plays bad cop. FBI officials describe Makol as a tireless worker and consummate professional who is skillful at one of the most difficult jobs in law enforcement: getting criminals to give up their lives of crime.

"An asshole," was how one person with firsthand knowledge of Makol's methods describes him. His main tactic, though, is surprise. Makol is most effective when he catches the target doing something ordinary—getting a bagel or sitting at a restaurant and then shocking the person into submission. Being told while you're walking your dog that you're going to jail both underscores that your life as you know it is about to change dramatically unless you cooperate and also ensures that you have no time to prepare yourself for the psychological and emotional onslaught.

Makol did his homework on Slaine. He knew he was a trading desk legend based on the issues with his temper—the trading desk fights, including one allegedly over whether a colleague stole some of his french fries, and another when he allegedly coldcocked his friend and supervisor at Galleon, Gary Rosenbach, while they sat in the sauna after a grueling day of trading.

The truth of both incidents was more complicated, and they shed further light on Slaine's complex personality, friends say.

The fight at Morgan was less about french fries and more about a long-simmering feud with a coworker of equal size and heft. One day they were discussing a client matter in a conference room when all hell broke loose. "I was in the room next door and I thought they were about to crash through the wall," said one person with firsthand knowledge of the incident. That person and five others soon broke up the melee.

As for the other fistfight, Slaine clearly lost his temper with Rosenbach, who was pressuring him on his performance and, as Slaine would say later, something more troubling. The two were once close friends and accustomed to speaking freely with each other, though Slaine had been under tremendous pressure at work to churn out bigger returns, as just about everyone was at Galleon or any hedge fund in the business. That pressure came primarily from Rosenbach who "continually gave David shit," according to one person with knowledge of the matter.

After they finished working out one afternoon and both were seated in a steam room, Rosenbach began taunting Slaine once again. According to friends and supported by a *Bloomberg* News report, Slaine would later tell the FBI that his anger was fueled when Rajaratnam bet against a stock he was holding using insider information, but Rosenbach's demeanor angered him further. At one point, during the encounter, Rosenbach put his hand up to Slaine's face; Slaine responded by slapping it away and slapping Rosenbach's face as well.

The altercation revealed something else about Slaine: He may have been a crook, but at least initially he was a somewhat reluctant one, who used insider trading not simply to make a lot of money, but because he had to in order to keep his job. Something else made Slaine flippable. Friends recalled that Slaine's attitude toward the business was more cynical than anything else. In his mind it was a business where friendships didn't matter; when you leave a place like Morgan Stanley or a big hedge fund like Galleon and you need a favor, your friends quickly forget all the favors you have done for them, he told people. Not exactly the type of people you go to jail trying to protect.

Makol and Chaves doubted that a guilty conscience alone would make him switch to the side of the angels. But something else would. They believed they had strong evidence against him that could put him in jail for a long, long time, and of course, the element of surprise. And they planned to use it to rattle a guy who seemed to have the rest of Wall Street rattled for years.

Chaves and Makol had narrowed the best evidence to a series of trades including one involving an insider tip on a UBS upgrade that Slaine used to earn more than $500,000, punishable under the sentencing guidelines by about twenty years in prison.

Makol approached Slaine twice, including a second more extended visit to his apartment a few days after their first encounter on the street. This time Slaine was seated with his wife Elyse, with whom he had just separated, and was attempting reconciliation.

After presenting the evidence, Makol reminded Slaine several times that he faced many years in prison because they had an airtight case, according to people who know Slaine, and said, ominously, "You will probably never see your family and daughter again."

The words about his daughter "scared David" is how one friend put it. Makol underscored his anxiety by asking Slaine to look through the eyes of his daughter—around twelve years of age, with a bright future that would be considerably less bright if her dad were in jail.

"David was going to receive more jail time than for rape," is how one friend described the situation, which isn't that much of an exaggeration. For more than a decade, law enforcement authorities have been steadily ramping up the penalties for various white-collar crimes to the point where they match or even surpass those mandated for violent robberies and rapes. Under the federal guidelines, the maximum sentence for insider trading is nineteen to twenty-four years, while a rapist could get fifteen years to life in prison.

What was most surprising to FBI officials was how easily Slaine flipped when confronted with his actions and the price he would have to pay. There were no histrionics, no crying, and no "Fuck you, I'm innocent" moment, just a quiet resignation that he had been caught, and was ready to make amends.

Slaine's friends offer a different version of Slaine's decision to become a cooperator. According to their accounts, following Makol's second visit, Slaine met with a series of attorneys who explained his options. The case against him was good but not airtight. The witnesses against him, including Erik Franklin, were conflicted individuals, but juries convict people all the time based on evidence supplied by murderers. Franklin had even worn a wire to secretly record Slaine about his trading activities.

And Makol was right about one thing: If he fought and lost, they said, he would lose big. The government would stop at almost nothing to put him in jail for a long time.

In the weeks leading up to the decision, some people who know Slaine say his decision to cooperate was made easier by the advice of his older brother, Mason Slaine, a longtime publishing executive who didn't share his brother's interest in weight lifting, fighting, and stock trading, and instead made his mark, according to the financial website Minyanville, as "a business entrepreneur and private investor."

A Harvard graduate who was once the CEO of Thomson Financial, Mason Slaine was regarded as a man of integrity who wouldn't cheat on his taxes, much less trade on an illegal inside tip. David Slaine is said to admire his brother, and according to one person, it was Mason's influence that finally convinced David to cooperate and get on with his life.

Elyse Slaine has told people that the government's interest in her husband appeared to begin innocuously a few months before the FBI came calling, with an official notification that a few of his trades were being questioned. It was something that David Slaine seemed to take in stride as a routine matter.

Of course, it all depends on your definition of innocuous, as the next five years of Slaine's new life as government informant CS-1 would demonstrate.

• • •

Chaves took a simple approach with potential cooperators. There would be no guarantees on the all-important issue of jail time. But if the witness delivered, so would the FBI. It is, after all, the most important law enforcement agency in the country and maybe the world. And it can make things happen for friends and against foes; at least that's what the statistics show.

Time served in prison for the average insider trading defendant is less than two years, but that's only because so many cooperate. Nearly half of those who cooperate *never* end up in jail. Those who don't cooperate, people like Sam Waksal, often spend more than five years behind bars.

Faced with those odds, Slaine vowed to live up to his end of the bargain and his end, according to the government, was pretty simple: Once he signed on he was compelled to provide the feds with everything he knew about insider trading on Wall Street and doing what they asked him to do to catch the bad guys.

With that, government officials have said, Slaine wasted little time leading them to one of the most important insider trading rings uncovered during Perfect Hedge: a cluster that began with Craig Drimal, his old workout partner. People who know Slaine say Drimal was already on the government's radar. Either way, Slaine pointed to Drimal as a trader, with sources at various places on Wall Street and one who relied on inside information to make a living.

Slaine had mentored Drimal early on and had helped him meet the Galleon brass in the late 1990s. Drimal had been a valuable asset at the hedge fund in part because he was a personal trainer, and he devised workout programs for various Galleon executives. Through the years, Drimal continued as a high-end trainer for hedge fund pros, and in exchange, Galleon allowed him to use its offices to trade stocks. He wasn't an official Galleon employee; people who worked with him directly say he mainly hung out, answered telephone calls for the real traders, and sucked up whatever market insight he could get.

Slaine and Drimal were once close—"Craig idolized David" was how one former Galleon trader described the relationship. But by the time Slaine had become a government witness, their relationship had cooled somewhat. Some people with knowledge of the relationship say a rift developed because Drimal kept borrowing money from Slaine, and over the way Drimal paid it back. Slaine gave Drimal access to his brokerage account so Drimal could repay the money simply by crediting to Slaine any profitable trades he had made. Drimal may have been a good personal trainer, but he often lost money trading and was frequently low in cash, people who know him say.

People close to Drimal say the rift had more to do with the way Slaine left Galleon. His fight with Rosenbach made it impossible for Drimal and Slaine to remain tight, though they continued to remain friendly. Which is why, despite these tensions, government investigators believed Slaine could easily ingratiate himself with Drimal for the greater good of the case, and, of course, for the greater good of avoiding a long jail sentence.

CHAPTER 8

THE FEDS MIGHT BE LISTENING

It is a common misconception that the feds need a court order to put a recording device—known as a *wire*—on a cooperating witness. Not so. The federal law on so-called one-party consent is a loophole in the privacy laws that the government uses with great regularity. It allows the government to have a cooperator clandestinely tape just about any potential target, either by wearing a wire or by having a recording device attached to the cooperator's telephone, with the government listening to every word.

A court order is needed to tap into the conversations of potential targets who are not cooperators, of course, and such decisions to pursue wiretaps have been rare in the pursuit of white-collar crime. (That would change as the insider trading investigation progressed.) But once cooperation is established, one-party consent kicks in, allowing the feds to secretly plant a wire on person A and tape person B without the approval of a federal judge.

Chaves wanted Slaine to be person A.

Chaves began by testing Slaine's dedication to truth and justice with a long debriefing. He asked Slaine to tell him everything he knew about the places he worked, and the people he dealt with, which included traders at both Galleon and SAC Capital. Slaine said, for example, that he had evidence that SAC was the recipient of early word of an analyst downgrade involving Amazon.com. It was among the many tips and leads Slaine would provide investigators over the next three years.

The next step was to send Slaine into the line of fire and have him secretly record and entrap Drimal. Slaine may have introduced Drimal to Wall Street, at Galleon no less, but Drimal was now an experienced trader with access to what Slaine told his FBI handlers was a circle of friends that surpassed anything he had ever assembled.

There's an old saying among FBI agents, often attributed to the legendary federal judge Jack Weinstein, who at ninety-one years of age still presides over a full docket of cases that run the gamut of federal law, from mob murders to class-action lawsuits: "Nothing breaks the bonds of loyalty like the threat of imminent incarceration."

Weinstein was said to have been opining on the facts and circumstances surrounding witness testimony in a mob case. The witness was a former mobster himself, who had finished testifying against a former partner in crime.

In the late fall of 2007, the buzz at FBI New York headquarters in Foley Square was noticeable, and it mostly involved two criminals—Roomy Khan and David Slaine—who, agents claimed, had "found religion." In other words they decided, when faced with imminent and lengthy incarceration and two FBI units racing to come up with the insider trading case of the century, to out their circle of friends.

The internal competition was said to be fierce between the two FBI groups assigned to the insider trading probe—C-35 run by Chaves and Makol, and C-1 run by Jacobs and Kang. Prosecutors could feel the tension during meetings where both teams were present, with each side trying to take credit for an advance in the investigation. Chaves bristled when he saw in the press that the Galleon investigation was also being referred to as Operation Perfect Hedge, the name he had come up with for the probe that he and Makol were running. He alerted the FBI's press office to begin correcting the record.

In the race to make white-collar law enforcement history, Jacobs and Kang held the early lead. For now, the case against Rengan Rajaratnam was set aside. That's because agents were focusing on his older, richer, and more corrupt brother and the hedge fund empire he had created. Much of the Raj Rajaratnam case centered on what Roomy Khan could bring. She was well on her way to offering full cooperation in the investigation, while the feds were taking their first steps in getting the necessary court approval to tap Rajaratnam's cell phone, over which, they believed, he conducted the vast majority of his information gathering for his various insider trading schemes.

Sanjay Wadhwa at the SEC wasn't far from the action, either. He had been promoted and attained a new status as a team leader, someone his supervisors had looked up to when it came to complex cases. He had also done something else: He convinced the FBI that not all SEC investigators are dumb.

There has been friction between the FBI and the SEC that dates back to the 1980s cases. The SEC believed the FBI glommed on to the commission's work and got all the headlines for arrests and convictions. The FBI simply believed the SEC would screw up any case.

Kang saw Wadhwa as a partner, and vice versa.

Once Khan was cooperating, it was up to the bureau and the Southern District prosecutors to get as much information from her as possible—and figure out, at least in her case, what was fact or fiction. She said she was working for a hedge fund, Trivium Capital Management, where she was buying and selling stocks on tips she received from Rajaratnam and her circle of friends, including a money manager named Doug Whitman, who lived in a nearby mansion.

Whitman's hedge fund, Whitman Capital, wasn't the powerhouse that Galleon had become, but they shared a similar trait. Whitman was said to have had one knockout year, and in order to keep his returns up and keep the investor money from fleeing, he became an expert in trading on insider information. As he explained it to Khan one day, "What value do you have if you're not a slimeball?"

Khan took Whitman's advice. She earned close to $350,000 that year, she confessed, by trading on these tips. She described her relationship with Rajaratnam as part friendship and part business. The friendship part stemmed from a common ancestry. The business part was all about insider trading. She was a key member of Rajaratnam's inner circle, giving him information on stocks she had an "edge on," which was market slang for inside information.

She didn't come clean at least initially about the Hilton trade and stuck to her tale that it was the press attention and increased investor focus on the company's stock after Paris Hilton's legal issues that prompted her well-timed decision to buy shares rather than advance knowledge of the Blackstone takeover.

But her story finally unraveled in April 2008 when she confessed that the trade had had nothing to do with Paris Hilton and everything to do with Khan's own circle of friends. She got her edge on the stock, she finally conceded, through a junior analyst named Deep Shah, who was a friend and a roommate of her cousin, and then shared the edge with Rajaratnam

Shah worked at Moody's Investor Service, the big ratings agency, which had advance knowledge of the $26 billion unannounced takeover. Khan paid Shah roughly $10,000 a tip, in an arrangement where the money would be funneled through her cousin.

The lies continued to pile up as Kang debriefed Roomy Khan. Kang discovered she had deleted emails on issues that involved the investigation (in other words, had destroyed evidence) and began using a new cell phone so she could speak to Deep Shah about the circumstances of the investigation into the Hilton trade, before she came clean with the truth.

She lied about where she received inside information on shares of Cisco, pointing to Doug Whitman when in reality it was someone else.

Whitman, she told investigators, would exchange insider tips with her on other stocks, which made her lying seem even more absurd. Khan wouldn't fess up to the totality of these misdeeds until after six sessions with the FBI and the Justice Department, and only *after* she began working for the bureau sharing inside information with Rajaratnam while the FBI quietly listened.

If the feds had a second thought about using such a conflicted person—a convicted felon, no less—in the pursuit of someone who wasn't even an alleged felon, they didn't show it. In the end, she just knew too much about too many people they wanted to see in jail more than her.

The act of wiretapping involved the use of an "extraordinary investigatory device," because the courts have held that it places an "invisible policeman" at the scene of an alleged crime, sweeping into his path not only the guilty but the innocent as well.

It's unlike wearing a wire because it invades privacy more directly than by, say, a taped meeting between an informant and a target at a place of doing business. The cell phone is personal property, and a wiretap records all conversations on it, both those germane to the investigation and those purely personal. Because of that, the courts have set a high standard for using phone wiretaps, largely permitting them in extreme circumstances involving organized crime (or terrorism) where either life or death is on the line and/or the conventional law enforcement tools to break up these conspiracies are limited and ineffectual.

Any wiretap application must meet the legal standard that it is complete, in that all known materially important information should be included so a judge can determine if the wiretap is necessary. Probable cause—the notion that the government has good reason to believe the wiretap will uncover illegal activity—is a given.

Lauren Goldberg and B. J. Kang knew they needed a wiretap on Rajaratnam's cell phone, for several reasons. Just taping the calls Khan placed to him wouldn't uncover his larger circle of friends. Rajaratnam may have liked Roomy Khan enough to trade information with her, but not enough to give up his information pipeline.

And Rajaratnam, they believed, may not fall for an in-person meeting to share information with Khan, since all they did was speak over the telephone. It would have been a red flag, a reason for him to clam up and possibly finger Khan as a cooperator if she broke from her routine and showed up at Galleon's New York offices.

In 2008, wiretapping was still a rarity when it came to white-collar targets. Title III of the Federal Wiretap Act was adopted in 1968 and expanded in the coming years, mostly to crack organized crime and terrorism rings, not circles of friends involving insider trading.

That detail would prove to be a weakness at trial. Attorneys for Rajaratnam would undoubtedly make the case that when Congress passed Title III, it specifically *excluded* white-collar crime because such a direct invasion of privacy was meant for only the most heinous of illegal activities, including murder committed by criminal organizations. Insider trading was far from murder, they would argue, and Galleon wasn't the Mafia.

It wouldn't end there. Wall Street might be sleazy, but it's a heavily regulated industry, thus hardly impenetrable. Rajaratnam's lawyers would try to show that the government hadn't exhausted other investigative tools. As proof, Roomy Khan was still helping them with the Rajaratnam case, with a recording device on her telephone that didn't need a court order since she was already cooperating.

Even so, the courts have been slowly warming to an expansion of wiretapping into the white-collar realm. In fact, former prosecutors say they used wiretaps of telephones to crack down on penny-stock fraud during the 1990s, which included insider trading. As financial fraud grew during the 1990s stock market boom, the legal system adapted and judges increasingly showed less distinction between the typical gangster from Mulberry Street versus the one on Wall Street.

That was at least part of the case Kang and Goldberg made to Judge Gerald Lynch to tape Raj Rajaratnam's cell phone in March of 2008.

The other stuff involved establishing probable cause through the information Roomy Khan was dishing about Rajaratnam's activities, which involved everything from his Hilton trades to Rajaratnam's ramblings about his market exploits, including how the guys at tech company Xilinx were giving him a lot of guidance.

With the wiretap on Rajaratnam's phone, the unprecedented phase of the crackdown was about to unfold, though if Judge Gerald Lynch thought he was making history or something close to it when he reviewed and granted the wiretap request, he didn't show it.

It was a pretty perfunctory affair. The application stated that the government believed it couldn't obtain the information to make its case any other way, though it left out a key detail: that Rajaratnam had been a focus of the SEC's investigations for years and had turned over millions of documents to government officials.

It was a mistake, and later, Rajaratnam's attorneys would add it to their list of complaints and argue it was a deliberate attempt to mislead the courts into granting the request and hiding the fact that the government failed to meet its very high bar to obtain the wiretap, namely that it had exhausted every other means before resorting to the ultimate invasion of privacy.

But for now it didn't matter. On March 7, 2008—the same day it was submitted—Judge Lynch granted the application and the taping of Rajaratnam's phone began.

Slaine, meanwhile, was well into his FBI-sanctioned espionage work by this point, having met with Drimal several times and recorded their conversations. At least initially, Slaine didn't think recording people was part of the deal he had cut with Makol and his other handler, assistant U.S. Attorney Andrew Fish, people who know him say. Maybe so, but it would soon loom large in his new life as a cooperating witness.

Documents show that some of the first evidence Slaine gave the FBI involved Drimal's trading in the stock of ATI Technologies. That trade had also caught the attention of Slaine's new bosses at the FBI because it appeared that Slaine had made it right before a market-moving corporate event. But Slaine said it wasn't his. It was one of the trades Drimal had placed in his account to repay the money Drimal had borrowed.

That was just the beginning, Slaine pointed out. Even though the relationship between the two men cooled, Drimal remained in awe of Slaine, and, some mutual friends say, Drimal still wanted to impress his mentor, reminding him that the guy who used to be a doorman at a nightclub now had his own trading relationships.

That would be Drimal's fatal mistake. Slaine pointed to those relationships immediately, explaining how his old weight-lifting partner now had a pretty sophisticated circle of friends and used them to make dirty trades.

According to people who know Slaine, the feds were clearly interested in Drimal as a starting point to unravel what they believed was a well-orchestrated scheme to trade on confidential information. They wanted to know everything about him, from his work life to his private life. Drimal's work as nightclub doorman in the 1980s helped him make connections with Wall Street traders looking to get into some of the city's hottest clubs.

By 2007, Galleon was one of the hedge-fund world's biggest players, putting it firmly on Wall Street's radar screen—and the phones were ringing constantly, with Wall Street trading desks begging for Galleon business, and the commissions they produced for completing trades.

Drimal was in the middle of what one former trader there described as "the wild west of the hedge fund business." Unlike competitors such as SAC Capital, there were few rules, and no overarching investment strategies at Galleon. Fiefdoms developed between Rajaratnam's people—namely the firm's analysts—and the traders who reported to Rosenbach. Some of Rosenbach's traders would place huge bets against the same stocks Rajaratnam was touting as a buying opportunity and vice versa.

Galleon traded so much that it produced around $250 million in yearly commissions for Wall Street's brokers. One of its stars, Todd Deutsch, earned the name "Rain Man" both for his awkward temperament and his remarkable ability to keep track of hundreds of different trades at the same time. Galleon was also a hub of information, with Rajaratnam bragging about his sources in the technology community who gave him guidance about the direction of stocks, and the Wall Street brokers handing market intelligence to the firm's traders.

Drimal was no Todd Deutsch, who once earned approximately $25 million in a year. In fact, he was never officially hired by the firm, but over the years he managed to understand the value of information and find his niche at Galleon, where he was known to all by the oddly effeminate nickname: "Ruby."

"It was a name of an old girlfriend, or something," was how one person who knew Drimal described his trading-floor moniker.

But he was now married—ironically to a former prosecutor in the Manhattan District attorney's office and living in the New York City suburb of Weston, Connecticut, a far cry from his early days. Inside Galleon, Drimal thrived for another reason: He had a penchant for skirting the law, Slaine told his handlers, which fit the FBI's working knowledge of his activities in the hedge fund business.

Makol and Fish weren't the lead investigators on the Galleon investigation, which was headed by Kang and Lauren Goldberg, but Slaine was such a treasure-trove of industry knowledge they also began to probe what he knew about Rajaratnam. Slaine had left Galleon many years earlier so his information was a bit stale. But what he knew fit what the government had begun to uncover as well: Galleon was a place where trading on inside information wasn't uncommon. In fact, Slaine claimed at Galleon there was significant pressure to crank out big returns even if that meant crossing the line into illegality.

But Slaine's knowledge of Galleon was considered a secondary matter; Makol and Fish were most interested in building a case against Drimal and uncovering one of the most convoluted circles of friends FBI agents had ever witnessed—a probe that would ultimately snare numerous traders and lawyers and expose the seedy world of expert networks, including a wannabe hedge fund star who was known by his cohorts as "Octopussy," because he had so many friends radiating out from his particular node in the circle.

"Hey, how's it going?" Slaine asked Richard Dickey, his old friend from his days at Morgan Stanley, as they casually crossed paths outside the swanky Delano Hotel in South Beach Miami where Dickey had been vacationing with his family. The two hadn't seen each other for years, though Dickey, like most people who knew David Slaine, also knew the legend: a street-smart brawler who made it big in the hedge fund world. In fact, Dickey was one of the Morgan executives who broke up the alleged French fry fight at Morgan Stanley, and he could attest to both Slaine's strength and his good-guy status on Wall Street.

What Dickey didn't know when they crossed paths was that Slaine was not merely a hedge fund trader; he was in fact a key government cooperator going underground to snare friends and their circle of friends. "He just said hello and said he was doing some trading and we agreed to get a drink and that was the last I heard of him," Dickey recalls.

That's because Slaine had bigger things on his mind than getting a drink with an old pal. The months following his cooperation agreement with the government were a difficult time for Slaine. Whereas lying to Rajaratnam seemed to investigators almost second nature for Roomy Khan, Slaine's betrayal of past friends and associates caused him great emotional pain. People who know him describe it as an excruciating experience, particularly during the first two years of his undercover work where his efforts were most intense.

The biggest emotional hurdle for Slaine was wearing a wire and secretly recording other targets, including, most prominently, Drimal. Being a rat was "humiliating for David," is how one friend described Slaine's life working undercover. At several points Slaine asked Makol if he could stop because of the emotional stress of spending much of his days as an imposter. Slaine's wife even threatened to personally alert Drimal that he was being recorded as she witnessed the emotional toll wearing a wire took on her husband.

Slaine reported the threat to his FBI handlers, who confronted Elyse Slaine on the matter. It's unclear exactly what the FBI said to prevent Elyse Slaine from following through, but people who know her say she made it clear to Makol that she believed her husband had done enough, and that the punishment, in her view, didn't fit the crime.

"How much more do I have to do!" Slaine screamed during one particularly tense meeting with Makol. As Slaine's friends recount it, Makol reminded him bluntly of the threat he made when they first met, that if he didn't cooperate, "You'll never see your daughter again."

The threat was incentive enough to keep moving until his new masters were satisfied and Slaine knew that slapping them in the face wasn't going to work. What would work was agreeing to help them fully uncover what the government believed was a formidable circle of friends.

It started with Drimal, whom he began recording in September 2007. But within a year Slaine had led the FBI to many more possible targets, helping establish enough probable cause for Chaves and Makol to get court orders to start their own wiretapping of other targets' telephone calls.

Slaine and Drimal appeared to re-establish many of the personal bonds they'd had in the past. Slaine was a notorious Wall Street tough guy, but he was also smart as he lured Drimal into the FBI's web. Drimal, meanwhile, dealt with concerns that Galleon people would notice him hanging out again with the guy who once slapped Rosenbach by meeting Slaine outside the hedge fund's offices. It was worth the chance, given Slaine's own reputation as a proficient trader and as someone Drimal could use to advance his own career.

During the Boesky-Siegel era, meetings at the Harvard Club in Midtown were par for the course. But the new breed of insider traders had no problem passing lucrative tips at more lowbrow establishments, such as Burger Heaven, a cafeteria-style burger joint on Forty-Ninth Street and Madison Avenue.

It was here as well as cafés like Pret A Manger, just around the corner from Burger Heaven, that Slaine helped the FBI nail Craig Drimal by unlocking his extensive network of insider trading accomplices, both in the Wall Street trading community and at law firms. Slaine's first recorded conversation with Drimal didn't disappoint. Makol took pains to make sure Slaine knew what questions to ask—and how to ask them—he put a recording device on Slaine's telephone and one on his suit. And it worked. Drimal began sharing insider tips with Slaine immediately, according to federal investigators with firsthand knowledge of the matter. Drimal at times appeared nervous; he often balked at talking over the telephone because he said the feds could be listening, but thanks to his trust in Slaine he agreed to meet once again and personally share something with him.

In preparation for Slaine's face-to-face meeting with Drimal, Makol had placed what's known as a "body wire" directly on Slaine, one so small it couldn't be detected. By now federal agents had gotten creative in their use of listening devices, placing them on candles in restaurants, on watches worn by informants, and even creating microphones that look like hotel key cards.

When they met, Drimal revealed that a big deal was at hand: Bain Capital was going to take electronics manufacturer 3Com private. The deal would be announced at the end of September. How did he know this? Drimal said he had a source named Zvi Goffer—the trader who would later be described as Octopussy—who had a source at a law firm named Ropes & Gray, which was representing Bain on the deal.

Slaine had seen many guys like Zvi Goffer during his twenty-five-year career; a relative kid in his early thirties with a vaunting ambition to make money. The scheme Drimal offered was indeed an easy way to make money even if Drimal added ominously, that he wasn't sure why the lawyer was risking jail by passing on what was so obviously illegal inside information. But Goffer was paying the lawyer for the information, which has always been enough incentive to commit a crime.

The old David Slaine would have made a crude remark or a joke, but now with the FBI listening and the threats of jail time in his head he just let his old friend dig himself into a deeper and deeper hole.

The insider tips didn't end there. Like Rajaratnam, these guys also traded on inside information involving Hilton Hotel's takeover, Drimal said. Meanwhile, Drimal's initial statements were enough for Chaves and Makol to obtain a court order to wiretap Drimal's telephone and eventually many others in the scheme.

Zvi "Octopussy" Goffer certainly lived up to his name; Slaine told Makol that while Drimal was well-connected inside Wall Street's seedy underworld, Goffer's connections were even better; he appeared to have sources of information everywhere.

Drimal didn't know who it was at Ropes & Gray who had provided the 3Com leak. In fact, the cat-and-mouse game would last most of the next two years, with Drimal providing insider tips to Slaine and then Slaine infiltrating the circle of friends directly, attending meetings with Drimal, Goffer, and others and piling up the evidence to bury them all.

Drimal and Slaine had come a long way since their days working out at the Vertical Club in Manhattan, and Slaine certainly yearned for his old life versus the one he had now as a cooperating witness. Yet for all his misgivings about being a rat, Slaine proved an adept one. He prodded and pushed the ever-growing circle of friends for information—and for the sources of their information. At one point he convinced Drimal to set up a meeting with Rosenbach, his old Galleon friend and later nemesis. "Tell Gary I want to see him, I miss him," Slaine told Drimal, who passed the information to Rosenbach.

Rosenbach demurred, Drimal has told people, after speaking to his wife who said it wasn't a good idea to get involved with someone who had nearly ripped his head off in a steam room. It's unclear how valuable Rosenbach would be to investigators in any event. Rosenbach may have been a tough boss, but former Galleon employees say Rajaratnam went to great lengths to hide key details about the hedge fund and how he obtained trading information from Rosenbach, who has not been charged by investigators. Others weren't so lucky, because, as Chaves and his team would determine, Slaine was a natural. He could mingle and elicit incriminating details about insider trading schemes from people he had never met before, and because of that the circle of friends now included not only Drimal and Zvi Goffer, but also Zvi's brother Emanuel, a trader named Michael Kimelman, and in a short time, many more.

"It's better for everybody" if you don't know our source, Zvi Goffer advised Slaine one afternoon in late August 2008 as they sat for one of their many meetings while the feds listened in from another location. Before this meeting Goffer and Drimal had approached Slaine about the possibility of a business venture—that the group would start its own hedge fund. Slaine was asked to invest $2 million to start the venture, but first he had to know the source of the insider leaks.

"A construction worker," was Goffer's first answer. Slaine was unimpressed at the time, but Goffer was adamant: It pays to know less, just in case Slaine were ever caught by the feds. "It's the guy fixing the pothole," Kimelman then joked, before turning to other matters. The government couldn't determine based on the evidence at hand whether Kimelman knew or didn't know about the source of the inside information on 3Com and a host of other stocks that Zvi Goffer and the circle had traded on. At this point they didn't care as they made final preparations to close in on the guy who undoubtedly knew all: Goffer, the so-called Octopussy, and the name had nothing to do with the James Bond movie of 1983.

He earned the handle from FBI agents on the case because he seemed to embody all that was wrong with Wall Street—only more so. In 2008, he had just got a trading job at Galleon, but his real aim was to establish a presence at a major hedge fund, share tips with Galleon chief Raj Rajaratnam, and then make the big bucks trading at his own hedge fund and keeping the lucrative fees for himself.

Goffer had "balls," was one way investigators described the thirty-one-year-old trader, the more they listened to his conversations on tape.

He openly discussed ways to cheat the system as well as ways to evade being caught. He once purchased a cell phone for one of the sources and had programmed two telephone numbers labeled "you" and "me" so they could communicate secretly, at least in his mind. After the 3Com deal, he broke the phone in half, keeping one half and telling the source to destroy the other.

In fact, Goffer constantly cautioned his cohorts to be careful, because you never know when the government is listening. He openly called himself paranoid, but he thought that his paranoia and all those steps he took to protect the source of his deal leaks would save him. Of course, they wouldn't. By mid-2008, Goffer's telephone had been tapped for more than six months, with government investigators listening to everything from his dinner dates with business prospects, trips to Madison Square Garden to watch the Knicks, to his attempts to game the market through trading on and passing along inside information.

By late 2008, Chaves and Makol believed they were sitting on a gold mine of potential cases—but they wanted more. The telephone wiretaps had already been in place on Drimal's telephone thanks to the probable cause evidence Slaine had come up with, and as Chaves and Makol kept listening, the list of targets grew, leading to a series of other wiretaps that enlarged this circle of friends even more.

As good as Slaine was as a spy, nothing could replace the wiretaps for effectiveness. Because Goffer's telephone was now bugged, and because of Slaine's recorded conversations with Drimal, the feds soon uncovered the source of the leaks: a thirty-one-year-old lawyer named Jason Goldberg, who had a friend inside Ropes & Gray, a thirty-three-year-old lawyer named Arthur Cutillo.

Cutillo made a good living as a corporate lawyer, a living made even better because he aided the Goffer circle of friends by passing along nonpublic deal information, such as the Bain Capital purchase of 3Com, and much more. His price: kickbacks of cash for passing along the deal information to Goffer, who would then pass the information "downstream" to others like Drimal.

As Makol and Chaves sat and studied the activities of this circle of friends, they realized just how brazen the participants in this scheme were: young lawyers and traders looking to make money and doing whatever they could to meet that end.

They also realized it was probably standard operating procedure in the hedge fund business. Zvi Goffer was hardly a criminal mastermind. In other words, he had learned the business of insider trading from someone else, so there had to be many more people like him out there.

They would have liked to have arrested Goffer on the spot, based on what they knew, but really big cases aren't made that way. They're made by moving up the ladder; you start small, targeting one cooperator, and move upstream until you nail the ringleader.

Upstream movement would put Craig Drimal next in line, but that too would have to wait, as the probe kept leading investigators to an ever-widening array of bad guys.

"Amazing," is all Chaves thought as he studied a large whiteboard in his office in late 2008. His cluster of suspects had numbered to over a dozen—but with so many wiretaps going at the same time, he and his team had come up with scores of leads and potential targets. And based on the leads Slaine had provided, the possible targets seemed endless.

CHAPTER 9

ODD COUPLES

"Hey, so did you hear anything on Xilinx?" Roomy Khan matter-of-factly asked Raj Rajaratnam one afternoon in early 2008.

The call was no different than the dozens of other conversations the two had had since they began their business relationship of sharing market intelligence years earlier. Only this time, Khan was a cooperating witness for the government in its probe of Rajaratnam.

Even better, the feds were listening to every word of the call. They could rewind and replay the tape to their hearts' content.

"I think this quarter is okay. Next quarter not so good," Rajaratnam said, adding: "I haven't made the call I have to make. I got to call a couple of guys there at Xilinx."

To be sure, the call in and of itself wasn't enough to bring charges against Rajaratnam, but as Rajaratnam's lawyers would even concede, it was a great start for the FBI. Later the FBI would track down one of the guys: Kris Chellam, the technology company's chief financial officer, who would eventually settle civil fraud charges and pay a hefty fine that amounted to nearly twice the $1 million he had earned for passing along tips as a key member of Rajaratnam's circle of friends.

But that would have to wait. Meanwhile, Roomy Khan was turning out to be an excellent accomplice in their effort to bring truth and justice to the markets, particularly if you could look beyond the messy details of her cooperation.

Khan's phone lines showed calls to a vast array of Silicon Valley insiders, people who, she would later admit, were part of her own circle of friends that she had never let go of even after being caught by the FBI years ago. Doug Whitman was described as a "putz" by one of his competitors, a one-trick pony who started his fund with some lucky picks and then fell back on his circle of friends to keep returns high and his investors from bolting. He and Roomy Khan were longtime friends and remained key partners in her various schemes, the government discovered. Another one of her best sources of insider tips was a top executive at the tech firm Polycom, who was a neighbor. They often shared illegal information at the local coffee shop.

Still, criminality was turning out to be a tough habit for Khan to break even as she took her second turn as a government informant. She 'fessed up to most of her illegal trading activities, but the government kept finding more. In addition to deleting email messages from Deep Shah, the Moody's analyst who tipped her off to Blackstone's purchase of Hilton, she also used a cell phone listed in her gardener's name to cover her tracks as she continued to talk with Shah. That is until she eventually gave him up to the feds on their way to building the case against Rajaratnam (and through these wiretaps, many of his associates).

To put it plainly, she was still violating the law while she was cooperating with the FBI. She wasn't quite on the level of infamous Boston mobster Whitey Bulger, who was killing people and dealing dope even while he was ratting out his fellow mobsters. But Khan's ongoing shenanigans might well make her toxic on the stand, particularly against the legal firepower Rajaratnam would assemble, even if they made her essential to entrapping Rajaratnam in his own words.

And entrap she did, in the same casual banter she had used with the Galleon boss for years. "What's going on with the earnings this season? Are you hearing anything on Intel?" Khan asked Rajaratnam matter-of-factly in 2008.

"Intel I think will beat the current estimates by, they'll be up like nine to ten percent and then guide down eight percent," he shot back.

After Khan asked for more "color," or more exact data on the company's profit margins, he replied: "Margins I think will be good this quarter but next quarter will be below. . . . I'm not trading Intel anymore. . . . They're a fucking pain-in-the-ass stock."

David Slaine had told people that his work in developing evidence against Drimal and the rest of this circle made him physically ill. He fought with his government investigators incessantly; both David Makol and Andrew Fish took turns berating him on what would happen to him if he stopped doing what he was told.

With the strain of going under cover for so long, Slaine lost weight, looked sickly, and before long he would break up with his wife, albeit amicably.

The thing that kept him going was the horrible alternative of not seeing his daughter for twenty years. Roomy Khan, meanwhile, was a great liar, Wadhwa and Kang discovered—perhaps the best they'd seen so far in the investigation. She did it so effortlessly, without a hint of despair or apparent remorse.

"This is amazing," Sanjay Wadhwa said as he was briefed by Kang on what Khan was producing, not just from her recorded conversations but through other records. Kang kept Wadhwa in the loop on most matters, but there were limits, particularly when it came to wiretaps. Conversations from Rajaratnam's phone were off-limits to anyone outside the Justice Department, and that included the SEC, as was the brief detour Kang made in the middle of the Galleon hunt to return to his first love, Steve Cohen.

Little is known about exactly how Kang got the court order to tap the Steve Cohen's telephone which began, according to one investigator, sometime after the 2008 Rajaratnam wiretaps were launched (Kang declined repeated requests to be interviewed for this book). But according to senior law enforcement officials with direct knowledge of the matter, Kang had to prove both a reasonable suspicion that Cohen was doing something wrong and that he couldn't get the information using other types of investigative techniques.

That, as it turns out, was the easy part. Much more difficult was finding something to incriminate Cohen on. When the Cohen wiretaps began, Kang could have received his probable cause from any one of a number of sources, including the suspicious trading that Funkhouser's computers detected. Kang had interviewed Patricia Cohen as well, and Slaine's information about the inner workings of the big hedge fund didn't hurt.

The judge granted his request, and for a period of time described by one law enforcement source as a few weeks, the federal government was listening to Steve Cohen's business affairs as conducted on his home telephone.

Cohen often holds a Sunday conference call with various traders to discuss market bets and other ideas from his home telephone. It was a grueling affair, at least according to those who took part in the weekly meeting. Traders would be grilled on their positions, and mostly their "conviction" level on stocks, meaning how strong they felt about a particular trade.

Kang believed that listening to these calls was one of the best ways to determine if Cohen really wasn't playing by the rules. But Cohen didn't bite. "There was a lot of noise," was how one government official with direct knowledge of the wiretap conversations described what investigators discovered.

In the end it was a frustrating experience, particularly for Kang, people say. The calls provided no clear-cut evidence that Cohen knowingly or intentionally traded on illegal tips. It's unclear exactly what was said, but Cohen is known to speak in his own code, often about "conviction levels," and to bullshit incessantly about various stocks. All of which is a far cry from hard-and-fast evidence that shows he engages in insider trading or condones it below his rank,

Or as one former Justice Department official put it, "In the end, we really didn't get shit."

The question of why the wiretap came up empty became a huge debate within law enforcement circles. Maybe he was just that good a trader, and maybe the people he hired were for the most part incentivized to do their jobs legally by receiving huge pay packages to play fair. Since SAC was such a massive fund, trading billions of dollars in stocks every day, even the suspicious trades by a few bad players in its ranks when put in this context were just a small fraction of the fund's overall business.

But others in government believe their suspicions are valid and that something dirty was clearly happening at SAC. It was becoming increasingly difficult for FBI officials and people in the Justice Department and the SEC to believe Cohen ran a completely honest business amid so much trading that touched off so many of their alarm bells.

The conclusion among other investigators was that Steve Cohen was just smart enough to see it all coming, trusting his trader's gut to ramp up his compliance systems when he knew the scrutiny of his trading practices became more intense. People at the FBI had come to possess an odd respect for their ultimate target, as making a case against him, at least for the moment, appeared nearly impossible. According to someone involved in the matter, when Chaves heard the results of the Cohen wiretaps, he muttered one word: "Brilliant."

Cohen was indeed a man of contradictions. He was an information junkie, and SAC was a veritable information factory. But he appeared to take pains to stop his addiction when it came too close to home.

He loved his privacy, but investigators also came to understand that Cohen's media image as a total recluse who lived behind large walls, protected by twenty-four-hour-a-day surveillance, was something of a caricature. Yes, he and his family sought a large degree of protection from the outside world, much of it warranted given his wealth. But Cohen didn't exactly hide from the world.

And in 2007 he weighed turning SAC into a public company. A few hedge funds had done so to raise capital and use stock to keep their best performers from jumping to other firms. He didn't in the end, but according to one person who briefed Cohen on the matter, it had nothing to do with secrecy. Rather he had nixed the idea because the financial crisis had roiled the markets.

Agents heard he liked Italian food enough that he ate at two of the New York area's biggest hot spots—Il Polpo in Greenwich, and Campagnola in Manhattan. He was a fat cat who didn't always hang with the fat-cat set.

He could dine with anyone in the world, and managed money for the likes of private equity honcho Stephen Schwarzman of Blackstone, but one of his frequent dinner partners was former New York City cop and private investigator Richard "Bo" Dietl, whose claims to fame included a book about his exploits as a New York City detective and his regular appearances on the *Imus in the Morning* radio show.

Cohen, the government investigators were beginning to conclude, also had a surprisingly limited circle of friends, which meant he was either innocent or just very skilled at covering his tracks.

Contrast that with Rajaratnam, who seemed to talk to *anyone* who could give him a market edge and never seemed to tone it down, even after being deposed by the SEC. His circle included everyone from the former chief executive of McKinsey & Co., Rajat Gupta, who appeared continuously on his telephone logs, to more junior executives such as Anil Kumar, a McKinsey executive vice president.

Wadhwa had joked that Rajaratnam's circle of friends was Wharton-based and that the feds should indict the entire class. But Wadhwa, himself of South Asian descent, also believed that ethnicity played a role in the criminal conspiracy: They were people largely from the same continent and felt comfortable doing business with one another, even if that business was illegal. Cohen epitomized the typical Wall Street career path: middle-class childhood in Long Island, business school, then intense trading desk work, and like Slaine, a certain disdain for the motives of people he was working with. That disdain didn't save Slaine and the circle he was busy making a case against, but it appeared, at least to government investigators, to have saved Steve Cohen.

The ethnic aspect of the Rajaratnam investigation was both unavoidable and unsettling, as far as Wadhwa was concerned. Many of the best mob investigators, people like Rudy Giuliani, were Italian American. They were among the most zealous prosecutors of the five big crime families because of the obvious taint the mob's activities brought to Italian Americans, the vast majority of whom are honest and hardworking.

Wadhwa felt much the same way in his pursuit of Galleon. Matters of race and ethnicity aside, this group of conspirators orbiting around Rajaratnam also exhibited the same disgusting criminal traits that are common across all ethnic lines, including one in particular: greed. And Wadhwa believed they were tainting a culture built on hard work. Wadhwa was born in India, came to the United States as a teenager, and always appreciated the opportunities his adoptive country had given him and his family. He had left a lucrative job at a corporate law firm for the long hours and low pay of government work, because he believed he was doing the right thing, and the right thing was worth a lower paycheck. That was what stung him the most as he watched Rajaratnam and his countrymen do the wrong thing for a buck.

It also made Wadhwa all the more motivated to take the case to the next level. By now, he was working with the FBI almost daily, listening into Khan's conversations (except for the Title III wiretaps) and sharing what he and his team were coming up with, namely their own mosaic as to where Rajaratnam was getting his tips.

These tips were, as Wadhwa discovered, centered around certain stocks, many of them the tips that Khan had provided. All were involved in technology of one sort or another, including companies like Polycom, AMD, and Google, to name a few. (Khan herself traded many of these companies.) For Wadhwa, AMD stood out because it was so obviously a dirty trade nearly from the moment he began looking at Rajaratnam's business.

AMD's 2006 purchase of a chip-making firm named ATI came out of the blue. The Street barely saw it coming and there were no leaks to the press. But Rajaratnam saw it coming. He snapped up ATI just before the merger, earning him more than $20 million, and it had little to do with his vaunted "mosaic."

The reason for his good timing, as the wiretaps would show, was the executive at McKinsey, Anil Kumar, who was doing consulting work for AMD and feeding Rajaratnam his inside tips for a "consulting fee" of $125,000 every quarter. The Kumar-Rajaratnam deal wasn't known by the feds, at least not yet. That would come later, as would others, the result of the wiretaps on Rajaratnam's and Kumar's phones.

Roomy Khan was good, but investigators were seeing the limitations in their arrangement. For all his bluster and networking, Rajaratnam's conversations with Khan didn't yield the wider circle of friends the government was now tracking because of the wiretaps on Rajaratnam's cell phone.

Targets and potential witnesses piled up by the dozens. Most of them, like Kumar, Kris Chellam of Xilinx, Rajiv Goel of Intel, or Danielle Chiesi, a hedge fund trader, weren't household names even in the Wall Street community, but a few were. Rajat Gupta, the former McKinsey partner and Goldman Sachs board member, eagerly shared inside information with Rajaratnam, just like everyone else. By establishing there was a conspiracy, prosecutors were able to get wiretaps on other phones as the case exploded in size. In the end, they had recorded thousands of conversations involving Rajaratnam's circle of friends including the so-called consensual recordings made by the various cooperators.

Somewhat unknown to Kang, Goldberg, and the rest of the government's insider trading bureaucracy was a bigger story. Indeed, much would happen on Wall Street after March 10, 2008—the date Judge Lynch granted the wiretap application to bug Rajaratnam's phone. Just four days later, the Wall Street firm Bear Stearns collapsed, setting off a chain of events that would lead to the demise of Lehman Brothers and the rest of the financial system before the government spent billions bailing out the remaining big banks.

Over this period of time, the Justice Department asked a series of federal judges to extend Judge Lynch's wiretap application, as many as seven times, while also granting permission for the wiretapping of other culprits caught as a result of Rajaratnam's taped conversations.

FBI agents described it all as a costly affair. Running wiretaps requires tremendous manpower. No one in the Justice Department would provide an estimate on the total costs, but a report issued in 2009 from the administrative office of the federal court system sheds some light. A single wiretap or recording for a federal investigation costs an average of $62,552 for a period of roughly thirty days. Since the Rajaratnam case lasted far longer, it's easy to see how the costs added up.

But government investigators will claim it was all worth it as each member of Rajaratnam's entire circle of friends was eventually revealed through the vast tangle of recordings. People involved in the investigation of Rajaratnam tell me there was no discussion to divert resources toward mortgage fraud and the disclosures from the big banks about their financial condition through 2008, from the time Bear Stearns imploded right through the government bailouts.

In fact, just the opposite was true. "We received an increase in funding and people," an FBI official says, "after the financial crisis and the Madoff scheme."

At the SEC the sentiment was largely the same. The current chairman was an appointee of President Bush: Chris Cox, a former Republican congressman from Orange County, California. Cox was regarded as a true believer in the free market. One of his first reads among the morning newspapers: the *Wall Street Journal* editorial page, which had over the years questioned the validity of insider trading as a crime.

And yet Wadhwa was alerted by his supervisors to keep pressing forward. A common misperception, buttressed by the allegations of Gary Aguirre, was that the SEC had gone soft on the bad guys, ignoring the Madoff scandal or the dangerous amount of risk being taken by the banks out of their zealousness to protect the "free markets." As part of this misperception, Cox, the free marketer from California, is held in particular disdain.

SEC officials say the real story was more complex. The SEC was once a lean operation with some of the best attorneys in the business at the helm. It was now a bloated bureaucracy, and like most such creations, was always pressing for increased funding. Also, as with any bureaucracy, it measured performance in absurd ways. Staff attorneys like Wadhwa were judged by the number of cases, not necessarily by the impact of the crime against the average investor, and it led attorneys to think twice about pursuing a Bernie Madoff or a boiler room of penny stock crooks who worked at one firm since both would be counted as one case. Commission lawyers were urged to make numbers and do so in areas that generated the most publicity, rather than what various enforcement chiefs over the years referred to as more routine "slip and fall" cases.

In the Rajaratnam case, the SEC saw a perfect storm: numbers *and* big publicity impact. And they wanted more. Wadhaw had always believed the SEC faced limitations precisely because it lacked the tools that were available to the criminal authorities—namely the threat of jail time—and the ability to wiretap phone lines, or even listen to these so-called dirty calls once court authority was established. (SEC targets face civil charges: fines and industry bans, not jail time.) Thus they could listen to Roomy Khan's calls to Rajaratnam, but they could not listen, or even know about, what Rajaratnam said on his wiretapped cell phone.

Around the time of the Rajaratnam wiretaps, a tense meeting with Assistant U.S. Attorney Lauren Goldberg took place in which attorneys for the SEC and the Justice Department hashed out the possibility of equipping the SEC with the ability to wiretap—or at least listen to the wiretapping. The general feeling was that in the current statute, under

Title III, nothing specifically prevented the commission from listening to conversations or even seeking approval. The biggest question: What if a defendant like Rajaratnam with the resources to hire the best lawyers mounts a successful challenge? It could pollute the entire case, causing a judge to throw out all of the wiretap evidence.

With that the decision was made to fight this particular fight another day.

Raj, you better listen to me . . . let me make a little bit money too okay. . . . Akamai . . . please don't fuck me on this. . . . They're going to guide down. Just got a call from my guy. I played him like a fine tuned piano."

Notwithstanding her colorful language, Danielle Chiesi's little chats with Rajaratnam were all business, though, as the FBI was discovering, she wasn't against using more than a whiff of sexuality to woo tippers of inside information if it would benefit her and the Galleon chief.

Officially, Chiesi, known inside her circle of friends as "Dani," was an analyst for a hedge fund called NewCastle Partners, a subsidiary of Bear Stearns, the big Wall Street firm with a history of bending securities laws to reap enormous profits. That history, of course, came to an abrupt end in March 2008, when Bear became insolvent, a victim of its own recklessness, and was taken over by J. P. Morgan.

The big bank would eventually spin off NewCastle, but not before Chiesi and her boss, Mark Kurland, had been snared through the wiretaps on Rajaratnam's cell phone, and eventually a wiretap on their own telephones. Bear had long suspected that NewCastle, and Chiesi in particular, were dealing in dirty information. It had blocked attempts by Kurland to get its own trading desk—as opposed to using the one at Bear Stearns—for that very reason. But keeping in its tradition as one of Wall Street's most legally challenged outfits, it kept the subsidiary alive because it was extremely profitable.

All along, Chiesi and Kurland were each key elements of Rajaratnam's circle of friends, and through their conversations, that circle would soon include nearly two dozen others, some of whom were paid directly by Rajaratnam, while others, like Chiesi (and for that matter Roomy Khan), maintained a quid-pro-quo relationship with the Galleon chief to be privy to his tips.

For the government investigators, Chiesi revealed a couple of things about Rajaratnam's network. He began Galleon by leveraging relationships with technology executives whom he knew from earlier in his career and were original investors in the fund. Those relationships over the years began to lose their effectiveness, particularly in helping Rajaratnam bet on the direction of stocks. That's when he began to create a separate circle, which included people he knew from his days at Wharton, and others like Chiesi, whom he met at a technology conference and who impressed him with her knowledge of stocks and her ability to get information. What would astound investigators about Rajaratnam's new circle was not only that it went deeper into corporate America than expected, but also that it brushed up against people with whom a billionaire wouldn't usually be caught associating.

Galleon was, of course, one of the nation's biggest hedge funds. It dealt with all the blue-chip firms and was a major client of Goldman Sachs. And yet a lowly analyst, albeit a connected one at a mid-sized hedge fund, was regularly speaking with Galleon's founder.

Over the course of the next year or so, the feds would record scores of conversations between the two, confirming a tip that David Slaine, himself a Galleon trader before he became a cooperator, had provided investigators. Makol asked Slaine at one point whether Rajaratnam "liked pretty girls." Slaine's response: Of course he does. In the case of Chiesi, he liked them better when they helped him make money trading.

A former beauty queen with blue eyes and a Jayne Mansfield build, Chiesi was quite the topic of conversation among the traders and company executives she dealt with—though at forty-four years of age, her beauty was slowly starting to fade. Unlike Rajaratnam, Chiesi didn't go to Wharton or even to graduate school. But as the investigation showed, she was street-smart and had one of the best brains for obtaining and leveraging inside information. She came from a middle-class background. Her father was an insurance company executive. She attended the University of Colorado, was a sorority queen, graduated with a degree in economics, and then set her sights on Wall Street. Friends described her as outgoing and generous. The feds who were listening to her conversations thought she was a hardened white-collar criminal who had learned through her twenty years of working up the Wall Street ladder the game of developing sources that could provide insider tips. Along the way, she met Kurland, and when Kurland came to NewCastle in 1996, he brought her with him.

The Wall Street hedge fund trading community is one of the last nearly all-male bastions in corporate America, but Chiesi knew how to fit in with the boys. She dressed provocatively and wasn't bashful about flirting, former associates said. She also could curse like any of the guys, as the feds discovered from their wiretaps.

She might not be Ivy League material, but she was brilliant at the dark arts of insider trading, developing relationships with key executives all over the hedge fund and technology worlds and expertly prying information from them. It was a cat-and-mouse game for Chiesi; for people like Rajaratnam she offered a quid pro quo in terms of shared information. For people like Robert Moffat, an executive at IBM, it was sex, or possibly love.

Moffat was one of IBM's rising stars. He was so close to CEO Sam Palmisano that many people inside the company thought he would replace him, which is why he was a perfect friend for Chiesi. How or when the sexual part of their relationship began was unclear to the government investigators. Chiesi, government investigators say, had a real emotional bond with Moffat, but her first love was the information he brought her. Moffat, friends have said, initially liked Chiesi mostly because she was a real player in the technology world with relationships that included major investors and top CEOs.

Moffat, who was married, soon became a key member of Chiesi's circle of friends, passing along tips about earnings announcements to

Chiesi, who would then pass those tips along to others, including Rajaratnam. As investigators were discovering, Kurland encouraged his subordinate to use any means necessary to squeeze tips out of these sources—in fact, Kurland and Chiesi had had their own fling over the years.

One of Chiesi's skills, it seemed from the wiretaps, was her understanding of why each source needed to talk to her. Rajaratnam spoke with her because it was lucrative. And Chiesi spoke with Rajaratnam for the same reason. She said she "loved" him, but it was mainly for the love of insider tips he passed back to her.

Likewise, Hector Ruiz, chairman of chipmaker AMD, initially needed Chiesi because NewCastle owned shares of the company, and Chiesi needed Ruiz for the obvious reasons, though less obvious ones would develop over time. Ruiz had attended one of Chiesi's soirees at her apartment in Manhattan's Sutton Place, and the two began what some people described as a close relationship. Ruiz denies that the relationship was anything but business.

Chiesi, meanwhile, sprinkled her information—some of it acquired legally and some not—around to the various people in her circle of friends, but as the wiretaps showed, she saved the best stuff for Rajaratnam, and for obvious reasons. She knew he had an even better circle of friends and the information that went with it.

One of the best examples that investigators were looking at involved the circle's trading in shares of AMD. Initially it was Roomy Khan who was Rajaratnam's AMD source, but by 2008 he was getting much of his information from two other players in his circle, Anil Kumar, the McKinsey consultant who worked on projects for the company, as well as Chiesi, through her dealings with Ruiz.

Chiesi's AMD trades had already drawn interest from Bear Stearns compliance, though they dropped the matter and the firm's implosion prevented further action. Meanwhile Chiesi smelled a big score, as the feds had found out. Not long after Bear's demise in the summer of 2008, AMD was ready to strike a deal with a Middle Eastern sovereign wealth fund, Abu Dhabi's Mubadala Development Co., to create a joint venture. IBM had a role in the deal as well because of technology it was providing AMD.

The deal represented the best of both worlds for Chiesi, given her dual relationship with Moffat (the point man for IBM on the deal) and Ruiz. It was an insider trading version of a ménage à trois; Chiesi bragged to her boss Kurland that she was going to "triangulate" the relationship with her pals Ruiz and Moffat to get more details, which she did. She sat in on meetings with Ruiz and Moffat as she discovered that AMD and the fund were entering into the joint venture that would lead to a spin off AMD's chip manufacturing business into a separate entity.

The fund would hold a 50 percent stake and the result, they believed, would be positive for AMD's stock. AMD had struggled in chip manufacturing, and unloading a chunk of it to a well-financed partner could boost shares.

Chiesi and Kurland moved quickly, as did Rajaratnam, who kept his end of the bargain, alerting Chiesi that someone in his circle had provided further proof the deal was a go. An additional tipper was Rajaratnam's source Anil Kumar, the McKinsey executive who was also working on the transaction.

"We've got to keep this radio silent," Rajaratnam told Chiesi after he presented his own piece of the puzzle. The information he had was so good that she shouldn't share it with anyone, "not even to your little boyfriends."

"Believe me, I don't have any friends," Chiesi answered, adding "Love you," before hanging up.

Chiesi did love the arrangement she had with the billionaire hedge fund manager, and the feeling, at least according to the wiretaps, appeared to be mutual. On its face, the AMD deal seemed so esoteric that it would barely attract notice from the regulators as a material event once the friends began snapping up shares before it was made public. That is, unless, the feds had wired someone's telephone, which they had. In any event, NewCastle began aggressively buying shares of AMD, as did Galleon, amassing a position of 8 million shares, while NewCastle held 2.3 million. By this time in the summer of 2008, the growing financial crisis was forcing hedge funds to unload stocks for the safety of cash. Even Steve Cohen, by the crisis's September height, was largely selling stocks, not buying. The AMD deal also turned out to be a rare loser for Rajaratnam, Chiesi, and the entire circle, and not just because the feds were recording their activities. The broader market hated the deal, and the financial crisis made stocks a bad bet with or without insider tips. Still, the episode was instructive to government investigators as they pieced together the cluster's wiretaps and trading records. Rajaratnam did indeed employ the mosaic theory of investing, albeit with illegal inside information, and one losing deal did little to break up this circle of friends.

It was also instructive for Rajaratnam, who continued to rely on Chiesi because, more often than not, she delivered.

"He just called me talking about the family," Chiesi breathlessly explained to Rajaratnam during the summer of 2008, about a call she had just had with Kieran Taylor, a family friend but also a mid level marketing executive at tech company Akamai. She had just finished "playing [Taylor] like a fine-tuned piano," she said about the details of the company's earnings announcement.

At this point, Bear Stearns no longer owned NewCastle, and the financial world was just a few months away from its cataclysmic collapse. But Chiesi was focused like a laser on how best to beat the markets, and in so doing help Rajaratnam beat them, too.

It "took a little time" for Taylor to trust her with Akamai information, Chiesi told Rajaratnam as the feds listened. In fact, it is still unclear if Taylor even understood that what he was telling her could be used to profitably trade on Akamai shares. Unlike Chiesi and most of the rest of her circle, Taylor hasn't been charged in the matter. In an interview Taylor says he gave Chiesi nothing of substance—he wasn't high enough up in the company to do so.

But as Chiesi explained it, she had subtly slipped in her request for some insight into Akamai's pending earnings announcement, and at least based on what she was telling Rajaratnam, it had worked.

"People think it's going go to twenty-five," she said. Based on what she was able to discover, Akamai insiders believed the earnings number would be so bad that the stock could crater 25 percent.

With that, she implored Rajaratnam to short the stock steadily in the days leading up to the announcement but not to share the information with other traders on his team. Keeping it quiet would be more worthwhile, she said, because without so many others playing the same trade, she and Rajaratnam would both be virtually printing money.

During the call, Rajaratnam said the trade was "an easy one for you."

Always the charmer, Chiesi responded: "Honey, you know it's for us. I could very easily short it without telling you. I wouldn't do that because we share everything . . . we need to be a team."

Akamai's guidance conformed with the information Chiesi had given Rajaratnam. The company slashed its profit forecast and shares cratered by the 25 percent Chiesi was predicting, showering millions of dollars of profits on NewCastle and Galleon.

CHAPTER 10

SOMETHING GOOD IS GOING TO HAPPEN

Another reason Danielle Chiesi was such an effective player in the Rajaratnam circle of friends was that she put pressure on others to become better at breaking the law. Keep in mind, Chiesi wasn't paid directly by Rajaratnam with cash, or at least investigators didn't find evidence of money directly changing hands. She was paid with information.

Like Rajaratnam, Chiesi understood that the mosaic they were trying to assemble often required several pieces of inside information assembled from various sources; the compensation was in the sharing of that information until the mosaic was completed.

And she seemed to stop at nothing to meet that goal. Anil Kumar, the executive at McKinsey & Co., felt the most pressure in Rajaratnam's circle to live up to her example.

Unlike with Chiesi, whom Rajaratnam liked, his relationship with

Kumar was somewhat strained. First, Kumar worked for money. Even more, Rajaratnam considered him an Indian version of a WASP, with his Ivy League pedigree and family background. Later the relationship faltered because Kumar, for all his book smarts, couldn't match Chiesi's talent for gathering inside information.

That didn't cause Rajaratnam to cut Kumar off—far from it. Despite his complaints about Kumar that were picked up on tape, Rajaratnam knew that it was always good to have friends in high places who were willing to break the law. And given Kumar's position at McKinsey, there were few places higher.

McKinsey's tentacles extended into every corner of corporate America, and if Kumar wanted to earn money from Galleon, he would be competing with the likes of the feisty Chiesi to provide Rajaratnam with the most valuable of that information.

Kumar and Rajaratnam, of course, shared many attributes aside from their education at one of the world's best-known business schools. They were immigrants: Kumar from India, and Rajaratnam from Sri Lanka. They were both ambitious, Kumar in a quiet, analytical way, while Rajaratnam boasted a macho approach to trading, calling himself a "warrior." He once told Kumar that trading during the 2008 financial crisis was like "fighting Muhammad Ali; I know he's stronger and faster but you're in the ring with him."

And they shared a love for making money, as the wiretaps so vividly displayed. That said, Kumar was a reluctant addition to Rajaratnam's circle of friends. "Raj seduced Kumar into doing insider trading," was how Wadhwa believed the relationship took hold. The facts bear that out to a certain extent. Kumar was looking for a legitimate business relationship with Galleon, offering the consulting services that McKinsey is known for, and was seduced by the trappings of Rajaratnam's success—the private planes, the houses, the expensive trips—and of course, his enormous wealth.

Once he decided to join the Rajaratnam circle, Kumar was paid $500,000 a year and offered a $1 million bonus in return for what Rajaratnam described as "valuable" information. Rajaratnam even had an idea on how to hide the obvious illegality of the arrangement. He suggested that Kumar set up a dummy company in Geneva, Switzerland.

Rajaratnam would arrange to have the bulk of the Galleon payments to Kumar delivered to something called Pecos Trading. The money would wind its way to Pecos from a Galleon account under the name of Kumar's housekeeper, Manju Das.

Then, once the money started to flow, the mind games with Kumar began. "Your value to me is a little bit diminished because there's now another source coming directly from the CEO," Rajaratnam told Kumar one day, referring to Chiesi's relationship.

"I'm giving him a million dollars a year for doing literally nothing," Rajaratnam complained to a mutual friend. That wasn't true at all. Indeed, as the growing web of wiretaps showed, Kumar was furiously supplying Rajaratnam with information on AMD, including the timing of the proposed spin-off of the manufacturing arm.

No character portrait of Rajaratnam is complete without an appreciation of just how well he understood the criminal mind—his own and others. His arrogance led him to believe he would never get caught, which people who know him say is the main reason he blathered so much on the telephone.

But his knowledge of the white-collar criminal mind was sharp and he knew that at bottom, all of them, from Anil Kumar to Rajat Gupta to people like Danielle Chiesi, were motivated by vaunting greed and—perhaps even more astutely noted on Rajaratnam's part—the need to please. They would do anything he asked if he could press the right button.

That's why Kumar was so valuable despite Rajaratnam's complaints. For that $1 million he helped steer tips Rajaratnam's way, and as investigators discovered, served as a recruiter as well.

In fact, it was Kumar who introduced Rajaratnam to Gupta, one of corporate America's leading statesmen and soon to be co-conspirator as one of the most important members in Rajaratnam's circle.

Wadhwa and the SEC were on to Gupta from the minute they got hold of Rajaratnam's telephone records; they also knew that Kumar and

Gupta had founded a business school in India together and that the two remained close. Kumar considered Gupta his mentor, and on paper it's easy to see, given their mutual corporate pedigree.

But it took some more digging to determine just how low Gupta, an icon of the business community, had sunk. This was, after all, a man who counted as friends Kofi Annan, then secretary-general of the United Nations, and Microsoft cofounder Bill Gates. Gupta raised millions of dollars to fight AIDS, malaria, and tuberculosis across the globe. As it turns out, Gupta's record at McKinsey held some clues for why he turned bad. The white-shoe consulting firm had for years been a place for high-quality services delivered in specialized fashion. Gupta, according to people there, changed the dynamic. McKinsey began to ramp up the fees and hired more low-level talent to pitch more work.

McKinsey, as the *Financial Times* once pointed out, had a tradition that ran counter to the "sins of self-enrichment and self-aggrandizement" that could be found all over Wall Street. Gupta's tenure was controversial, according to some former partners, because the firm operated more like a bank; it embraced both of those sins as a way to ramp up fees and profits at the expense of its clients. Yes, the Gupta years were profitable, and huge bonuses were awarded to senior executives, obviously including Gupta himself, but the drive for more money changed the firm's culture—some would say for the worse.

Yet Gupta's drive to make money held obvious value to Rajaratnam. Gupta had sat on the board of directors of several firms since he left McKinsey in 2003, including Goldman Sachs and Procter & Gamble, and he knew just about every major CEO in the country and many around the world.

He was worth an estimated $100 million at sixty-five years of age, but by all indications he wanted more. So, not long after leaving McKinsey in 2003, he reached out to Kumar to set up a meeting with Rajaratnam about creating a hedge fund.

The fund never made it out of the starting gate, but the Gupta-Rajaratnam relationship flourished, as he too became a member of the Rajaratnam circle. Over at the FBI, the connection became apparent the minute they began taping Rajaratnam's calls. One key moment came in 2008, as the financial crisis started to accelerate and Gupta began feeding Rajaratnam confidential information about Goldman board meetings.

Rajaratnam called to tell Gupta that rumors were rampant that Goldman was looking to buy a commercial bank like Wachovia, which was run by former Goldman executive Bob Steel. There were obvious benefits to Goldman in such a purchase, as Wall Street slowly slipped into crisis mode during the summer and fall of 2008. A commercial bank, unlike a traditional investment bank, has consumer deposits. These deposits could be drawn down to fund the firm's operations if Goldman's own lenders ended up pulling back, if and when the crisis became more acute.

Gupta's answer: "Yeah. This was a big discussion at the board meeting." However, he added that he would be surprised that the firm's desire to splurge to buy a bank was "imminent." For one thing, Goldman had no funding problems just yet.

Was that enough to nail either party? Not by a long shot. The information wasn't acted upon, and in and of itself, knowing that Goldman was considering something that was rumored in the market took away from the standard of nonpublicness that a dirty tip would have to meet.

But it was a start, and given Gupta's apparent comfort level and ease in sharing with Rajaratnam board discussions that were supposed to remain confidential, the investigators were sure better stuff awaited.

That better stuff came a few months later, in September 2008. Lehman Brothers had just filed for bankruptcy and the entire financial system was in turmoil. A massive government bailout was unfolding, one that would inject tens of billions of dollars into the remaining investment banks.

And still it wasn't enough to calm the jittery markets as investors continued to sell the shares of financial firms and refused to lend them money to finance their operations. For Goldman, buying a commercial bank like Wachovia never looked so good except for the fact that

Wachovia was now in trouble as well. It was about to fail, as its investments in housing-related securities tore into its balance sheet (as similar housing bubble deals did to the rest of the banking system).

But Goldman being Goldman, historically one of the savviest and most creative firms on the Street, came up with a solution—a $5 billion infusion of cash from legendary investor Warren Buffett.

The Buffett investment was controversial for several reasons. Some critics would say he traded on something similar to inside information, knowing that Goldman was being bailed by the federal government through various post-crisis programs, including the Troubled Asset Relief Program, or TARP. The same charge would be made against several lawmakers who traded in and around the crisis. Yet such moves were perfectly legal under the law. Buffett and these lawmakers may have had an informational edge against the average investor but it was in the type of information that was legal—it wasn't misappropriated from any company, just possibly the massive rumor mill known as the U.S. government.

Goldman, meanwhile, was less focused on any insider trading around its stock than it was in surviving the tumult as investors began dumping shares and closing lines of credit to a bank that had until now avoided the worst of the financial crisis. In exchange for the money, Goldman agreed to Buffett's extortion-like albeit perfectly legal terms: Lloyd Blankfein, the firm's CEO, said Buffett would provide Goldman with an immediate $5 billion in cash in exchange for preferred stock with a 10 percent dividend, as well as warrants to buy shares at $115, which were good until 2013. The investment, Blankfein knew, would ensure Buffett a huge payday, $500 million annually, or as Buffett later boasted, "we're getting fifteen dollars a second from this investment."

Rajaratnam, thanks to Gupta, didn't do too shabbily, either, though unlike Buffett's, his methods were far from legal. The Buffett deal was sealed during a board meeting on September 23, which Gupta attended via conference call; he dialed in from an office that he still had at McKinsey's New York headquarters.

Then he called Rajaratnam with the news before it was made public. Goldman now had the blessing of the world's most prominent investor; shares would almost certainly spike when that was announced the following day.

The conversation wasn't recorded because rather than calling Rajaratnam's cell, Gupta called his office phone, which wasn't wiretapped. But investigators had a trace on Rajaratnam's phone records and trading account. The Goldman board meeting ended around 3:50 p.m. and a few moments later, records indicated, Gupta called Rajaratnam. Just before the markets closed, Rajaratnam began snapping up Goldman shares.

He would earn a quick $1 million on the trade, and as he would explain in a telephone call that was recorded with a Galleon trader, "I got a call, right, saying something good might happen to Goldman."

The "good" that was happening wasn't confined to Goldman's bailout. It also included the increasingly airtight case against Rajaratnam and his cohorts. By the end of 2008 and into early 2009 dozens of people were facing charges in one form or the other from the Kang investigation, and dozens more were being developed separately by the Chaves/Makol squad, with Wadhwa in the middle.

One irony still lost on the government apparatus assembled to take down Rajaratnam and Gupta and possibly larger players in the future was that the biggest insider trading investigation in the nation's history was coming together at a time when the public couldn't care less about insider trading.

Investors were now shell-shocked by far bigger issues; between the end of 2008 and March 2009, the country would go through wrenching change, including a new president, after Barack Obama, a junior senator from Illinois, beat his Republican challenger, Senator John McCain of Arizona.

Even during the height of the financial crisis, Obama was receiving huge contributions from the big Wall Street firms and many hedge fund players—in part because he was the likely winner, after a Republican had held the office for two terms, and in part because in private meetings he seemed very smart on economic matters.

But within a few weeks of his election investors saw something else in the new president: He was a novice when it came to the economy. That realization began to set in when he selected an unsteady bureaucrat, Timothy Geithner, then the president of the New York branch of the Federal Reserve, to be his Treasury secretary.

The markets initially cheered when Geithner was appointed because he was seen as one of the architects of the bank bailouts and had knowledge of the financial system. But it wasn't long before he started making public statements about the economy and the banking system that gave investors just the opposite reaction, sending the Dow Jones Industrial Average to around 6,000—its lowest point since 1996—in March 2009.

It didn't help, of course, that Obama and Geithner and the SEC had the financial crisis to contend with, or the Bernie Madoff scheme to unravel. But one thing is certain: Investors made it clear that their lack of trust in the economy or the markets was grounded in simple concepts: They didn't believe in the health of the financial system or the acumen of the new administration enough to jump back into the markets.

Insider trading, much less Rajaratnam, Steve Cohen, or any of the other traders on the government's unofficial white-collar crime most wanted list, wasn't on public investors' radar.

Yet even with a new SEC chief, Mary Schapiro, and her new enforcement chief, a former prosecutor named Robert Khuzami, the insider trading investigation rolled on. For a few months after joining the commission, Khuzami decided to "recuse himself" from the Galleon portion of the investigation. Before taking the SEC post he had been general counsel of Deutsche Bank, which did business with the hedge fund. But not Schapiro, who was appointed SEC chief by President Obama, approved by the Senate, and shortly after held a private meeting with Wadhwa on what he had been doing for the past two years.

Wadhwa was said to be impressed with the show of additional support. He had never met Chris Cox, and he wasn't even sure Cox knew about the Galleon probe. But Shapiro did, it appears, almost immediately when she started to run the agency.

The reason was simple: Word of Wadhwa's success filtered through Washington, and for the political types who run the SEC, insider trading was viewed as the easiest way to restore the agency's reputation following the Madoff catastrophe and the image hit taken in the aftermath of the financial crisis.

The enforcement division of the SEC was known as an independent unit (within an independent agency), theoretically immune from political pressure by the presidentially appointed chairman. The reality is somewhat different.

The enforcement agenda is set by the chairman, a presidential appointee who bears the brunt of the political pressure exerted by the White House. Arthur Levitt, the longtime SEC chairman, appointed by President Bill Clinton, created the image of being a crusader for the small investor, installing rules that were supposed to democratize the release of company information among small and large investors. But he also ushered in an era of deregulation of the securities business—a move advocated by Clinton when he signed into law a bill that allowed commercial banks to merge with investment banks.

There would be much wealth creation in the Clinton years, of course, bolstered by the big banks that were created after the passage of the Gramm-Leach-Bliley "financial modernization" act. New megabanks like Citigroup used all their financial might to take greater levels of risk and developed new and more profitable investments. The collateralized debt obligation was a way to package all kinds of consumer loans, from mortgages to credit card bills, into a bond that had the practical effect of allowing banks to extend greater and greater amounts of credit to more and more people regardless of their long-term ability to repay loans. Through financial alchemy, risk was being reduced by having bonds that were sold to other parties and not held on the banks' balance sheets, or so the story went.

The banks created other ways to hedge it: The credit default swap (CDS) was an insurance contract that could theoretically cover any bond in the market. The holder of a CDS on the bonds of a big bank, for instance, would have a guarantee that the issuer of the contract (often an insurance company like AIG) would repay the bonds if the bank defaulted.

The conventional wisdom was that the banks wouldn't, that is, until 2008, when they almost did.

Between the mega-banks that created bonds based on loans that couldn't be repaid, and the insurance companies that created a hedge against the possibility that the financial system would implode, Wall Street became a tinderbox of risk. It was a bipartisan failure on the part of policy makers to understand the notion of risk and why and how it can spread.

However, many in the hedge fund business saw the house of cards for what it was, and they had the tools to make an easy killing. In 2007 and 2008, the best way to make a quick buck in the markets wasn't just by being part of Rajaratnam's circle of friends; there was a separate circle that involved calling a couple of your buddies and simultaneously shorting shares of bank stocks, and then buying the banks' CDSs.

With the financial system on edge, simply buying the CDS would drive shares of bank stocks dramatically lower as investors saw it as a sign of imminent doom. The run on Bear Stearns, the first bank to fail during the financial crisis, began with a sharp increase in the price of its CDS contracts.

Top executives at Bear complained publicly that the company stock was being manipulated to death—literally—through rapid-fire purchases of CDSs and the simultaneous shorting of its stock that crushed shares. A vicious cycle ensued. Lenders pulled lines of credit, and shares fell further, and CDSs would rise. In just one week in March 2008, that process would lead to the demise of the firm (what was left was sold to J. P. Morgan). A similar cycle would play out in Lehman Brothers' demise, and the rest of the big banks were threatened, too, before the bailouts saved the system.

The manipulation of the credit default swap became a brief and fleeting controversy during the financial crisis. It also exposed a form of insider trading that had a profound impact on the markets but went unaddressed by regulators. Bank executives like John Mack of Morgan Stanley complained to securities regulators during those dark days. To deal with it, SEC chairman Chris Cox banned short-selling of bank shares until the crisis had subsided. But the manipulation never emerged as an enforcement issue.

Of course, many factors led to the near demise of the big banks, but the fact remains that traders could make a quick and easy buck simply buying a credit default swap not for its intended purpose of hedging against a company's debt but in fact to drive shares lower and profit off a short sale.

Bob Khuzami, the general counsel for Deutsche Bank's U.S. subsidiary, knew as much about the practice as anyone in law enforcement even before he received the call from Schapiro to run the SEC's enforcement division. While an assistant U.S. attorney in the Southern District of New York, he was chief of the securities fraud unit and focused on high-profile white-collar crimes, including an investigation of improper trading on the floor of the New York Stock Exchange.

His reputation for diligence got him a key assignment as part of the team that prosecuted the so-called Blind Sheikh, Omar Abdel-Rahman, for the 1993 bombing of the World Trade Center. Beginning in 2002, Khuzami decided to cash in on his government experience, taking a job as general counsel for the U.S. unit of the German mega-bank. He did so at a time of great excess on Wall Street in terms of risk-taking that spread even among foreign firms and their U.S. units. Deutsche Bank was one of the top packagers and sellers of toxic mortgage-backed securities to other firms—instruments that were a primary cause of the 2008 banking collapse.

Khuzami was hardly on the ground floor of the bank's mortgage business, and as general counsel, he wasn't in charge of the bank's risk taking. But those untidy little facts were barely mentioned when Schapiro announced that Khuzami would now head the SEC's enforcement division, the agency's primary investigatory weapon against white-collar crime.

How well Khuzami fared is a matter of debate. Khuzami "moved heaven and earth" to bring cases involving mortgage fraud and the broader financial collapse, according to one senior SEC official. His record, according to the raw data, was impressive: During the Khuzami era, the SEC brought cases against 150 individuals for financial-crisis related activities and set new records for overall enforcement activity.

But the cases of CDS manipulation largely evaporated, as did major cases against executives from Lehman Brothers, Bear Stearns, and other big U.S. banks for broader abuses that led to the banking crisis. Brad Hintz, an analyst for Sanford C. Bernstein who covers brokerage stocks, had been called by government investigators just weeks after the September 2008 bankruptcy of Lehman Brothers about crisis-related fraud, but he never heard from them again.

In private moments with his staff and with reporters, Khuzami would explain the difficulties of bringing cases involving the financial crisis. The accounting gimmicks employed by Lehman during its final months were used elsewhere and received approval by major accounting firms. So, Lehman was simply listening to its auditors, who were interpreting accounting rules. No intent to break the law here.

A 2010 report by an auditor looking at Lehman's bankruptcy said there were "colorable claims" against the firm's senior executives for their crisis-related risk disclosures, but by early 2011, the SEC had all but concluded that it couldn't charge any of them for fraud; not even a parking violation.

Maybe the bank chiefs *really believed* their firms would survive when they made all those statements projecting confidence in the face of mounting evidence that they wouldn't survive, Khuzami explained at one point when questioned about the lack of cases. It's hard to press a fraud case of misleading the investing public unless there is clear evidence of intent to mislead.

Or maybe Khuzami knew that the political clock was ticking, with President Obama gearing up for a second term and declaring war on fat cats, even if those fat-cat cases were taking longer than desired. Thanks to the work of Wadhwa and the people at the FBI, they had instant gratification in the form of insider trading.

Okay, you got me," is how regulators describe the initial phases of Richard Choo-Beng Lee's confession to FBI agents after a week of tense negotiations with his attorneys, ending with his agreeing to be the latest rat to cooperate. Lee was a prize catch for investigators; he was a technology geek with degrees in science and business and even chip making. He knew Rajaratnam well, having worked with the Galleon chief while they were both analysts at Needham & Co.

More than that, Lee had worked at SAC Capital and he knew Steve Cohen.

Lee had been on the government's wish list for some time. Investigators simply referred to him as "CB." He ran a midsized hedge fund named Spherix Advisers, and as the SEC discovered through its maze of records and wiretaps, Lee had traded the same stocks that the Galleon chief had traded, and he had used some of the same illegal sources of information, including the same investor relations consultant who had alerted Khan to the Google earnings announcement.

But in the end, it was a Danielle Chiesi wiretap that finally did him in.

Lee and his business partner at Spherix, a trader named Ali Far, had as many connections as Chiesi in the Silicon Valley tech world, which is why she had kept them in her loop, and they kept her in theirs. Insider trading, the government had discovered, was like any other business in that information as much as cash was the currency that both parties relied upon. It was the quid pro quo that often mattered. With the government listening to various calls, the Lee-Far connection to the broader scheme became evident; both had access to the same Google investor relations executive from Market Street Advisors that Roomy Khan used. Meanwhile Chiesi shared with them tips she got from Moffat.

Kang made his first visit to Lee's Silicon Valley home and offered Lee a chance to cooperate and avoid jail time. As the Galleon probe progressed, its list of targets and possible cooperators had unraveled in bizarre ways. Far was actually approached first by the FBI, and alerted Lee that the government was starting to ask questions about their trading.

Lee listened intently as Kang explained the situation, providing Lee with a little taste of what the government had as evidence by playing some of the wiretaps. Lee seemed interested but let his attorney work the details before fully committing. When the attorney heard the tapes he gave Lee the following assessment: Cooperate or face jail time.

Lee was considered a great "get" by the government because of his obvious connections to the Rajaratnam circle of friends, as well as to Steve Cohen, for whom he had worked early in his career. Rajaratnam and Cohen might have been competitors in the markets, but they were fellow travelers in the hedge fund business. Far, for example, was a former Galleon executive who remained in regular contact with Rajaratnam. The wiretaps were making the case against Rajaratnam rock solid, even as the case against Cohen had stalled. But Kang considered Lee a possible game changer.

Once Lee began to fully cooperate, he explained in various sessions with the FBI and the SEC how he believed the famous SAC "edge" worked. "At SAC you are expected to develop an edge with information that no one else had," is how one government investigator present at the meetings described Lee's remarks. The takeaway from the government's discussions with Lee: SAC's trading environment was a breeding ground for insider trading.

Based on the Justice Department's review of the Cohen wiretap it was clear that the SAC chief didn't engage in Rajaratnam-like banter, at least on the telephone. So Kang settled on the next best thing. He planned to have Lee approach Cohen for a job, so the feds could plant someone inside the firm.

But first he needed a cover story. Because Lee and his partner, Far, were now government cooperators, they had to shut down Spherix. Kang knew the move would raise suspicions because insider trading actually works: The fund was doing well, posting returns of around 10 percent.

Even worse, the wiretaps were starting to show that the various people under scrutiny were growing suspicious about a possible rat in the circle. Chiesi for one opined that she might end up in jail just like "Martha fucking Stewart." Indeed, as soon as Lee and Far announced the closing of Spherix, the finance message boards began to speculate that they were in fact the rats.

Kang suggested a cover story to Lee and Far that went something like this: Tell clients and associates you had a falling-out over money, a move that might not raise suspicions in a world where people fight over money all the time. But it did, almost immediately. Rajaratnam, in particular, called Far first and asked if he was working with the government. Great traders have a gut feel for the markets and people, and Rajaratnam's gut was that Lee and Far were now government spies.

Far dodged the question with the cover story, but investigators were on high alert that their cover might have been blown and the authorities might have to move forward with arrests.

"Do you guys know about the expert networks?" Lee asked Kang one afternoon in the late summer of 2009. Up until now, the FBI and even the SEC thought the contingent of traders and analysts sharing and trading on illegal tips was doing so without buffers. But if Lee was to be believed, an entire shadow world existed where so-called experts in specialized fields, mostly in the tech field, sell to the highest bidder information about the companies they work at.

The arrangements were done through various firms, including one outfit known as Primary Global Research, which served as a broker for the information. On its face, the networks and the information-gathering system they said they employed appeared completely legal. What's wrong with an outside company employing executives from Apple or experts in the medical profession, including doctors, to provide insight into trends in technology or new drugs so a trader can better put together his mosaic?

But as Lee pointed out, hedge fund managers rarely wanted trend watching: They were actually looking for actionable material, such as early calls on mergers, earnings announcements, FDA rulings on new drugs—anything that would move a stock.

The experts were employed by just about every big hedge fund. SAC Capital often relied on a company named the Gerson Lehrman Group, which specialized in getting scientists and doctors with knowledge of drug companies to provide analysis of drug stocks, and at times relied on Primary Global. In late 2008, SAC's compliance department believed Primary Global lacked the proper controls on its consultants, and it was rejecting requests by fund managers to hire the firm's experts. The exact reason for the SAC move is unclear. Sometimes the information from the expert networks was like a view from thirty thousand feet—summarizing, for example, industry trends. But often the experts were handing their hedge fund clients confidential information as well. Still, SAC, like other hedge funds, thought experts were an integral part of the research side of their trading business. One such researcher was Dr. Sidney Gilman, a professor at the University of Michigan Medical School and an expert on drugs to combat Alzheimer's disease. Gilman, a Gerson expert, earned $100,000 from Gerson for his SAC work because the people there believed he was well worth it.

When these revelations made it back to the SEC, they shocked Wadhwa, who thought he had a pretty good handle on what was happening on Wall Street. Naturally he had heard about the expert networks but didn't realize just how big a business it had become—and exactly what type of "advice" it was peddling to the big hedge funds.

Many of the experts never revealed to their companies that they had cut these side deals, earning tens of thousands of dollars on top of their regular take-home pay, and it was clear, based on Lee's roadmap, that part of their function as part of these networks was to pass on insider tips.

The Galleon investigation was now three years old, and to Kang and Wadhwa it was still in its formative stages. Hearing about the expert networks was revelatory because it deepened their understanding of how illegal information flowed through the markets. In addition to the experts, countless other middlemen roamed through the hedge fund world, offering illegal inside tips disguised as good old-fashioned stock research.

Many of these individuals were former Wall Street analysts, who had looked at the expansion of the hedge fund business as a gold mine, particularly if they did more than crunch numbers, and passed along illicit tips that they managed to squeeze out of their contacts at the companies they once covered.

By Wadhwa's estimate, there were now literally dozens of potential targets on top of the investigation's big prizes, like Rajaratnam and possibly Cohen, who for all the attention remained elusive. That said, government suspicions about SAC were enhanced by the expert network revelations since no hedge fund would pay $100,000 to any single person without getting something in return.

The challenge wasn't in finding enough small-fry analysts whom the government could investigate and pressure to say something nasty about Steve Cohen and SAC; it was how to turn those cases into something bigger, like a conviction. Kang believed the time was right to plant a mole inside SAC, and Lee seemed like the perfect candidate, given his pedigree.

Lee had left SAC in 2004, but knew Cohen well enough for the SAC chief to take his call, which he did in 2009, and the two discussed Lee rejoining SAC. The conversation ended without a job offer. As one SAC insider put it: "People call Steve all the time looking for jobs." Yet, one reason why Cohen is so good at his job is that he follows his instincts. Something was definitely fishy about Lee, a trader who had just closed his fund down while it was producing 10 percent returns. Even to a casual observer, the odds were just too high that Lee had been turned.

With that, the urgency of making a move on Rajaratnam grew. In the late fall of 2009, the FBI was now following Rajaratnam daily. It had a car camped outside his spacious home in Greenwich, Connecticut, and one outside Galleon's offices in New York City. Kang was listening for any bit of evidence that might make him think Rajaratnam, with access to a corporate jet, contacts around the world, and billions of dollars at his disposal, might just leave the country and never come back.

That's about when Kang heard from the wiretaps that Rajaratnam planned a surprise trip to London. The official motive was to see the premiere of a movie he had invested in called *Today's Special*, starring Aasif Mandvi, a comic correspondent on Jon Stewart's *The Daily Show*.

Even more troubling was a report from U.S. Customs and Border Protection that Rajaratnam had bought a plane ticket to London. With his vast wealth, worldwide connections, and growing suspicions that the feds were closing in, leaving the country might be more preferable than spending more than a decade in a federal prison.

His return trip touched off even more alarm bells. He was coming back to New York. But it wasn't from London. Instead it was from Geneva, a place where he could conduct business as a fugitive.

For the Justice Department prosecutors it was a no-brainer—they should arrest him as soon as they could put together an indictment. If the tapes could hold up in court—and at least for the moment there was no reason to think they wouldn't—they would have enough evidence to put Rajaratnam away for many years. If they were to let him leave the country and he somehow made his way back to Sri Lanka, which does not have an extradition treaty with the United States, he could live very well for the rest of his life.

The wiretaps on the others in his circle would mean that he could be arrested, but so would the principal players in his orbit. Investigators didn't quite have their case on Gupta completed yet, but that could wait. Once arrested, Rajaratnam would be offered a deal that would include cooperation against Gupta or anyone else if he wanted to have a few years of his life outside of prison.

On October 15, 2009, early in the afternoon, Wadhwa was sitting in his office, looking over Galleon trading records, when he received a call from Kang.

"Sanjay," Kang deadpanned, "we're going to arrest him."

CHAPTER 11

POUNCE HARD

The FBI's standard procedure for arresting white-collar targets can best be described as law enforcement's version of the military's "shock and awe" tactic. Agents show up early, ideally before dawn. They allow the clearly dazed and confused target a few minutes to dress, but with minimal contact with family members. And then they apply the pressure, explaining the rigors of a life spent behind bars for many years.

Kang didn't deviate much from the script when he showed up at Rajaratnam's apartment, situated right off New York's East River in the exclusive Turtle Bay neighborhood of Manhattan at 6 a.m. on October 16, 2009. Rajaratnam's account of the arrest as told to *Newsweek* and confirmed by a close associate, goes someting like this: After announcing himself and his fellow agent, Kang began his shock-and-awe treatment. He told Rajaratnam to look at his children because it could be the last time he'd see them for a long time. You should take a look at your wife as well, Kang said. She's going to have a good time spending your money while you're away.

The ride to FBI headquarters at Foley Square in lower Manhattan took about a half hour. Rajaratnam was used to being in total control of every aspect of his life, but all that was about to change.

Once Rajaratnam was processed, and before his lawyer was present, Kang turned up the heat. For FBI interrogators, the hour or so they have alone with the target is the most crucial in convincing the latter to cooperate. Rajaratnam was a big catch in the eyes of the FBI—but there were bigger. Rajaratnam rubbed shoulders with heads of finance across the globe, so his cooperation would be enormously helpful in crushing the shadowy world of inside information.

They wanted him to tell them all about Rajat Gupta, whom they considered an even more important catch than Rajaratnam himself, given Gupta's position in corporate America. And they wanted Rajaratnam to tell them what he knew about other hedge funds.

Investigators by now understood that for all its size and power in the markets, the hedge fund business was really like a small town. There was an incestuous quality to its employment—traders would work for SAC, for instance, and turn around and take a job at Galleon, and vice versa. In a sense everyone knew everyone else's business.

Kang then launched into his routine. *Newsweek* reporter Suketu Mehta, who scored the only media interview with Rajaratnam following his arrest, described the interrogation: "Two FBI agents, wearing prominently displayed guns, played good cop, bad cop. They thumped tables . . . jumped up and down, told him, 'Just say you did it to one count'" of the various allegations they were hitting him with, namely trading on insider information in numerous stocks, as had been recorded on his cell phone or the phones of others.

They had a lot to work with. Agents told him the tapes had turned up dozens upon dozens of suspicious trades in shares of Hilton, Polycom, Intel, AMD, and many more. If he didn't cooperate, Kang told him, life as he knew it was over.

The people at the FBI give a different account. Kang, they said, was respectful and direct, and Rajaratnam was merely given his options: Turn in Gupta, and help them develop cases against others since Rajaratnam had contacts at every major Wall Street bank. Investigators subpoenaed Merrill, where he did the bulk of his business, and other firms for trading records. Surely he wasn't the only trader breaking the law. His other option: He could take his chances in court, which, Kang told him, weren't very good.

The arrests and charges made in the following days targeting the Rajaratnam circle took on the air of a circus. Rajaratnam was a billionaire, with friends like Goldman Sachs chief executive Lloyd Blankfein (who would eventually testify at his trial as a government witness, given the Gupta trades). And yet he made much of his wealth not through his high-class Wall Street contacts but through low-level minions like Dani Chiesi, who that very same morning had also been offered a chance to cooperate against Rajaratnam and others.

Staying in character, Chiesi was initially defiant when the FBI showed up that morning and was prepared for the consequences, namely going to jail. Although she was considered small potatoes in the grand scheme of things, she also held one of the keys to that grand scheme in her direct access to Rajaratnam, which is why she was targeted immediately as a potential cooperator.

FBI agents wanted her to start that very moment. Some people close to the investigation say the notion of cooperating to make a case against Mofat, who had also been arrested that morning, was jarring to Chiesi. But others say the agents wanted her to begin cooperating by placing calls to her West Coast circle of friends, which would have been recorded through the wiretap on her telephone. When she refused their offer, Chiesi didn't faint, as many targets do, but she did make it clear that it was too early (6 a.m. New York time) to be making telephone calls to the West Coast.

With that, the government placed her under arrest. She didn't even think to put on makeup before she was ushered into the FBI van parked outside her Manhattan apartment.

Before long she was in full view of the waiting cameras assembled outside FBI headquarters in lower Manhattan. Dressed in a white sweater and black coat, Chiesi looked a lot less glamorous than her Wall Street reputation would have suggested.

Moffatt was, indeed, the second of six arrested that day in one of the biggest insider trading busts in history, and the FBI had just gotten started. Mark Kurland, Rajiv Goel, and Anil Kumar rounded out the group.

Kumar actually did faint when the FBI announced his arrest, a sure sign he wasn't prepared for jail but that he was ready to spill the beans on Rajaratnam, which he eventually did.

In late 2009, the financial crisis was then barely a year old. The banks were recapitalized and the Dow had recovered from its low point reached in March—thanks to money being printed by the Federal Reserve. But all wasn't well on Wall Street. Small investors who continued to flee the stock markets could hardly be blamed for ignoring the mass arrests, or seeing it as yet more evidence that Wall Street plays by a different set of rules. Just weeks after the Rajaratnam cluster went down, Chaves and Makol made their move against David Slaine's circle of friends.

Craig Drimal, Slaine's old weight-lifting buddy, had to know it was coming. His wife Arlene, a former prosecutor for the Manhattan district attorney's office, noticed something strange in recent weeks: A car parked outside her home in a rural part of Connecticut with two men who at the time looked to her to be FBI agents. Then a few days later she found out they were when Makol knocked on her door and spent the next half hour with Drimal offering him a chance to cooperate, explaining that he had him on tape sharing inside information, and, by the way, he was facing a twenty-five-year jail term if he didn't. Makol also asked Drimal if he would help the feds build a case against Slaine, an attempt to keep Slaine's identity a secret once the arrests went down.

Drimal demurred, but he and his wife were terrified—and not just about the possibility that he could be in jail for a quarter century.

That's because the FBI also had a window on their private lives from those taped telephone calls, which included discussions between Drimal and his wife about marital difficulties, according to one person with knowledge of the matter. Knowing the FBI had heard the personal stuff in addition to Drimal's business affairs added a creepy dynamic to the turn of events. After Makol left, Drimal and his wife discussed the possibility of getting a prepaid cell phone so they could avoid the obvious wiretaps on their home telephone. That's when the situation got even more creepy. They heard from Makol again, this time on the telephone, warning that he knew what they were up to.

It's unclear if the FBI had placed a listening device inside the Drimal home. Arlene Drimal has said she believes the FBI used a nearby abandoned house to spy on the family. Given the advanced listening devices the FBI had been using, a bug could have been placed anywhere in the house or one could have been slipped into her husband's cell phone. In any event, Drimal would meet one more time with officials from the Justice Department and the FBI to discuss a possible cooperation agreement, including one where the ruse of setting up Slaine with Drimal wearing a wire was discussed. Again, Drimal said no, explaining to his wife, "I'm not going to sacrifice someone else's family to save myself."

A few days later, before the crack of dawn, Makol and a few other agents were back at Drimal's door, awakening him from a deep sleep and placing him under arrest for trading on inside information.

His wife didn't even have a chance to say goodbye.

He wasn't the only one to get the call from the FBI that morning. Less than a month after the Rajaratnam cluster went down, so did Drimal's entire circle of friends—all except one, David Slaine, who at least for now remained anonymous, only to be identified in charging documents simply as CS-1

It wasn't long before the Drimal circle figured out the identity of CS-1 since Slaine was the only member of the crew not to get busted. Slaine's old friends on Wall Street have characterized his work in helping the government as a betrayal, against Drimal and others who did nothing more than what Slaine himself had done, that is break the law to make a quick buck.

Slaine, for his part, was said to be devastated the day the arrests came down, comforted only slightly by the words of his government handlers—that he had done his part in making Wall Street a better place. Taken together, the wiretap on Drimal's telephone and Slaine's cooperation built cases against such people as the infamous "Octopussy," Zvi Goffer, who had finally fulfilled his wish to work at Galleon—thanks to Drimal, who had persuaded Rajaratnam to make the hire without Rosenbach's knowledge. That is until one day when Rosenbach noticed Goffer in the back of the trading floor.

But it was a short-lived stay at the firm. Goffer's arrest came nine months later just as Galleon was about to shut down. Authorities also rounded up Arthur Cutillo, the lawyer at Ropes & Gray who fed the cluster inside tips on mergers, and Michael Kimelman, the trader who was looking to set up a hedge fund with Slaine and pass around the same illegal information—along with ten others—were rounded up as well.

The Drimal case was fascinating for a number of reasons. His old friends at Galleon couldn't believe how someone regarded as a mid-tier trader often in need of cash had managed to create such an intricate insider trading ring. "Ruby was always complaining that 'things are tough,'" said one former Galleon trader. "He came across kind of pathetic, like he was looking for scraps from us, and then we saw this and we were blown away."

For investigators it was fascinating because the case provided a link between two different circles of friends. In assessing the information, FBI agents now realized that the wiretap on Drimal's telephone linked him to aspects of the Rajaratnam case. Before he went to work at Galleon, Zvi Goffer worked at a firm called Schottenfeld Group, where a trader named Gautham Shankar received tips from an analyst who regularly spoke with Roomy Khan.

Untangling the web of relationships was causing headaches for the government staff. The organizational charts began to look more like a Rorschach test than the neat, Mafia-like organization chart they had when they started. Relationships were overlapping, built on a mutual disdain for the law and love for making money.

Instead of two concurrent probes, the Jacobs-Kang and Chaves-Makol investigations were now being coordinated and combined. Stoking the investigators' suspicions about Steve Cohen's operation was the inordinate number of traders, money managers, and analysts who either worked for SAC or did business with the firm and could be found among the various clusters.

Another common element was the manner in which everyone seemed to operate: Their code of conduct was the good old-fashioned quid pro quo. They were essentially sharing information with people who would share back. Some of the information came through tips and some of it was paid for; the most disturbing part of what cooperator Richard Choo-Beng Lee told the government was that most experts never told their companies they were moonlighting as hedge fund employees. And why would they? The expert networks were really people who were busy stealing company secrets from the firms where they worked.

Through simple deduction, it was easy to see why the experts would stretch and provide not just advice but "color" that resulted in handing over secret, illegal data. Many hedge fund traders wouldn't even speak to experts unless the information resulted in a quick moneymaking event. If they wanted to get (sometimes literally) envelopes full of cash, they would have to push the figurative envelope and steal confidential information from their own company.

Places like Primary Global simply acted as brokers for the selling of the stolen goods.

Oh crap!" was the way Mark Anthony "Tony" Longoria reacted to news of the Rajaratnam arrests and government officials' boasting that more were on the way. Longoria was a midlevel supply chain manager at AMD. At least that's what he did during the day; his side job was moonlighting as an "industry expert" working with major hedge funds through the outfit Primary Global.

What worried him wasn't necessarily that he knew Rajaratnam or did business with Galleon—he didn't. But one of the stocks Galleon had profited on through illegal trading on inside information was AMD.

Longoria didn't know it at the time but this conversation and many others were being recorded by the feds as they extended their investigation into the seedy realm of the expert networks—the analysts, mid-level managers, and executives who were paid a fee by hedge fund traders for "actionable data" and advice about their companies. For the most part, the companies were kept in the dark about the practice, and even when they did disclose to their employers what they were doing, the experts described what they did in the most benign ways.

They were giving high-level advice, speaking in a general fashion about industry trends, providing context to help Wall Street better understand their business.

Lee's cooperation on these expert networks led investigators to Longoria, who was paid through Primary Global a rate of $300 per telephone call to discuss company business with traders throughout the hedge fund industry. He made about two hundred of these calls a year and he was often passing on tips about key events inside AMD before they were made public. That's why the Rajaratnam news was so jarring to him. His first call that day was to James Fleishman, his main contact at Primary Global. Fleishman conceded that he had seen the Rajaratnam news as well, though he seemed less nervous about its implications. "I saw that. . . . But I can tell you point-blank they are not a client."

"I was just really freaking out when I read that," Longoria shot back. "So there's no way they can tie them back to me. Because, oh my God!"

Fleishman replied, "Hopefully this will just kind of . . ."

"Blow over," Longoria muttered.

Longoria wasn't convinced. "Okay, okay, so there's no way they can tie them back to me?" he asked again, relaying a story from work that day. Someone in AMD's finance department mentioned that as part of the charges against Rajaratnam there was trading in shares of AMD. This person said Rajaratnam must have had a source inside AMD because he had an early read on the firm's revenues, which Longoria said "really freaked people out" inside the company.

Longoria was one of those people. As if he were looking to assure himself, Longoria stated he would "never speak in exact" ways that would cross over the line into giving specific company information. Or at least that's what he told Fleishman, who simply muttered, "Okay, okay, yeah," before hanging up.

Fleishman was right about one thing: Longoria's problem wasn't necessarily with Galleon. But that didn't mean either man was clean. That's because several months earlier Longoria had a conversation with Choo-Beng Lee, just after Lee shut down his hedge fund, in which Longoria provided detailed estimates about AMD revenues and financial numbers. That one piece of information opened up a new phase in the investigation of the expert networks, providing investigators with more than a few surprises over the course of the next year. They were finding a wide variety of people involved. Some were bookish technology nerds like Walter Shimoon, an executive at the technology company Flextronics, who sold inside tips through Primary Global. Others were more like John Kinnucan, a rogue of sorts, who, although he didn't work for the technology outfit, had more than twenty years' experience covering technology companies for Wall Street firms and so had plenty of contacts inside the Silicon Valley tech infrastructure. He also knew that hedge funds would gladly pay for his "expert advice."

Kinnucan's name came up in a number of places; several informants commented that he had one of the best rosters of hedge fund and mutual fund clients. He worked extensively with players such as SAC Capital, Citadel Investment Group, and even mutual funds like Janus and Friess Associates, the latter owned by hedge fund pioneer Foster Friess (as of this writing, none of those funds or their executives has been charged).

Kinnucan came onto the FBI's radar screen through a cooperating witness developed by Makol. With a little digging Makol was able to see how Kinnucan conducted business: He was plugged into the expert networks and had associates at hedge funds, often coming to New York "for a few beers," as he would say, with people at SAC Capital and other players. He also knew people inside technology companies.

He conducted business from his home in Portland, Oregon, which he shared with his children and his wife, Catherine. She was listed in incorporation documents as a partner in his venture known as Broadband Research. In reality the business revolved around her husband's contacts in the tech world. It was created in 2003 when regulators were clamping down on the Wall Street research business.

For Kinnucan, as regulators were closing that door, a bigger door was being opened: the sale of his "research" to hedge funds, which were growing in number seemingly by the day.

Makol received authorization to tap Kinnucan's telephone, but not with the goal of snaring Kinnucan and ending it there. In the government's eyes he was small fry. The bigger goal was to snare his client roster, which included the omnipresent SAC Capital.

Illegal insider trading is rampant and may even be on the rise," U.S. Attorney Preetinder "Preet" Bharara of the Southern District of New York said in a speech to a group of lawyers in October 2010. It was nearly a year after the Rajaratnam arrests, and two years after the financial crisis.

"In some respects, inside information is a form of financial steroid. It is unfair; it is offensive; it is unlawful; and it puts a black mark on the entire enterprise," he said during the speech to the New York City Bar Association.

"Some have asked why use court-authorized wiretaps in insider-trading cases?" he said, alluding to the debate around the expanded use of wiretaps to include not just drug cases but also those involving insider trading.

"The quick answer," Bharara said, "is that every legitimate tool should be at our disposal especially where, as in the case of insider trading, an essential element of the crime is a communication."

He even borrowed a page from the man who appointed him, President Barack Obama, and found a class-warfare argument to justify the wiretapping spree on hedge fund fat cats. "Disturbingly, many of the people who are going to such lengths to obtain inside information for a trading advantage are already among the most advantaged, privileged, and wealthy insiders in modern finance. But for them, material nonpublic information is akin to a performance-enhancing drug that provides the illegal 'edge' to outpace their rivals and make even more money."

The speech immediately found its way into the press (in this case the *New York Post*). It was, after all, a warning to the perceived bad guys or the already arrested bad guys like Rajaratnam, whose attorneys were preparing their fight to save him from serious jail time: The government was going to pounce and pounce hard.

The financial crisis may have escaped serious prosecution, but insider trading wouldn't. It was low-hanging fruit for federal prosecutors and SEC brass—much-needed proof to the public that the law enforcement community was serious about cracking down on financial crimes, even if this particular financial crime had very little to do with the root causes of the financial crisis and following Great Recession.

By October 2010, the Justice Department had concluded that the prosecution of financial-crisis-related crimes was never going to happen. Aside from some civil cases brought by the SEC, most notably one involving Goldman Sachs, which was fined a mere $550 million for unloading toxic securities to unsuspecting investors, the financial crisis was over from a law enforcement standpoint.

Just a few months later, Charles Ferguson, the director of *Inside Job*, a documentary about the financial crisis, accepted an Academy Award and echoed the sentiments of most Americans when he shouted that "not a single financial executive has gone to jail and that is wrong!"

Ferguson's statement was quickly seized on by the business media as proof that the federal government, even the allegedly reform-minded

Obama administration, wasn't up to the task. But a crackdown on insider trading might just change the subject, and perhaps even make Preet Bharara a law enforcement star.

It took about a year after being named Southern District chief for Bharara to tout the success of the insider trading crackdown he inherited. In doing so, he emerged as one of the most controversial law enforcement officials in the country. Harvey Pitt, the former SEC chairman, says Bharara deserves to take credit for the success of the probes even if they began under his predecessor, Michael Garcia. "He hasn't lost a case," Pitt says. "That's a huge achievement."

Others are less complimentary. "Preet's a smart gut and a very good lawyer, but he's also a publicity hound," a former Justice Department official said about the new U.S. Attorney from Manhattan, while a former law school classmate of Bharara (they both attended Columbia Law) described him as "the last guy you would think of as a modern Eliot Ness, much less Rudy Giuliani."

Preetinder S. Bharara was born in India, and came to the U.S. when he was twelve. By all accounts, he came from a family of overachievers. His brother Vinnie, an Internet entrepreneur, would ultimately become a dot-com success story by selling a company he started to Amazon.com for around $500 million. Vinnie's business acumen is a point Bharara makes often in speeches to show the Wall Street crackdown isn't anti-business, just anti-corrupt businesses.

Bharara attended Harvard College and Columbia Law School. After graduation he landed a job in corporate law, and then became an assistant U.S. attorney for the Southern District of New York. He is described by fellow attorneys as a good prosecutor but one who also excels at the political side of the job. His affable personality combined with political savvy enabled him to befriend people in the office with ties to New York's powerful state Democratic Party, such as Ben Lawsky, an ally of the senior U.S. senator from New York, Chuck Schumer.

Lawsky, himself a rising star in New York political circles, and Bharara have remained close associates through the years. When a job opened for the position of general counsel for Schumer, who was a ranking member of the Senate Judiciary Committee, Bharara got his shot at the big time.

Lucky break or not, he made the most of it. Schumer and Bharara led the committee's investigation into the Bush administration's firing of U.S. attorneys. The case made lots of headlines, but aside from a critical report, it produced no prosecutions. Even so, Bharara earned the trust of Schumer so much that when the Obama administration took over, Schumer's very important nod to fill the Southern District post went to the guy everyone simply refers to as "Preet."

Being in the right place at the right time has served Bharara well. The Southern District, as it is known in law enforcement circles, is a prosecutorial destination like no other. It is considered the most important of all the federal prosecutorial offices, primarily because its jurisdiction includes Manhattan—just about every trade, every financial transaction, has *some* link to a firm located in Manhattan. Consequently, a scam in Shanghai might be investigated by the Southern District because it had some roots in one or more of the big New York banks.

Over the years, the office has made good use of its power. One of its high-water marks came back in the 1980s, when another prosecutor from the Southern District, Rudy Giuliani, launched what was at that time the largest crackdown ever on white-collar crime.

That crackdown crippled that era's big players, such as investment banker Marty Siegel, arbitrageur Ivan Boesky, and ultimately junk-bond king Michael Milken. It also led to Giuliani's political career as mayor of New York and his subsequent highly lucrative career in the private sector, specifically the corporate security industry.

Bharara had to know what those cases had done for Giuliani and perhaps he was looking to create the same magic for himself. There were of course key differences. Giuliani actually led the office as it was making the white-collar crime cases of the 1980s; thus he was responsible for its successes and more than occasional failures (several of his high-profile indictments floundered in court).

By contrast, Bharara had inherited much of his good fortune from predecessors in the Bush administration, though you wouldn't know that from some of the rhetoric coming from the Southern District press office. To be fair, Bharara had little choice but to go public in a major way given the very nature of his job, which is to show the general public that law enforcement is addressing white collar crime, particularly following the excesses that led to the financial crisis. Moreover, a closer look at Bharara's remarks shows he often gave credit to the career prosecutors and agents who had developed the cases before he took the job.

That said, his press department wasted little time touting various arrests that came as a result of the crackdown on insider trading. Bharara clearly understood what he had stumbled upon. As an assistant U.S. attorney he brought cases against Mobsters. But when he joined Schumer's office he got a taste of how the Wall Street Mob worked. He was at the Senate Judiciary Committee when it championed Gary Aguirre's cause against insider trading.

With that the Southern District press machine went into overdrive. One story in the *Wall Street Journal* promised a wave of insider trading arrests that would surpass the size and scope of Giuliani's crackdown. The government had mountains of targets, and the press frenzy that followed sent the hedge fund business into disarray. Suddenly a guy, whose last name reporters had had a tough time spelling, was known across Wall Street.

Meanwhile, the takeaway from his now-famous speech heard all around the hedge fund world was unambiguous: Mass arrests in the insider trading probe were imminent. Or as one white-collar defense attorney with clients caught up in the expanding probe put it: "Preet believes it's gonna be like shooting fish in a barrel."

CHAPTER 12

NEVER LET A GOOD SCANDAL GO TO WASTE

"We did all the work," muttered a senior FBI official when he digested the *New York Post* story about Bharara's speech. By now senior FBI officials were convinced the speech was part of a broader campaign by Bharara's press office to take credit for the bureau's hard work.

The FBI is an office inside the Justice Department, but it's in many ways an independent agency. Its director is appointed by the president, not by the attorney general. FBI agents need U.S. attorneys to bring cases, but U.S. attorneys need the FBI to help them make those cases.

Now a battle over which part of the Justice Department deserved credit for the fruits of the crackdown threatened that relationship at a time when so much work was yet to be done. The expert networks and their role in funneling dirty information to the hedge fund business were now on the front burner at all the major law enforcement agencies involved in the insider trading probe. New informants were being brought forward, and wiretap authority sought. The pursuit of new targets was still an objective for all the government agencies.

Most of all, senior officials in the FBI worried about the agency's place in history. The FBI's early days include the secretive J. Edgar Hoover, but the modern version of "the Bureau" is one where image and PR count. Press releases touting arrests are routinely sent to reporters to make certain the public knows that all the money spent on investigations produces results. In fact the agency assigns at least one agent to protect its image in Hollywood, since criminals often develop their first impression of the bureau from seeing it in the movies.

Combating Bharara's PR blitz, though, would be a dicey matter. He was, of course, the U.S. attorney, and with that he had a bully pulpit not available to any FBI agent, or even to Janice Fedarcyk, the newly appointed head of the New York office of the FBI.

Eventually the FBI would get into the act, tipping off selected reporters to show up for high-profile arrests. But FBI officials complained that the Southern District had a big lead. A November 20 story in the *Wall Street Journal* added color and depth to the *New York Post* scoop about Bharara's speech. Citing people familiar with the matter, the *Journal* reported that "federal authorities, capping a three-year investigation, are preparing insider-trading charges that could ensnare consultants, investment bankers, hedge-fund and mutual-fund traders, and analysts across the nation," as well as the shadowy world of the "expert network business," where inside tips were passed from company executives moonlighting as researchers to big hedge funds.

The story sent shock waves across Wall Street. Seated at his usual luncheon perch, the San Pietro restaurant in Manhattan, John Mack, having just retired from Morgan Stanley, predicted that his old nemesis Gary Aguirre was behind the insider trading assault. Others at the exclusive Manhattan eatery believed it was an overambitious Obama Justice Department following the class-warfare message of their supreme leader.

Still others said the ultimate target was Cohen, whom the feds had been eager to grab for years. "But I bet they never get him," said one executive as he chowed down on his plate of thirty-dollar pasta. Hedge fund executives and their legal staffs read the story for detail and nuance to predict the feds' next move.

Cohen, meanwhile, wasn't specifically mentioned in the account, but no story about insider trading allegations would be complete without a mention of SAC Capital. In this case the mention stemmed from an FBI person of interest, John Kinnucan, the independent research analyst whom the FBI had come across as someone who used expert networks and other sources of insider information and passed them along to his clients, which included major hedge funds and mutual funds.

Kinnucan had done something unusual a few weeks earlier. It was after Special Agents David Makol and Edmund Rom paid a visit to his home in Portland, Oregon, and he sent a blast email to his clients, firms like SAC, Citadel, and other big hedge funds, alerting them that "two fresh faced eager beaver" FBI agents had showed up to his home, offered to play some tapes they had of him passing along and trading on inside information, and told him he could make the case go away if he wore a wire to snare some of his clients.

The way Kinnucan described his FBI encounter in a subsequent interview was more dramatic; he said Makol and Rom announced who they were, surrounded him, and after offering to play a recording of some of his illegal doings, began shouting threats about how long he would spend in jail because of his illegal activities. At one point they brought up someone else who had been found on the wiretaps—a sales representative from a technology firm that Kinnucan used as a source of information. The sales rep's son just died in a biking accident. "It's a shame if we put him in jail," Makol said, referring to the sales rep. "But we don't feel sorry for you."

Kinnucan held to his story, saying he had done nothing wrong—the information he received from the sales rep or anyone else "can be downloaded off the Internet."

Makol was unimpressed. "Come on, John," he shot back. "You know something is happening before it happens."

Kinnucan said it all went down as he was sitting in his kitchen, worrying about being arrested in front of his wife and children, who weren't home at the time.

Kinnucan declined the FBI's request to cooperate, and a few hours later he became among the more bizarre footnotes in the insider trading drama. His blast email was leaked to the *Wall Street Journal* and soon went viral, picked up by other media outlets, both print and television.

As any defense attorney will tell you, targets shouldn't antagonize the feds. The government, being the government, can always find something to charge you with, and they will do so if you rub their noses in it.

But that's exactly what Kinnucan did. He appeared on both Fox Business and CNBC to tell his story, not of a fat cat guilty of cheating the system, but about an average citizen unfairly targeted by the all-powerful federal government, waging a political vendetta.

Kinnucan described himself as a mere researcher, pushing information to his clients like everyone else does on Wall Street and in the hedge fund business. He penned a column in the Dealbook section of the *New York Times* titled "Why I Declined to Wear a Wire," and in it he wrote: "My personal belief is that much of this enforcement activity is politically motivated and will ultimately only serve to delay the return of confidence in our country, on the part of Main Street and Wall Street alike."

The question is, why? At the FBI, the guess was that he was desperate and that Kinnucan thought he could keep them at bay by having the media portray him as a victim. Others at the FBI simply believed Kinnucan was crazy, which appeared increasingly the case as his criticism of the government turned more bizarre.

Still, there was nothing strange or crazy about why the FBI believed Kinnucan could be an important witness. The *Journal* originally reported that the agents wanted him to focus on SAC. Kinnucan has said they were interested in another client, the Chicago-based hedge fund Citadel.

Either way, both were major clients, as were about a dozen other large hedge funds and a smattering of mutual funds.

Kinnucan's email, and its description in the press, had the practical effect of further putting the hedge fund business on red alert. The feds were ready to move and they were willing to do anything within the confines of the law to snare the biggest players in the business, including playing hardball with a witness and threatening to confront him in front of his wife and kids.

Most hedge funds just hunkered down, hiring press agents to manage the fallout when the subpoena arrived and its name was leaked. Such leaks often cause investor panic, and as the tally of hedge funds under scrutiny became known, investors reacted in kind. Suspects reacted in their own way. Some tried to keep a low profile. Former SAC trader Donald Longueuil was recorded describing how, after reading a story about pending arrests, he destroyed hard drives on his computer that contained trading data.

Longueuil was eventually snared the same way Drimal was caught: thanks to the cooperation of a friend. The best man at his wedding, Noah Freeman, a former SAC portfolio manager, wore the wire that led to Longueuil's arrest. Both were fired from SAC in 2010 for poor performance, which was hardly surprising to investigators given the sink-or-swim mentality that operated at SAC and how, they believed, it caused some traders to push the limits of acceptable conduct.

Freeman's odyssey from criminal to informant began when he was out of the hedge fund business for a few months, teaching at an all-girls school in Boston—that's when he was approached by B. J. Kang, who gave him the same choice he gave everyone else who came onto his radar: Cooperate or go to jail.

Freeman chose to cooperate, helping the FBI develop evidence against his best friend, and telling all he knew about SAC. Freeman's SAC experience was important to FBI investigators. He confirmed much of what they knew about the inner workings of the giant hedge fund, and how Cohen himself operated, namely by culling the best trading ideas from his money managers.

None of which is illegal, of course. Although Freeman said he had minimal direct contact with Cohen (he worked in Boston as opposed to Stamford), he also shed more light on how he believed illegality took place at SAC. A report in *Bloomberg News* citing an FBI memo said Freeman told Kang at one point that the pressure to give Cohen profitable trading strategies was immense, and that pressure led traders like himself to cross the line into trading on insider information.

Freeman conceded that he took steps to evade the firm's compliance rules. These included policies designed to curtail the passing of inside information by forbidding SAC employees from talking directly to executives of public companies through expert networks. Freeman also admitted he communicated by the video-calling service known as Skype rather than through emails on his computer because he said it wasn't checked by SAC's compliance team.

But Freeman also described a compliance system that was fairly easily evaded, and "willfully blind" to illegal activities, according to one person with direct knowledge of what Freeman told the feds. He pointed to his use of one Primary Global expert named Winifred Jiau, an American citizen who was born in Taiwan. Primary Global had been raising red flags at SAC where the compliance department was putting an end to its use. Freeman found a way around the ban simply by paying Jiau through trading commissions, rather than directly as a consultant, which would have brought on greater scrutiny.

With that, Jiau earned $200,000 a year dispensing inside information to Freeman, mainly from her contacts at technology companies like Nvidia and Marvell Technology. Jiau clearly had her quirks. To those who employed her services, she was bossy, high maintenance, and, according to Freeman, appeared to have a predilection for high-end seafood.

In addition to getting paid cash, Freeman felt obliged to provide Jiau from time to time with fresh lobsters, he said. Despite his disdain for Jiau, he jokingly referred to her as "Poohster" or "Winnie the Pooh." But what she was doing was no joke. Freeman's cooperation led to a wiretap, and at one point Jiau was recorded calling the money she received "sugar" to help complete the "recipes" of insider trading.

With Freeman's assistance, by late 2010, the expert probe had progressed well beyond Tony Longoria, the AMD manager, to include people like Jiau; Walter Shimoon of Flextronics; Daniel DeVore, a supply manager at Dell; and Kinnucan, who wasn't an expert, but rather a researcher who relied on experts to help him guide his clients at the hedge funds. Jiau fascinated investigators not just because she liked to eat lobster. She graduated from Stanford with a degree in statistics and was plugged into the nerd crowd throughout Silicon Valley, which like the traders in New York played a key role in the various insider trading clusters.

For all Jiau's outlandish requests, Kinnucan seemed to one-up her in the weirdness department as his media tour continued. "If they arrest me they will have to arrest the entire Wall Street research community," he said during one of his more lucid moments, since the information he traffics in—estimates of sales, and shipments of computer parts, etc.—is part and parcel of the research business.

Lee Ainslie, the founding partner of the hedge fund Maverick Capital, was allegedly ducking paying Kinnucan for some research before the trouble started, prompting this email outburst by Kinnucan one night: "Yo Lee homey, Sorry to break it to you, but looks to me likely that Maverick will soon be charged with insider trading. Just thought I'd let you know . . . Regards, JK."

Maverick eventually paid him some money, and Kinnucan's outbursts to Ainslie ended. Others, particularly those he considered his accusers in government, weren't so lucky.

In one email sent to various reporters, attorneys, and investigators, Kinnucan called Bharara "a limp dick Indian piece of shit."

The more Kinnucan spoke or emailed reporters and clients, the more he angered people at the Justice Department and the FBI, particularly Chaves, who believed he had given Kinnucan, like

Slaine, a second chance at a new life. They had a solid case against him for insider trading, and now he was trying to make the FBI look like the Gestapo.

Shimoon was now a cooperating witness and told the feds he had given Kinnucan inside information on Flextronics. Wiretaps indicated that Kinnucan received inside information on other tech companies and passed them to people like Freeman at SAC. His name came up from other sources and cooperators. He wasn't the biggest fish in the insider trading sea, but he was as guilty as Rajaratnam.

Kinnucan, meanwhile, continued to think of himself as a crusader against government overreaching as his emails—increasingly hostile and at times racist—suggested. That's when the feds came to the conclusion that Kinnucan needed to know what happens when you call one of the government's top law enforcement officials a "limp dick."

"Mr. Kinnucan will soon need some help and there will be no one around to help him," Chaves remarked at the time.

The government's boasting about the onslaught of new cases may have been good PR, but combined with John Kinnucan's own big mouth it had the practical effect of alerting at least some of the bad guys to stop doing what they were doing. Senior officials at the FBI openly fretted that the burst of publicity would cause some of the bad guys, mainly those born overseas, to try to flee the country rather than face arrest and prison.

Since so many of the suspects and targets arrested were of foreign origin, the government began to take measures to stop those they believed would most likely flee from doing so. Jiau, for instance, was immediately placed in custody and found herself in a series of federal prisons, including one in lower Manhattan for nine straight months following her arrest. Pretty harsh for someone who loved to feast on lobster, and things would get even harsher when she was sentenced to an additional four years in jail.

The feds weren't so lucky when it came to Deep Shah, who had tipped Roomy Khan to Blackstone's purchase of Hilton Hotels and was a key suspect in the probe. Shah had already gone missing, presumably fleeing to his native India before he could be arrested.

For now, that was the least of the government's problems.

In the fall of 2010, the Southern District staff was embarking on its prosecution of Rajaratnam, with a trial date set for spring 2011. Its choice to lead the case, a forty-two-year-old prosecutor named Jonathan Streeter who had made his bones in the Southern District dissecting, then simplifying and winning some of the most complex white-collar fraud cases. Streeter's most recent victory was against the infamous attorney Marc Dreier, convicting him of a massive investment fraud surpassed only by Bernie Madoff's Ponzi scheme in size and brazen disregard for the law.

Streeter was known for his affability and directness, and most of all, he wasn't a political grandstander, which is why he got along so well with the FBI agents while preparing for the trial. Something else also set him apart from those working on the inside trading investigations: He didn't think insider trading was the white-collar equivalent of murder.

To be sure, Streeter didn't buy the "victimless crime" excuse offered by academics (and those who had been caught during the probe) who suggested that insider trading had no practical impact on investor confidence. But he also saw limits to how much insider trading really did hurt the little guy particularly when compared to outright rip-offs. In Streeter's worldview, the long jail sentences often meted out under the sentencing guidelines should be reserved for people like Madoff and Dreier, rather than the typical insider trader.

But that didn't stop Streeter from taking on a case that was being regarded as a game changer for prosecutors who were still without a financial-crisis scalp to display as a trophy. First, Rajaratnam was no typical insider trader. The evidence showed him brazenly violating the law, basically thumbing his nose at the entire federal government just days after being questioned by the SEC with his Google and Hilton trades. Moreover, the Galleon investigation produced "one hell of a sexy case," Streeter said at the time, emboldened by wiretaps, cooperating witnesses, and larger-than-life characters—all the ingredients of a great movie. What prosecutor wouldn't want to try that case?

The trick was to assemble the evidence into a coherent narrative. As he listened to the wiretaps, and heard Rajaratnam incriminating himself in his own voice, Streeter, however, had two major concerns. First, since there was so much evidence, with all the various tape recordings, he could easily overwhelm the jury with information. He needed to narrow and simplify the evidence and that would take time.

He also needed to prepare for a major setback that could upend the entire case if Rajaratnam's defense team, now led by veteran litigator John Dowd, succeeded in its goal to convince the judge to disallow the wiretaps.

Dowd was somewhat of a surprise choice to lead the Rajaratnam defense. He hadn't been before a jury in a major white-collar case in years. His last big white-collar case was back in 1997 when he defended Fife Symington, the former Arizona governor who was accused of bank fraud (Symington was convicted, but later pardoned by President Bill Clinton).

But Dowd, a former Marine, was someone Rajaratnam wanted. Like himself, Dowd is a fighter who both knew the law (he headed the criminal defense department of Akin Gump, a large Washington law firm) and knew that the case against his client was weakest at precisely the strongest piece of evidence: the wiretaps.

As mentioned earlier, wiretapping phones was hardly unprecedented, but prosecutors have rarely relied on that tool to build white-collar cases. According to government statistics, in 2009 drug cases were the most prevalent type of case investigated through wiretaps, followed by homicides, organized crime, and, somewhere near the bottom, white-collar felonies.

The procedures to get wiretap authority are pretty strict, and given all the various applications in the case, Dowd's bet was that he could find more than a few procedural mistakes and begin to chip away at the wiretaps that showed Rajaratnam breaking the law all in his own words.

Streeter knew where Dowd and his people were heading. The government has "limitless resources," is the old saying, but Rajaratnam was a billionaire. In other words he had the resources to make the government look really silly if the wiretaps were declared inadmissible.

As the trial date approached, what looked like an easy win started to look somewhat less easy. For starters, Bharara, with his comments about the successful use of wiretaps, had made a crucial error: celebrating a victory that had yet to be won. It was a bad omen, and even worse, some government investigators worried it may have pissed off the judge, Richard Holwell, enough to get him to toss the wiretaps on a technicality.

A buttoned-down former corporate lawyer, Holwell was appointed to the federal bench eight years earlier by President George W. Bush. Holwell was known as a stickler for details, particularly when something as sensitive as a wiretap application was at issue.

Put simply, Streeter was worried that for all the mountains of evidence against Rajaratnam, the government could still lose by having the wiretaps thrown out of court. The implications were huge not just for the Rajaratnam case, but for the entire insider trading probe. Traditionally, insider trading had been difficult to prosecute precisely because it was hard to establish the exact nature of the communication between the tipper and the tippee.

Based on information uncovered by Cam Funkhouser's computers and those at the SEC, there were literally thousands of potential cases of insider information each year. The trades before major market-moving announcements, such as mergers and acquisitions, painted a fairly compelling picture of how rampant insider trading was in the markets. The problem was proving it. Even with witnesses testifying to the guilt of a tippee, he-said-she-said cases are rarely a slam dunk. Targets can always rely on the concept of a "mosaic," or a combination of various pieces of (public) information, as the real reason for a trade, rather than any specific piece of nonpublic information. In the Martha Stewart case, prosecutors went for the low-hanging fruit that Stewart lied about her suspicious trades to investigators, rather than the more difficult case of proving that her trades themselves were based on inside information.

The Rajaratnam wiretaps left no doubt about intent. They showed in his own words how hedge fund traders worried less about their mosaics and more about their access to inside information in doing their jobs. And they were costly. Each wiretap needs at least a half-dozen investigators monitoring calls around the clock. Because the feds had multiple wiretaps going on at the same time, Perfect Hedge was already possibly the most expensive white-collar investigation in recent history—and the biggest waste of money if the wiretaps couldn't be used.

John Dowd may not have tried a case—at least not a case of this magnitude—in a while but he proved to be a crafty litigator from the outset. The actual trial of *U.S. v. Rajaratnam* wouldn't begin for several months, sometime in the spring of 2011, but the case was basically being decided in federal court in October 2010 when Dowd and Streeter duked it out before Judge Holwell over whether the wiretaps of Rajaratnam's cell phone—the same phone he used to dish inside trading dirt with Danielle Chiesi and his broader circle of friends—should be suppressed during trial.

Dowd's argument was pretty simple: The feds had to show—had to have proved to Judge Lynch back in 2008—that they had exhausted other methods of investigating Rajaratnam in order to get his approval to initiate a wiretap, and that the invasion of privacy that is at the heart of every wiretap was the last resort in catching an alleged bad guy. It was a high bar, albeit not insurmountable given the difficulty of prosecuting insider trading.

Title III of the Omnibus Crime Control and Safe Streets Act of 1968 is the federal law that allows the government to wiretap private citizens. There are rules and procedures that must be followed before wiretap authority is granted by a federal judge, including utilizing all other investigatory techniques before going for a wiretap.

The problem for Streeter was, Dowd claimed, that those rules and procedures were not followed, at least not that closely. In Dowd's words, the "FBI went straight to tapping the phones" before fully utilizing conventional techniques to investigate their targets.

Streeter was well prepared to make the argument that the wiretapping was necessary since Rajaratnam had been investigated for years without success. It was harder to defend against a procedural mistake made on the part of Goldberg and Kang when in their initial wiretapping application before Judge Lynch they failed to even mention that the SEC was investigating Galleon Group—and had yet to conclude that investigation.

Worse than making it look like the government was hiding stuff, it helped make Dowd's argument, namely that the government was so scared about not meeting the Title III test that it left out what the court needed to know to render a decision.

Kang took the stand and did his best to try to explain why he would leave out a key fact—namely that he didn't see it as necessary since the SEC and Justice Department always work together on cases. Any federal judge would know that, so it was unnecessary to put it in writing. Streeter tried to pass it off as an innocent mistake and one that wasn't material in granting the application. "There was nothing nefarious about it . . . it would be bad government if we didn't work with the civil authorities."

When Holwell first granted Rajaratnam's request for a hearing on the wiretaps he said the government had "recklessly or knowingly misleadingly omitted several key facts" in the initial application. Streeter and Bharara had met at least once during this time. They agreed that despite Holwell's initial bluster—they were prepared to be "smacked around" a bit by Holwell—they weren't going to lose and the wiretaps would be safe. Streeter was confident that he had provided enough evidence to prove that nothing Kang and Goldberg had done was "reckless." It was a mistake, plain and simple, and there was no way Holwell would upend the biggest post-financial crisis white-collar case on a simple mistake.

What they didn't know was how close they came to being wrong and watching Rajaratnam possibly walk away free. Holwell is a judge who is hard to read. He displays little if any emotion when weighing evidence on such pretrial matters. Streeter and Bharara didn't know it but nothing Holwell heard during the hearing changed his initial assessment of the wiretap application. In fact, Holwell has told people it only reinforced the need to "suppress," or throw the wiretapped evidence out of court.

The hearings lasted four days, but they could have lasted four minutes as far as Holwell was concerned; he was ready to side with the defense and throw out the wiretaps. It would be a huge blow to the government. In a sense, if Rajaratnam's taped conversations were thrown out, one could make the case that most of the ensuing telephone wiretaps of all the other people investigated in the mammoth roundup were so-called fruit of the poisonous tree (and hence inadmissible in court) since they had grown out of an illegal wiretap.

"Okay, this is a real mess," Holwell thought as he began to scope out the reasons for upending what was possibly the biggest insider trading case in history. Without the wiretaps, the government had to resort to conventional means such as witnesses and circumstantial evidence, the stuff that makes insider trading so difficult to prove in court, since witness memories fade and markets are full of rumors that are hard to differentiate from inside information.

The government's efforts on the broader issue would be dealt a huge blow. Defense attorneys would be given a road map to have evidence thrown out of court. Forget nailing Rajaratnam; cases against lesser subjects could be thrown out, including those against many of the current cooperators. It was unclear how many of the other wiretap applications excluded the same information, but it was a good bet this wasn't an isolated example.

As Holwell prepared to suppress the best evidence against

Rajaratnam—indeed, possibly against any white-collar criminal in recent memory—he alerted his clerk, a bright Harvard Law grad named Justin Raphael, to start the work to prepare the opinion. In Holwell's mind, the courts were pretty clear when it came to anything that looked like government misbehavior: They don't tolerate it and evidence tainted by it is inadmissible.

Raphael was hardly an expert on the inner workings of Wall Street though as an undergraduate, he wrote a magazine piece where he tried to explain why so many college graduates chose a career there. While "money is the sole rule of the Street," he wrote, "it is far from its only allure." The essay went on to say that people on Wall Street love the "adrenaline rush" they get at work, and they "relish the competition" of deal making. Raj Rajaratnam couldn't have said it better.

Raphael graduated from Harvard Law in 2009, and now just a year later he was advising a federal judge whose decision could upend the biggest inside trading case since Ivan Boesky. Raphael knew that Holwell worried broadly about the invasion of privacy issues that wiretaps presented. He was also aware that wiretaps were rarely used in white-collar law enforcement. Insider trading might be bad, but was it worth trampling on the U.S. Constitution?

Title III appears to be pretty clear on one important matter: The government needs to show a federal judge that before it can invade a private citizen's *privacy* it has exhausted all conventional techniques. And at least in this case, the government left out a key piece of evidence. Simply put, Goldberg and Kang screwed up, and when it comes to privacy rights, you're not supposed to screw up.

That's when the twenty-five-year-old clerk pressed the sixty-five-year-old Holwell to reconsider what he described as the judge's antiquated notion of privacy. The notion of what is and isn't private has been changing in recent years. He urged Holwell to consider all the personal information that appears on the Internet, and accordingly to temper his views about privacy to reflect modernity; with technology very little of our lives is truly private.

He also urged Holwell to consider what a Title III application is all about and put himself in Judge Lynch's shoes: Would he have really said no to the wiretap even if he knew the SEC was still looking into Rajaratnam's trading? Of course not. The evidence against Rajaratnam was significant, maybe not enough to put him in jail, but clearly enough to approve a wiretap and a necessary ingredient to convict someone who might otherwise get away with fraud.

Insider trading is a crime of communication; if you don't know how Rajaratnam is making his communications, how can you properly investigate his activities? All told, maybe one in ten wiretap applications had been denied in recent years, Holwell discovered. Based on all of that, Raphael asked, was he really ready to let Raj Rajaratnam and countless others off just because of a procedural mistake?

In the end Holwell wasn't. On November 24, 2010, he issued his sixty-page decision denying the requests of Rajaratnam and his fellow defendant Danielle Chiesi to suppress the wiretaps as evidence in the case.

Holwell mentioned the failure of the government to cite the SEC's investigation in its wiretap application. But, he pointed out, the SEC's long-standing interest in Rajaratnam was *the reason that* a wiretap was necessary. Conventional investigative techniques had been used and "nevertheless," he wrote, they had "failed to fully uncover the scope of Rajaratnam's alleged insider trading ring and was reasonably unlikely to do so because evidence suggested that Rajaratnam and others conducted their scheme by telephone." Even if Kang and Goldberg had included the SEC probe in the application, "it would ultimately have shown that a wiretap was necessary and appropriate."

In the opinion, Holwell clearly sided with the government, but in granting approval, he put investigators on notice that they had better do things right if they wanted to tap a target's phone. In fact, the judge used the word *reckless* in his decision more than twenty times. Bharara read the decision with a mixture of anger and relief, according to people who know him. Anger because based on what he had heard this wasn't nearly the slam-dunk Streeter had predicted. His relief came because with the admission of the tapes into evidence, he was all but assured his biggest victory since being appointed as Manhattan U.S. Attorney, even if he had no idea his margin of victory (and Rajaratnam's margin of defeat) came thanks to a recent Harvard Law graduate who had once written an essay about working on Wall Street.

Jonathan Hollander had just left the gym, feeling the usual high that comes after a good workout, when he was approached by a couple of FBI agents, including David Makol. According to Hollander's account, they said he wasn't under arrest, but the agents also indicated he was under suspicion as a member of the "SAC crime family" engaging in insider trading.

The crime family reference wasn't hyperbole, Hollander would later concede. Hollander accompanied Makol to a nearby diner, as Makol so often takes his targets. They sat down and ordered coffee, and before Hollander took his first sip, Makol produced a piece of paper. It showed a chart in the style of those iconic depictions of Mafia families, with Steve Cohen's face displayed at the top and arrows pointing below to a host of other SAC people.

Hollander has told people the experience was jarring, particularly because Makol was clear and direct in his approach. They knew Hollander was trading on inside information.

Also jarring was the chart Makol handed him. He has told people it bore a startling similarity to one of those used to describe organized crime families with the *capo di tutti capi*, in this case Cohen, at the top of the alleged criminal enterprise, followed by his captains and soldiers. Hollander said he recalled seeing his own photograph somewhere near the bottom left-hand corner, as if he were a low-level soldier in the bigger criminal conspiracy.

SAC is actually a multitude of hedge funds operating in a semi-autonomous manner, though Cohen has final say over key trading strategies. One unit is said to be different: CR Intrinsic, a subsidiary inside

SAC that operates as Cohen's private hedge fund, where most of his money has been kept. Hollander had worked at CR Intrinsic for four years.

Cohen had managed money directly for the fund where a chunk of his net worth has been held. Analysts like Hollander and traders know they receive their biggest bonuses by funneling investment ideas to Cohen and cranking profits for CR Intrinsic. An analyst or trader who works for this division could have direct access to Steve Cohen himself.

In late 2008, Hollander left SAC after his supervisors told him he was laid off to save money following financial-crisis related losses that led to SAC's first down year since its inception. Not long after, the FBI came calling. If the intent of the meeting was to scare Hollander into some kind of cooperation agreement, it was successful. Makol said the proof of Hollander's insider trading was significant; an informant had led them to trades in Hollander's personal account in shares of Albertson's food store chain.

The informant, an investment banker at the firm UBS, said that he had witnessed Hollander being given a tip about Blackstone's pending buyout of Albertson's. Hollander made an easy $3.5 million by snapping up shares of Albertson's in his personal account.

Hollander ultimately agreed to two "proffer sessions" with government investigators. Such interviews with law enforcement allow the target to speak freely; the testimony receives immunity, and it's an indication that the feds are interested in bigger fish.

In this case, there was little doubt who the feds were interested in as Assistant U.S. Attorney Reed Brodsky quizzed Hollander not just on the Albertson's trade (Hollander said he hadn't shared that tip with anyone at SAC) but on the inner workings of the hedge fund, namely how information flows from traders and analysts to the man at the head of the organizational chart.

Unlike Streeter, who had focused on other white-collar cases before taking in the Rajaratnam prosecution, Brodsky had been working on insider trading cases for years. He was in his early forties, and had joined the Southern District after a stint in private practice. He's known as a tireless and smart worker. If he has a fault it's in his overpreparedness, which can hurt him at trial, where juries respond best to simple, linear cases from prosecutors.

But this wasn't a trial, merely an attempt to get Hollander to tell him everything he knew about Cohen's operation. Overpreparedness didn't matter. Brodsky knew going into the proffer sessions the key elements of how SAC worked. Cohen, of course, ran things, but many buffers stood between him and the information source. It was known as a *hub and spoke* structure, in which portfolio managers and analysts fed him the best ideas that they were trading on.

This happened all day, every day, since Cohen rarely took a day off. The competition was fierce to get Cohen's attention, Brodsky knew, because of the rewards for profitable trades. SAC bragged that it had created the first stand-alone compliance department in the hedge fund business. By the time Hollander was approached by the government, the compliance unit was among the hedge fund industry's largest such operations with 36 people watching its trades. Brodsky, like others involved in the probe, believed SAC's efforts to detect dirty trades weren't enough given all the trading at the firm, and they probably came too late. After spending some time on the Albertson's trade, prosecutors seated across from Hollander made it pretty clear what they thought of the hedge fund by asking their witness to tell them "everything you know, firsthand or secondhand about insider trading at SAC," according to a person who was present.

This person said the investigators asked about Cohen's knowledge of dirty trades as well. "They asked John 'what do you know about Steve?' " this person said. "They were clear that they wanted to know about whether Cohen himself did anything."

During his two sessions with Brodsky and Makol, Hollander said his interactions with Steve Cohen were pretty nonexistent. "He said he was ten rungs below Cohen," said the person who was present during the interview. That said, he observed a lot during his time at SAC. He told Brodsky that the tone of the firm was set from the top and the message was emphatic: Do whatever it takes to make money. Insider trading, despite the firm's compliance efforts, occurred frequently, he said.

By the end of the discussions, Hollander had given enough evidence to escape jail. A short time later, Hollander would provide the same information to the SEC during another proffer session. He paid a $220,000 fine for trading shares of Albertson's, settling an SEC civil penalty that included a five-year suspension from the securities business, and, most important, serving no jail time.

Hollander would later say that, based on his questioning, he believed Brodsky and the government agents in the room were convinced SAC used dirty information to profit in the markets. It may not be the only reason for SAC's stellar returns since its 1992 inception and the fact that it never lost money except during the cataclysmic year of the 2008 financial crisis. But at least according to Hollander's interpretation of the questioning, government investigators thought inside dealings played a significant role in the fund's performance. Since 1996, SAC had produced annual returns of 25 percent for investors, though in recent years as the fund has grown and as its compliance efforts have increased, those returns have trailed off. Still, SAC's performance compares very favorably to the roughly 8.5 percent returns cranked out by the great Warren Buffett, not to mention the S&P 500's relatively paltry 5 percent return, during that time period.

Cohen's supporters contend that SAC's traders are just better than Buffett and the markets. Brodsky indicated to Hollander that no one is that good. The only question was how to prove it.

CHAPTER 13

THE LUCKIEST MEN IN LAW ENFORCEMENT

On the morning of May 9, 2011, after the grueling two-month trial of Raj Rajaratnam for insider trading had gone to the jury to decide, Jon Streeter had a nightmare. The jury hadn't come back with its verdict now for almost two weeks, and Streeter woke up in a cold sweat after dreaming that the foreman had read the long-awaited verdict in one of the most high-profile insider cases ever, and Rajaratnam was acquitted on all fourteen counts.

This, despite the mountains of evidence—from wiretapped conversations of the Galleon chief discussing how he used confidential inside information to make money trading stocks, to cooperators explaining how he gamed the system, to trading records showing how he traded time and time again with absolutely pinpoint accuracy right before a major event, all of which allowed him to own homes around the world and fly in his own private jet. All this while Americans slogged through a nasty recession created by Wall Street risk takers, and the jury still believed Rajaratnam was an innocent man.

What was so scary about the dream was that the jury deliberations made it seem like it *could be true.* Streeter had gone into the case believing it was a slam dunk and a guilty verdict on all counts could be delivered in twenty-four hours. Streeter's ten-plus years as a prosecutor taught him how to read a jury and try to see the world as they saw it. Most of them were middle-income people, caught in the vortex of the financial crisis and the bad economy that followed, with daily struggles that the Rajaratnams of the world didn't have.

They were fair-minded people and the looks on their faces, Streeter determined, showed disgust for what Rajaratnam had done by cheating the system. During the trial Streeter hammered home that point, with the help of more compelling evidence than he ever had in any case during his career—maybe any prosecutor ever had in such a high-profile matter: dozens and dozens of wiretaps, plenty of cooperating witnesses, and hundreds of shady transactions.

Having been in front of so many juries, Streeter knew they demanded simplicity. He narrowed the list to the best stuff: forty-five telephone calls, three cooperators, and about twenty dubious transactions, including the most sensational of them all, the notorious Goldman Sachs trade. That's where Rajaratnam bought shares of Goldman stock just minutes after he received word from Goldman board member Rajat Gupta that Warren Buffett had extended a lifeline to the firm in the form of a big investment.

Goldman shares, of course, shot up when the news became public the next day, but that was after Rajaratnam bought Goldman stock and earned a quick $1.2 million. That doesn't count the roughly $3 million he saved a month later when he was alerted by Gupta that the firm was about to post its first loss as a public company, and he sold his shares.

Gupta had yet to be charged, and some in the media and others in academia opined that the feds had a difficult case against him since they couldn't find any direct payments in exchange for these well-timed tips. But Streeter had a different theory pointing to Gupta's guilt.

Gupta's compensation from Rajaratnam didn't come in the form of wads of cash or bags of lobsters. They exchanged something with more long-term value: access to each other's circle of friends.

Streeter and his team had come across a speech Gupta had given to the 2010 graduating class of the Indian School of Business, where Gupta gave the following advice, which he had adroitly followed during four decades at the highest levels of finance: "try to make other people successful. You will work in businesses; you will work with lots of people. Try to make them successful. The reason for that is simple. You know, no matter how good you are, how brilliant, how fantastic, by your own efforts you can only achieve so much. But if you work on making other people successful, they will in turn make you successful beyond your dreams. There will be lots of people working to make you successful. And that in the end is how I would see a successful career."

It was all great stuff, and Streeter thought a jury would eat it up when it was Gupta's turn to face the music. But his more immediate concern was Rajaratnam and why the jury was taking so long putting this guy in jail.

Streeter believed he had assembled as good a team as he had ever had in a case to present. SEC investigator Andrew Michaelson came over to assist—not just for his courtroom acumen, but because he had been trailing Rajaratnam longer than anyone alive except perhaps Sanjay Wadhwa.

Reed Brodsky had a reputation for being a smart and able prosecutor, but also one who was so well versed in facts that at times he tended to get lost in mind-numbing details. But Brodsky kept with the program laid out by Streeter: Rajaratnam and those like him broke clear rules of conduct, he argued, and they were getting rich illegally while the average guy was following the rules and getting poor. Putting him in jail was necessary to make sure that the markets *are fair*, or, as Brodsky put it in his closing remarks to the jury: "The laws against insider trading are designed to protect the investing public against cheating. The stock market is supposed to be an even playing field."

People who know Streeter will attest that he comes across as the most self-confident man in the world, and yet his dream exposed a certain level of self-doubt, possibly about the crime of insider trading and how the government approached the Rajaratnam case.

Sure, Rajaratnam was guilty as charged, as was Gupta, a man Streeter believed had built a career by fostering relationships with powerful people, and then later finding ways to make money from those connections.

But in an era where a single Ponzi schemer like Madoff can steal billions from average people, who exactly were Rajaratnam's or Gupta's victims? Whoever was going to buy what Rajaratnam was selling, was going to buy it anyway. In a sense, they were victims of their own market calls. Rajaratnam just happened to be a more informed seller, albeit one with the advantage of illegal information.

Or maybe the jury had somehow taken a liking to Dowd, and bought his convoluted defense strategy in which Rajaratnam didn't take the stand to defend himself. Dowd asked the jury of eight men and four women to ignore the government's many witnesses because they were forced to say bad things about his client to save themselves from going to jail. He also asked them to believe that at bottom, Rajaratnam relied on his mosaic, rather than any piece of confidential, nonpublic data to make winning trades.

As the jury deliberated, it wasn't just the prosecutors who had a growing sense of unease, but people at the SEC as well. Wadhwa and his close-knit team had spent more time on the Galleon case than anyone in government; a loss would be devastating to them and their broader effort to clean up the markets. And yet it kept nagging at them that two of the best people in white-collar law enforcement had screwed up on the wiretap evidence—a mistake that Dowd had tried to exploit and might well exploit on appeal.

Maybe the jury was coming to that same conclusion, or maybe it saw Rajaratnam through the prism that Dowd had also attempted to construct; that he was a good businessman, albeit a well-connected one, who would never risk his fortune, well into the billions of dollars, for what the government said was just a few million dollars in dirty trades.

Such was the risk in Streeter's approach to the case, of course: Simplify and narrow the argument so he and Brodsky could tell a story about a man who brazenly cheated the system, even if that meant minimizing the raw number of dirty trades Rajaratnam had profited from. He thought it would work going into the case, but now he wasn't so certain.

"I'm starting to believe the jury didn't believe me," Streeter lamented one afternoon, as he told Reed Brodsky about the bad dream of how a case that should have been a layup was actually lost.

What scared him even more was Brodsky's response. He was worried as well; in fact, Brodsky said that he had just had the very same bad dream.

Raj Rajaratnam once told a reporter for *Newsweek* that he had been sitting at home in early 2007 when he received a telephone call from his sister Vandani, who was vacationing in Singapore. While Raj and his brother Rengan went to college and then launched careers on Wall Street, their sister had taken a different path. She was into yoga and believed in mysticism. That's why she was calling. A psychic had told her that a woman with a mole on her face, an Indian woman at that, was going to betray him.

At the time Rajaratnam didn't pay much attention to the remark. But not long after the day the FBI came knocking on his door in late 2009 and placed him under arrest for insider trading, Rajaratnam recalled that Roomy Khan had a mole on her face, and it made him seethe with anger.

No case is made with just one informant. All in all, the feds recorded a multitude of conversations Rajaratnam had had with as many as 130 people. Some were friends such as Rajiv Goel. The former Intel executive had also agreed to cooperate and help the feds wiretap the Galleon chief accepting and then trading on illegal insider tips.

One call from Goel underscored how the system worked, and worked against Rajaratnam. Goel began by asking Rajaratnam if he got his "message [that] you're a good man."

Rajaratnam was initially skeptical, responding "that's highly suspicious . . . you don't just call and say 'Hi, I'm just calling to say you're a good man' unless of course you want something," adding with a laugh, "You're a good guy, too. When I see you I'll give you a kiss on the cheek."

Goel, of course, did want something: more incriminating evidence for the government, which he received. He alerted Rajaratnam that "the Sprint thing [a reference to a transaction between Sprint and Intel] isn't happening in the short term" and that the company he worked for, Intel, was also having a confidential board meeting. Also, another matter of importance to Rajaratnam was "not happening today," he said.

Rajaratnam responded, "Thank you," and ended the call.

He should have ended his call earlier with Goel, with Anil Kumar, and of course with Roomy Khan. But he didn't; the allure of money was just too great to think twice that he might be getting set up by his circle of friends.

The six-week trial of Rajaratnam had some tense moments, of course, with Dowd trying to bully witnesses and an occasional reporter. The long jury deliberations led to some sleepless nights for Streeter and Brodsky.

But after Dowd failed to get the wiretaps thrown out, the case was pretty perfunctory, and in the end Streeter's and Brodsky's joint nightmare proved false. On May 11, 2011, the jury handed down a verdict that convicted Rajaratnam on all fourteen counts. The biggest insider trading case of all time (to date) was finished.

"I guess they believed us," Streeter told Brodsky after getting word of the verdict. Brodsky just smiled. They felt like the luckiest men in law enforcement, for many reasons, but most of all because they didn't blow a case that had more good evidence against the accused than maybe any other in the history of insider trading.

There weren't any smiles in the Rajaratnam camp, but there was some fingerpointing at Dowd over whether his demeanor made a tough case even tougher.

Armed with just circumstantial evidence such as phone records and trading patterns, prosecutors always face a difficult challenge proving if someone intentionally traded on "material nonpublic information." But Rajaratnam basically convicted himself. The wiretaps, once admitted, left little to be interpreted. Rajaratnam and his cohorts, such as Chiesi, were heard brazenly bragging about how they were getting their hands on confidential information and making lots of money trading on it.

To be fair, Dowd did have his moments. He managed to get Judge Holwell to criticize Kang and Goldberg for their sloppy handling of the wiretap application. He did a formidable job assembling evidence that the Justice Department was looking to put a man in jail for crimes that amounted to a mere $70 million in illegal profits—a scapegoat, so to speak, for the much bigger and yet to be prosecuted crimes of the financial crisis. Rajaratnam was worth billions, and Galleon managed $7 billion in customer money. So even if he traded on some dirty information here and there, it was small potatoes—immaterial to both his net worth and the overall size of his fund.

But Dowd's tough-guy tactics never caught traction—and a few of his stunts became a sideshow that made Rajaratnam's case appear even more desperate than it already was, including one where Dowd emailed a reporter he thought provided biased coverage and asked, "How long are you going to sucks [sic] Preet's teat," in a reference to the now-famous Manhattan U.S. attorney.

He fired his well-connected PR spinner, George Sard, for someone more to his liking, the attack-dog flack named Jim McCarthy, who, along with Dowd, went on the offensive against the government's leak machine. Dowd wrote to the Obama administration's Attorney General Eric Holder (and Bharara's boss) to complain about a "continuing pattern of unconstitutional conduct" by attorneys and others representing the three agencies involved in the Galleon problem—Bharara's Manhattan U.S. attorney's office, the FBI, and the SEC.

His central message was that the leaks of stories and the government's use of the press had violated Rajaratnam's civil rights to a "fair and impartial" jury trial.

McCarthy, who had a long record of sparring with reporters for their use of anonymous sources, went after the press, mainly the *Wall Street Journal* for running stories based on anonymous tips. Both Dowd and McCarthy made some good points about the leaking: in a way it was the government's form of insider trading. The leaks against Rajaratnam would allow the FBI and Bharara's prosecutors to benefit by controlling the public debate about the size and scope of the investigation and the guilt of the accused. And some of the leaks were sickeningly obvious: Reporters somehow knew when people would be getting arrested so they could take pictures of the FBI at work in a timely fashion. Both witnesses and targets were outed.

Yet it was a lost cause from the outset. McCarthy was acting as if the *Journal* was the first paper in the history of journalism to rely on anonymous sourcing. It wasn't and most of the stories about Rajaratnam and those that exposed the various people snared in Perfect Hedge turned out to be accurate. More fundamental, without the use of anonymous sources, investigative reporting that exposes corruption at the highest levels of government and business would largely cease to exist.

Dowd's complaints, meanwhile, prompted a broader examination of the leaking—and a meeting between the Manhattan U.S. Attorney's office and the FBI to try to stop it. But it all had little practical effect for the simple reason that the government needed good press to tout its bigger goal—that it was holding Wall Street accountable for its sins.

Dowd's bullying inside the courtroom backfired as well. A classic instance occurred during his cross-examination of Anil Kumar, the former McKinsey consultant. Kumar had set up an offshore brokerage account in the name of his housekeeper to hide the money that poured in from his illegal arrangement with Rajaratnam. Dowd, in turning the screws on

Kumar, finally got him to admit that he was a crook, and how his "wife did not know how adept" he was at lying and scheming for money.

For a moment, it seemed like Dowd had, finally, cast doubt on the truthfulness of a key witness, or at least shown the jury the unfairness of convicting someone like Rajaratnam when all these equally guilty stool pigeons were walking around free.

That is, until Streeter turned the tables, having Kumar state simply what the account was for: a holding place for his illegal payoffs from Rajaratnam for supplying illegal inside information in what Kumar, now a crook with a Wharton MBA, said was his "eternal regret." In the end, it looked like Dowd was bullying a sympathetic witness, albeit one with a criminal record.

But most of all, the jury never seemed to connect with the case Dowd was trying to make: that Rajaratnam's mosaic, rather than his access to various pieces of confidential information, was responsible for his decisions to buy or sell or short stocks. In his own words, Rajaratnam was showing that just the opposite was true: It was the various pieces of illegal information that made the mosaic, which at bottom was assembled through a network of like-minded criminals.

Rajaratnam may have been a good guy surrounded by bad people like Roomy Khan, who were ratting him out to save their own skin, as Dowd argued. Indeed several government officials working on the Galleon probe said they had grown personally fond of Rajaratnam, based on listening to the wiretaps. Take out the illegality and Rajaratnam, with his worldview of the markets as a battle to be fought every day, seemed like the type of guy they would want to have a beer with. But if Rajaratnam was such a mensch, what was he doing hanging out with avowed liars like Roomy Khan or with second-tier traders like Danielle Chiesi (also soon to be convicted and headed for jail) unless of course they were sharing insider tips?

Put that all together, and after the six-week trial and two weeks of deliberations, the jury came back with a solid guilty verdict on all fourteen counts. That was more than enough to put Rajaratnam away for a long time, which Holwell had no problem doing.

The federal judge known for his deliberate approach to the law handed down what could be a death sentence for a fifty-four-year-old man suffering from diabetes, as Rajaratnam was: eleven years in a federal prison, the same one in Butner, North Carolina, that houses Bernie Madoff and mobster Carmine "the Snake" Persico, for a crime that Holwell described as a "virus in our business culture that needs to be eradicated."

Later, Dowd told reporters that the case was his last one, and that Rajaratnam would appeal. His new defense team at Akin Gump began pulling every piece of evidence they had, every court precedent in an attempt to somehow disqualify the wiretap evidence. Such a strategy could take years if successful, and there's no guarantee it would be successful.

Still, the Rajaratnam legal team noticed a few openings. Just before Rajaratnam's sentencing another federal judge sentenced Zvi Goffer (part of David Slaine's circle of friends) to ten years in prison, which set an unfair precedent, they could argue. How could any judge give Rajaratnam even a day less than someone most people have never heard of?

But their biggest card was the government's much-publicized missteps in the wiretap application. The law was intended to amass evidence against suspects who operate covertly and who refuse to cooperate, and a case could be made that there was nothing secretive about Rajaratnam's business, unlike the mob or terrorist cells. He had been on the SEC radar for years. His instant messages and emails were a matter of near-public record, and hedge funds were a regulated industry.

But Holwell didn't rule the way he did by thinking that he would be overturned on appeal. He knew there would be questions that the jury had agreed to convict Rajaratnam as a scapegoat for Wall Street crimes he had nothing to do with, such as those that led to the financial crisis. Accordingly, he asked the jurors if "the fact that the case involves the financial industry, Wall Street executives, hedge funds, mutual funds and the like, makes it difficult for anyone to render a fair verdict." They agreed it didn't.

He also did his own homework and double-checked the reasoning of his clerk that despite the missteps, the wiretaps were still legal under the Title III test, namely that the government couldn't establish Rajaratnam's guilt without them. His conclusion: "Insider trading is a telephone crime." In other words, there was no other way to prove Rajaratnam's guilt than to have access to his private telephone conversations.

James Comey, who held Bharara's job during the Martha Stewart investigation, had made nearly the same assessment a few years earlier. Recall that Stewart didn't face criminal insider trading charges because the government couldn't come up with solid proof that Stewart knew she was trading on illegal information when she began selling her shares of ImClone just before the news broke that tanked the stock. There were no wiretaps in the Stewart case, just her word and some suspicious trading records.

Those days are done. Over the years, other traders have explained away various regulatory inquiries of suspicious trades just before market-moving events by pointing to their "mosaic" of information that produced the stock pick. No more, law enforcement officials say. As proof, they point to the sharp decline in expert network business, which had supplied hedge funds with the necessary fillers for their alleged mosaic. Primary Global had all but closed down when the Rajaratnam verdict was delivered. Gerson Lehrman was still around, but many hedge funds were not employing expert networks anywhere close to the levels they were prior to the investigation.

Maybe traders would stop talking on the telephone when passing along tips in a post-wiretap world. Or maybe, just as the mob does, hedge fund executives would start patting each other down to check for wires before discussing business, give up talking on the telephone all together, and do what crime bosses have resorted to doing: meet at public places but speak with their hands over their mouths so FBI cameramen can't read their lips.

Either way, wiretaps were here to stay.

After the Rajaratnam verdict, people like Kang and Wadhwa slowly went back to work; both would receive promotions and accolades inside their respective agencies, as would Makol and Chaves. Brodsky and Streeter took their bows, albeit privately, and would leave the government for the greener pastures of private practice.

Just a few weeks after the Rajaratnam verdict, Bharara appeared at a symposium on white-collar crime at the City College of New York. The event was sponsored by the Financial Writers Association—a group that represented the very same journalists who were critical to the government's strategy of using the media to get out the message that Wall Street was finally being held accountable for its behavior.

During the speech, he made certain to point out that despite the attention his office had given to insider trading, his prosecutors were hardly one-trick ponies. They have aggressively pursued fraud of all types, including more than one hundred cases involving mortgage fraud, which was at the heart of the financial crisis. And to counter the widely held belief that no big firm was charged with a crime related to the crisis, he recounted how his people fined Deutsche Bank more than $500 million.

Still he was also clear and unapologetic about the resources he had dedicated to eradicating insider trading. The list of people under investigation, including those convicted like Rajaratnam and those cooperating after reaching plea deals, made the insider trading probes the largest and probably most expensive investigation ever in the history of white-collar law enforcement. More trials were on the way, including Rajat Gupta, and the investigation into SAC was about to rev up. Much more money would be spent on these cases (the Justice Department says it doesn't keep a tally), and according to Bharara, it was money well spent.

"First, it should be clear by now to anyone other than the most obstreperous academic and stubborn editorial page writer," he said, "that insider trading of the type and nature that we have now charged dozens of times over is an insidious offense—it neither advances the market nor is it victimless nor does it fall into a hazy gray area as some suggested before they ever had a chance to see the actual allegations we made and the actual proof we collected."

That "stubborn editorial writer" may have been this author. No matter. Bharara was undeterred by the criticism and what he was now hearing from some people inside the Justice Department and in broader legal circles over what they believed was his exploitation of an investigation that was well underway when he took over as U.S. Attorney.

The internal criticism grew loudest after a lengthy profile of Bharara appeared several months later. Bharara's face blanketed the cover of *Time* magazine with the headline "This Man Is Busting Wall Street." The story opened with a fascinating anecdote illustrating how the U.S. attorney had played a direct role in the investigation, actually listening in on a wiretapped conversation of insider trading information being shared between two of the guilty parties in the probe. If only the anecdote were true. Indeed, government officials were listening in on the conversation. They were FBI agents, not Bharara, and not even one of his top lieutenants.

In 2011, while giving a speech before a federal law enforcement group filled with former bureau agents, he wore an FBI shirt. During the speech he explained that just a few days earlier he had been wearing it and someone mistook him for an agent, which was the "biggest compliment I could get."

That gesture alone was hardly enough to quell the hurt feelings as the *Time* profile made its way around the federal law enforcement offices in lower Manhattan. To be fair, when *Time* fact-checked the story, Bharara's spokeswoman Ellen Davis has told people that she objected to the characterization that he was doing the actual listening to the wiretaps, but the reporter said he wouldn't take out the anecdote because it was broadly factual—the U.S. attorney's representatives were doing the listening.

It's unclear if the reporter understood the difference or if Bharara understood how much anger from the FBI was now being directed his way. Of course, every government agency likes to boast about its successes, and Bharara's press office wouldn't be the first to work with reporters to tout the success of a given initiative. Eliot Spitzer was a master of such tactics, using the bully pulpit as the New York Attorney General to generate enough headlines to make him governor. And, there was plenty of leaking and political grandstanding during Rudy Giuliani's reign as Manhattan U.S. Attorney, much of it involving Giuliani himself as he prepared to run for New York City mayor.

Bharara is said to bristle at the notion that he has used the bully pulpit in a Giulianiesque manner. He has even done some research on the topic, pointing out to anyone who questions his motives that newspaper stories from the 1980s show how his predecessor used the media in a more overt manner than he ever has and how he has shared credit for the success of the various insider trading probes. And he does have his fans who say Bharara deserves to take credit for running a law-enforcement agency that so far has a perfect record in convictions.

Still, people inside the Justice Department and particularly at the FBI have found many of Bharara's media moves distasteful and have felt they diminished the role agents and career prosecutors have played and, in their eyes, were designed to advance his own career. By the time the Galleon investigation had put Rajaratnam in jail, speculation swirled that Bharara was in line for Eric Holder's job as Attorney General or that he was weighing a run for political office.

Not coincidentally, profiles of FBI officials involved in the insider trading crackdown sprung up in the press. Chaves came up with the idea of getting Michael Douglas, the actor who played maybe the most infamous (and fictional) insider trading crook, Gordon Gekko, in the movie *Wall Street*, to tape a public service announcement about the evils of insider trading.

Douglas agreed because he said he was astonished how many Wall Street types he met loved his character—maybe too much. The short segment showed footage from the film with Gekko, dressed in his trademark suit, his dark hair slicked back, delivering to an audience filled with investors one of the film's most famous lines: "Greed, for lack of a better word, is good."

The commercial then cuts back to Douglas more than twenty years older. His hair is much grayer now and he has a simple message: Greed *isn't* good. "The movie was fiction," Douglas says about insider trading, "but the problem is real." He then urges people with knowledge of insider information to contact their local FBI office.

Bharara was said to be angered by not being part of the media event. Later that day he held a meeting with Janice Fedarcyk, the head of the FBI New York bureau to discuss his concerns mainly with some of Chaves's comments during a briefing with reporters to unveil the Douglas spot. According to people close to him, Bharara was annoyed that Chaves appeared to have mocked him during the briefing. "Nobody over here would do that to you," he told Fedarcyk. According to FBI sources, Fedarcyk said some people in the bureau believed Bharara's press office had planted stories that failed to mention the FBI's contribution to the case. Bharara said taking credit for the success of the investigation was never his intention.

In the end, both sides called for a truce in the publicity battle. The cheaply done video, meanwhile, had some impact; people at the FBI say they received a couple of dozen insider trading tips.

Sanjay Wadhwa was a mere spectator during the Rajaratnam trial and the publicity war that broke out between the FBI and Justice Department, but that didn't mean he wasn't busy. He was no longer a staff attorney. Thanks to his work on insider trading, he had been appointed an associate regional director in the New York office of the SEC, meaning he was one of a handful of officials in charge of various investigations.

His star was certainly rising. Wadhwa now held meetings with the new SEC chairwoman, Mary Schapiro, and with Bharara as well. His meeting with Bharara was said to be wide-ranging and included a discussion about how two South Asians like themselves handled the obvious fact that they were busting up criminal conspiracies that dealt with people of the same heritage.

Wall Street is a big place, and Wadhwa's teams looked beyond insider trading for white-collar crimes. He had a case brewing against the New York Stock Exchange for allegedly providing better access to information to big hedge funds that trade through the exchange than to other investors.

But his main focus was insider trading, where he had a laundry list of potential new targets that he hadn't even made a dent in yet, a list he once described by separating his hands a yard apart, a smile on his face.

Many of the cases related to mopping up what was left of the Rajaratnam circle and investigating the expert networks. Others involved SAC Capital and trades flagged by regulators as being suspicious, including some heavy trading in drug-company stocks.

Wadhwa's star was rising and it was his turn to get some good publicity for it. The normally understated investigator agreed to cooperate for a long profile in *BusinessWeek*. With that, the backstabbing that once was directed at Bharara from the Justice Department and the FBI now focused on Wadhwa. Some people inside the Justice Department openly began to downplay his role in the investigations, as if he and his team had never met Rajaratnam and had never brought his case to the FBI in the first place.

Truth be told, there would be no investigation without Wadhwa and people like Michaelson at the SEC, and many FBI agents and federal prosecutors owe at least part of their government careers to his efforts.

Add enforcement chief Robert Khuzami to that list. "Look what we did to [Angelo] Mozilo and Goldman Sachs," Khuzami snapped after reading a column about how the SEC had focused on the low-hanging fruit of insider trading while bigger white-collar criminals went free.

Khuzami had come to the commission more than three years earlier vowing to restore the agency's former status as the gold standard in the federal regulatory system. In late 2012, he was now ready to step down and return to a highly lucrative job in the private sector, but the commission had barely made a dent on many key issues.

Khuzami did much to restore the SEC's *image*. The sin of missing the Bernie Madoff scam was still hanging over the SEC, and will never be fully expunged from its history, but Khuzami at the very least made it a sin of the past.

The new and allegedly reinvigorated SEC, with Khuzami leading the charge, raked in record numbers of enforcement cases. Khuzami's investigators took on Goldman Sachs and Angelo Mozilo, the former chief of the company that sold many of the toxic mortgages at the heart of the banking crisis, Countrywide Financial.

Yet the markets were still fractured, with technology issues more than occasionally disrupting the normal flow of trading. Facebook's IPO was a disaster after a trading meltdown on the Nasdaq stock market caused more havoc than any insider trading scheme. That fiasco was immediately followed by another trading malfunction at Knight Capital. The phenomenon known as a *flash crash* was a few years old by now but regulators at the SEC were no closer to figuring out how to stop them. Small investors appeared oblivious to how much time Rajaratnam was spending in jail; fearing the next meltdown, they kept buying bonds and gold.

The abuse of credit default swaps—where traders could buy these contracts (a bet that a company might default on its debt), short a company's stock, and profit from the market fear it would produce—went unaddressed as if the financial crisis in which they played a part had never happened.

And for all the SEC's chest-thumping regarding the Goldman case and charging Mozilo, not a single major bank chief was charged in a financial-crisis-related crime. Even MF Global's Jon Corzine, whose bets on risky European debt led to $1 billion of his customers' money being lost, escaped prosecution.

But Khuzami had insider trading. In 2011, his division filed more enforcement actions than ever before, and came one shy of the record in 2012. Much of that spike was the result of insider trading, and Khuzami rarely missed an opportunity to tout how the SEC was back to being the tough cop on the beat of Wall Street, even if the cases could be traced to his predecessor, the allegedly listless Chris Cox.

And he may be doing it by expanding the definition of what constitutes a dirty trade. Many of the defense attorneys representing clients snagged in this probe say he has. They point to a 2012 speech by an associate director from the agency's New York office, David Rosenfeld, who, according to people present, put traders on notice not to have private, one-on-one meetings with company officials because of the chance that nonpublic information might be shared. Rosenfeld even suggested that any working relationship with an expert network—even one that doesn't involve swapping nonpublic tips—will raise suspicions among prosecutors and regulators.

An SEC spokesman said in response that Rosenfeld was just alerting people "to be careful," as was his boss Khuzami, who in interviews with reporters explained how the SEC was cracking down on this vice "that is baked into the business model of many hedge funds." Khuzami has made a good case that the SEC, being a government agency, has limited resources, so it can only file insider trading charges for activities that are clearly illegal.

Still, an even bigger perceived threat came in March 2011 during congressional testimony, when Khuzami appeared to set his own standard for what might prompt an investigation of suspicious trading. "We're now doing things like canvassing all hedge funds for aberrational performance."

Khuzami had ordered his troops to be "proactive" in looking at fraud including suspicious trading after all the screwups in recent years, from Aguirre to Madoff. As a result, he defined such performance as when funds beat "market indexes by three percent and [are] doing it on a steady basis."

He might as well have said, "Note to Stevie Cohen: That means you."

CHAPTER 14

STEVIE IS WORRIED

I've had a rough six months," Steve Cohen told *Vanity Fair* magazine in a lengthy July 2010 piece written by veteran business writer Bryan Burrough, the author of *Barbarians at the Gate*. The best-selling book is considered a classic. It chronicled the epic takeover battle of RJR Nabisco, and the insanity of the 1980s takeover mania in all its gory details.

But Burrough was also the author of one of the worst business articles ever written about the 2008 financial collapse, a long *Vanity Fair* feature on the demise of Bear Stearns, the first firm to implode during the crisis. He pinned the firm's collapse not on its CEO, James Cayne, who spent much of his time playing golf, attending bridge tournaments, and smoking weed, nor on the firm's hyper-aggressive, risk-taking culture, or even its senior management team, regarded as the weakest on Wall Street.

In Burrough's opinion, Bear's implosion was the result of media bias: reporters (this author included) who were only too willing to report all the bad stuff about Bear, and none of the good things, until a market frenzy developed that crushed the firm's stock price, caused lenders to pull lines of credit, and drummed a once-great firm out of business.

This odd critique (Joe Nocera of the *New York Times* called it an "apologia" for Bear's feckless management) may have been the reason why SAC's media adviser Sard Verbinnen welcomed the news that Burrough wanted to do a profile of Cohen. Finally, Cohen's flacks had found someone who might accept the most positive spin on an increasingly difficult set of circumstances faced by the SAC chief.

Sard Verbinnen was no stranger to media challengers. The firm, and its top executive George Sard was Martha Stewart's press adviser when she was charged and stood trial in 2004 for lying to investigators about her suspicious trade of ImClone stock. Based on the facts at hand, it was a pretty open-and-shut case. At least that's what the jury thought, convicting Stewart after a relatively short deliberation. But Sard's aggressive counterattack had much of the media coming to her defense, describing Martha as a successful businesswoman battered by prosecutors looking for some cheap headlines in the aftermath of the tech meltdown in 2000 and 2001.

It would be hard to make Steve Cohen a victim of a sexist vendetta, but the firm's advice to Cohen was along the same lines: Go on the offensive, start making some public appearances, and open up to a friendly reporter. Burrough became that reporter.

The PR problem Cohen had was pretty obvious. People who had heard of Cohen—including average people who sit on juries—would know the characterization of him mainly from what *60 Minutes* reported back in 2006: He was a shadowy, secretive multibillionaire who lived in a secluded mansion, collects art, and does sleazy things to make a buck.

The reality was somewhat different. He wasn't quite the recluse the media made him out to be, and he was far from greedy. He and his second wife, Alexandra, raised tens of millions of dollars to fund a pediatric wing for New York Presbyterian Hospital in the immigrant-heavy Manhattan neighborhood of Washington Heights, where Alexandra grew up. He has given millions more to the North Shore-Long Island Jewish Hospital to fund another pediatric care center.

This reality, and little else, is what Cohen's media handlers wanted portrayed in the article. Burrough is, of course, a smart and gifted writer, and his long piece contained a rare interview with Cohen as well as a few interesting revelations about SAC. Cohen's trading desk operates without telephones that ring (which would distract his traders) and the room is kept at a temperature of 68 degrees so traders remain alert. He also said that investors shouldn't expect those blowout years they had in the past, where SAC cranked out returns above 50 percent. "We're not going to generate those larger numbers now that we are bigger," he said. After all, it's hard to crank out such large numbers when you're managing $14 billion in assets.

Maybe the biggest takeaway: Burrough made it clear that Cohen believes he has been made a scapegoat by a media gone mad over insider trading. Cohen told Burrough he hated being put in the same category as crooks like Rajaratnam, and rightly pointed out his fund's pristine regulatory record. If individuals at SAC have been responsible for bad conduct, that's because they violated company policy. The firm itself hasn't been touched.

"I could not understand it," Cohen said, referring to the media interest in his firm's trading. "What the hell was going on. It was like a circus, a fucking circus."

The article, however, was short on new details about the firm and how the various investigations were circling around SAC and the simple fact that regulators kept coming up with suspicious trades flagged out of the hedge fund, or even how Cohen's returns defied their logic—namely because it's impossible to beat the markets that consistently. Warren Buffett doesn't do it year after year, so why should Stevie Cohen?

Speaking about "Stevie," Burrough quoted Cohen saying he hated the name by which he's been known during his nearly thirty-year Wall Street career. "I mean, they still call me 'Stevie,' and I'm fifty-four years old. It drives my wife crazy." The article also said that Cohen was thinking about getting out of the hedge fund business sometime soon—something that his PR people would later retract.

"There's a lot of other things I can do," Cohen told Burrough. "I've been to the top of the mountain, and there's not much there. My dream is to liberate myself. So is that a midlife crisis? Or is it just being fucking smart? I don't know. But it's exciting." It was a bizarre statement coming from a man known equally as a control freak and as obsessed with investing, somewhat reminiscent of the weird comments he made the last time he opened up to the press during his brief and unfortunate career in tabloid TV about twenty years earlier.

But if the intent of the article was to humanize Cohen enough to give regulators second thoughts about pursuing him, it failed miserably. In fact, it only whetted their appetites. The media only cared about Cohen and SAC because reporters' sources in the SEC and the Justice Department had made the hedge fund a priority in the insider trading crackdown.

His remark about returns now falling back to earth only suggested to prosecutors in the Southern District that SAC knew it had problems and was taking steps to ensure complete compliance with insider trading laws after years of ignoring them. The increased compliance meant fewer dirty and profitable trades.

The "circus" Cohen complained about would only get crazier in the coming months. In fact it got so crazy that Sard couldn't possibly find any reporter whom he could get to bite on even a semi-positive yarn about the trader and the company that had so obviously become a leading figure in the eyes of the federal insider trading police.

Of course there were other players in the ever-unfolding enforcement drama, which the government agencies were fighting to take credit for no matter how lowly the analyst being arrested and charged. Some, of course, weren't so lowly. By October 2011, Rajat Gupta was finally arrested in what the feds were calling the most significant insider trading bust since the 1980s crackdown yielded junk bond king Michael Milken. Signing his indictment papers was one of the last major things

Streeter did before going into private practice. Gupta's lawyer, Gary Naftalis, a former assistant U.S. Attorney in Manhattan and longtime white-collar attorney, proclaimed his client's innocence. Rather than antagonize the prosecution, he immediately reached out to his adversaries and promised a professional fight.

Gupta wasn't without his friends in high places, and they could, Naftalis promised, all testify to his unblemished record in the private sector and his substantial charitable acts during his long career, he told prosecutors. Unlike Rajaratnam, his client wasn't obsessed with making money. He received not a dime from Rajaratnam no matter how much talking they did. Gupta was a good man, and juries generally like good people.

By now the government team was touting Gupta as a bigger get than even Rajaratnam, who was a mere trader compared to one of the most prominent businessmen in the world. They would show that good people sometimes do bad things, and that juries don't take too kindly to Wall Street crooks no matter how much moral support they can get from UN chiefs or prominent businesspeople.

Gupta's trial was set for early 2012, and based on the government's record, the odds of a conviction were high. On Wall Street the question wasn't conviction—that was largely a foregone conclusion. The betting involved whether Gupta would serve jail time (and how much), or whether the judge would show leniency to someone whose profit motive in sharing inside tips was having friends in high places rather than earning direct returns from his illegal activities.

Meanwhile, the investigation was taking a much-needed break from its frenetic pace. Most of the bad guys from Perfect Hedge had been rounded up. The few who hadn't wouldn't make big headlines. The expert network business had been put on notice while Primary Global was shut down as its clients in the hedge fund business began to cut ties with dozens of experts under investigation.

And with good reason: Several, such as Tony Longoria and Walter Shimoon, were cooperating with the government to avoid jail time and to implicate others. The independent analysts who used the experts and their access to inside information, such as John Kinnucan, were just waiting for their arrest.

But that doesn't mean the investigation came to a halt, particularly when it came to SAC and Cohen.

"The way I understand the rules on trading on inside information, it's very vague," Cohen explained one afternoon in early 2011 during a deposition taken not by any one of the federal agencies now investigating his activities, but by lawyers for a public company that believed he had broken the law.

Cohen was dressed uncharacteristically for him; gone were his trademark khakis and sweater. Today he was dressed in a dark suit and tie. He sat uncomfortably in the offices of his longtime outside counsel, Willkie Farr & Gallagher, flanked by his attorney Martin Klotz as the grilling began.

The deposition involved a case brought against SAC by an insurance company named Fairfax Financial Holdings. The lawsuit, filed in New Jersey Supreme Court, alleged that SAC conspired with the other hedge funds to drive shares of Fairfax down through rumors and other types of market manipulation to profit off a massive short position on Fairfax stock.

The details of the case were almost a second thought for officials at the SEC and the other regulatory agencies involved in the insider trading probe. They had already decided to drop an inquiry into Fairfax's claims, and in a few months a judge would dismiss the lawsuit against SAC altogether.

But what became must-reading among the government sleuths eyeing SAC and Cohen was his deposition and the parts where the SAC chief described his own belief system about what is or isn't a dirty trade.

In Cohen's mind, it seemed insider trading is a lot like pornography: You know it when you see it.

The questioning was being done by attorney Michael Bowe of the Manhattan law firm Kasowitz, Benson, Torres & Friedman. Bowe and the rest of the firm had by now made a small fortune representing companies that had a beef with SAC, namely Biovail and Fairfax. He and a PR handler named Michael Sitrick were behind the unflattering *60 Minutes* portrayal of Cohen.

Now they were ready for round two. Bowe knew of the feds' longstanding interest in SAC and had met with both government cooperators and with B. J. Kang at the FBI to share what he had found in discovery. The case being alleged by Fairfax didn't involve insider trading per se. But the company was ready to argue it was all part of a business model that makes money by playing dirty.

Bowe interviewed a number of people with knowledge of SAC's operations including Jonathan Hollander. Aside from their largely uniform description of how SAC was run like a money-making machine, with Cohen calling the shots either directly or through a few trusted people, what struck Bowe was how in awe they were of "Mr. SAC." He was described in almost superhuman terms as a man who knew everything, and could do just about everything. Bowe had never met Cohen, but as the two shook hands just before the deposition began, he was completely underwhelmed at least by his physical appearance: The bald head, the glasses, and the pudgy physique hardly equated with his reputation as a master of the universe.

Bowe began the deposition by trying to rattle Cohen, calling him "Stevie," which prompted an angry outburst by Klotz, who called Bowie's choice of words an "obnoxious, deliberate use of Stevie in addressing Mr. Cohen." Bowe said it was a "mistake" before moving on to the heart of the case: SAC's alleged manipulation of Fairfax stock.

Bowe had reviewed SAC's marketing material, boasting of the alleged SAC "edge" it has in the markets. SAC describes this edge in company marketing documents as the sum total of its ability to find talented traders, analysts, and portfolio managers to cover various industries, execute different trading strategies, and leverage its research.

The marketing materials also didn't hide the fact that SAC's advantage is derived at least in part because the hedge fund is a "major commission generator" for Wall Street firms. As a result, it receives "priority treatment" from Wall Street. Being everyone's biggest customer has its advantages in terms of market knowledge and insight.

But regulators increasingly believed the edge also involved the use of inside tips to profit—and Bowe wasted little time pressing Cohen on what turned out to be a sore subject. "I hate that word," Cohen explained, even as his spokesman conceded that he approved the use of the word for SAC's promotional brochures. (The word *edge,* I'm told, no longer appears in such material.) Bowe pressed the obvious hot-button question, namely what does having an "edge" really mean. Does it mean SAC knows "something everyone else doesn't"?

"You know, I think that's an over—I think that's an incorrect characterization of the word."

In Cohen's mind, at least during the deposition, having an edge is far less nefarious. It simply means "somebody believes that in a particular situation . . . that somehow their expectations are different than either investors' expectations or Wall Street's expectations."

For the remainder of the three-hour deposition Cohen appeared more annoyed than rattled, that is, until he explained that he wasn't all that familiar with something every SAC employee is supposed to be familiar with: his firm's own compliance manual and what it says about insider trading.

"The answer is when you're trading securities, it's a judgment call," Cohen explained, adding that "whatever the compliance manual says, it probably doesn't take into account every—every potential situation."

Bowe, sensing an opening, pressed Cohen even further, and Cohen's answers became more convoluted—and potentially more problematic. He said that while he had read the firm's compliance manual, which strictly forbids insider trading, he didn't "remember exactly what it says."

He explained correctly that there are times that legal trades can be made based on nonpublic information—and that he leans on his legal staff, not his compliance manual, for the final say. In Cohen's view there are "circumstances" where utilizing information that some might consider confidential is perfectly legal, which is true given the murky nature of the insider trading rules.

Cohen, who never went to law school, said one such instance occurs "where if you believe that even if you were trading on the same side as a—as a recommendation, if you felt or if you knew that would have no impact on the stock, then I can theoretically suggest that trading on that stock, even—while I might refrain from trading on that stock, if you believe that would have no impact on the stock, that therefore, I—theoretically, you might be able to trade on that stock if you knew that was coming out."

At bottom, he said that his understanding of "the rules on trading on inside information, it's very vague."

It's unclear if Cohen knew how his convoluted definition fit with what was being professed by the SEC or Justice Department or the FBI, where the use of any nonpublic information was at the very least something that might touch off alarm bells with the government.

But the feds obviously picked up on the difference. The SEC subpoenaed the deposition as part of its ongoing investigation into trading at the hedge fund, and Bowe shared it with just about anyone else interested in SAC. Simultaneously, Senator Grassley was back on the insider trading trail, this time demanding an accounting as to how many referrals Funkhouser at FINRA had made to the SEC about suspicious trades, and how many were acted upon.

The message to the SEC was direct: Get moving on an SAC case or be ready for more bad publicity. And the message was received. The SEC started to look deeper at nearly 100 SAC trades flagged by FINRA as suspicious. Investigators turned up the heat on Cohen as well. Within a year after Grassley began making noise about SAC, the commission decided to find out exactly what Cohen knew about some of the trades. For the first time in more than two decades, he was deposed.

During the deposition, Cohen didn't recall much about the events in question, according to people with knowledge of the matter. The FBI wiretap on Cohen's home telephone was largely a bust as well, or in the words of one investigator with direct knowledge of the matter, "It didn't turn up shit."

But by now investigators had begun to change tactics. Their modus operandi was to nail enough people around Cohen with the hope that someone facing lots of jail time would flip and explain how the guy at the top knew about the insider trading of his underlings, and either condoned it or possibly took part in it.

The possibility of someone talking to investigators was something that Cohen himself openly worried about to friends, including Bo Dietl, then-retired New York City police detective and private investigator.

Amid the frenzy that surrounded his firm, Cohen wasn't about to do another media interview, but he needed to make a public statement in order to at least give the appearance that things at SAC were running close to normal. Aside from the whispers about the various legal probes, his investment returns were strong—around 15 percent in 2011, but that only goes so far. One large hedge fund targeted in the probe, Level Global was on the verge of being shuttered as investors feared losing their money and began redeeming shares.

Cohen's fear was that if the government scrutiny intensified, the same might happen at SAC. After all, Cohen was more than a casual spectator in Level Global's demise. That fund was run by David Ganek and Anthony Chiasson, both former SAC traders and both under intense government scrutiny.

For that reason, even Cohen who had defied the media for so long, and who tried to ignore it except under very controlled settings, knew that out of necessity, appearances mattered. That's why he agreed to attend and participate in a high-profile hedge fund conference sponsored by his friend Anthony Scaramucci, founder of the investment company SkyBridge Capital.

SkyBridge is a "fund of funds" company, meaning that it invests in other hedge funds on behalf of its own clients. SAC was one of those funds offered by SkyBridge, and its conference is known in hedge fund circles as possibly the most important single event, at least from a media standpoint, of the year. Aside from nearly a thousand guests—

most of them high-profile traders and investors—Scaramucci signs up an A-list of speakers from the political world. The 2011 attendees included President George W. Bush and former Secretary of State General Colin Powell.

But the marquee name for this Wall Street crowd was Stevie Cohen.

Being interviewed by Scaramucci and not a reporter meant Cohen was in friendly territory. Other than explaining how "nobody likes that type of media scrutiny" and that SAC takes "compliance very seriously and the reality is we are going to cooperate with any and all investigations," Cohen didn't make much news. He sat with his legs crossed, dressed in a dark suit and tie. He seemed poised and at ease, explaining how he plans to be doing what he's doing for a long time, just the opposite of what he said the year before in Bryan Burrough's *Vanity Fair* piece.

Cohen also seemed to downplay the chatter about the government's interest in his activity. Among his biggest concerns involved stuff like the growing federal budget deficit, which the markets will demand fixing, he said.

Offstage, though, he was less self-assured, at least according to Dietl, who flew with Cohen to the conference on a private jet. It was somewhat of an odd admission because for the past year, he and his people, including his longtime president Tom Conheeney, have been assuring investors and selected reporters that they knew very little of the government's interest in SAC, and that whatever it was, the firm would survive because of its vaunted compliance program.

But Cohen, at least according to Dietl, knew the government's investigation into SAC was now real, and that there was considerable interest in flipping one of the handful of SAC targets who had either been arrested or had agreed to cooperate.

"One of those guys caught on tape" could easily "say something about me" to cut a deal, Dietl recalled Cohen telling him, and act not unlike a mob rat to save his own skin, even though, as Cohen explained, he "did nothing wrong."

"That's why," Dietl later said, "Stevie's worried."

• • •

By early 2012 the various government agencies investigating insider trading had a pretty good idea of how SAC operated, thanks to the growing list of cooperators they had assembled during the past five years.

David Slaine, who didn't work at SAC, knew people who did, and investigators say he pointed them in the direction of at least one suspicious trade that involved the hedge fund. Investigators believed Jonathan Hollander provided great details about how SAC works on a day-to-day basis. The information provided by Richard Choo-Beng Lee was even better. He worked at SAC for six years earlier in his career and led investigators not just to the seedy world of expert networks but also to a compromised former SAC portfolio manager named Noah Freeman. Rather than face a long jail sentence, Freeman began cooperating as well by ratting out the best man at his wedding, another former SAC portfolio manager Donald Longueuil.

An ex-SAC analyst named Jon Horvath would soon join the cooperation club. He was indicted for suspicious trading in a number of stocks, including shares of Dell. The insider trading trail provided by Horvath led the government to one of the highest-ranking portfolio managers at SAC Capital, Michael Steinberg. Then there's Wesley Wang, a junior analyst at SAC who began cooperating in 2009 rather than face a similar long prison term for insider trading.

Still none of them had delivered evidence that led to charges against Cohen. Not even close.

There are people in our industry that are rogues," Anthony Scaramucci said on the business channel CNBC. "I don't think Steve Cohen is one of them."

As the world seemed to turn against Cohen and SAC Capital through 2011 and well into 2012, Scaramucci remained a loyal friend, not just as an investor in SAC (Scaramucci's fund of funds kept its money in SAC) but as an unofficial spokesman.

Amid the ever-intensifying media scrutiny, senior executives at SAC had grown increasingly frustrated with the work of Sard Verbinnen particularly after the Fox Business Network ran a chart of SAC that made Cohen look like Carlo Gambino, according to SAC insiders.

Scaramucci, a Harvard Law graduate and former Goldman Sachs broker, was now pitching in on the PR front. In recent years he had built SkyBridge into a formidable presence in the hedge fund business, which meant people listened to him. His message about SAC was straightforward: SAC's compliance wasn't lax at all. Based on his knowledge (and he monitors hedge funds for a living), it was one of the most robust systems in the business. SAC now employed more than two dozen compliance people to make sure that the rules were being followed by its traders. Seminars on exactly what kinds of information crossed the boundaries of illegality have been common for a number of years.

SAC was now monitoring trades around market-moving events in much the same way regulators do. When recommending trades to Cohen, traders and portfolio managers, known inside the firm as "PMs," were pressed about their conviction level rated inside SAC on a scale of 1–10, with 10 being absolute certainty.

Aside from what Scaramucci said, people close to SAC described the beefed-up compliance system as a gradual system of improvements where SAC's in-house general counsel, Peter Nussbaum, and others began reacting to demands by the SEC—and the scrutiny over insider trading.

Regulation Fair Disclosure, an SEC edict, was passed in 2000, making it illegal for companies to give selective disclosure to just certain investors. Cohen himself conceded that what worked in 1992 from a regulatory standpoint wouldn't pass the smell test in 2012. "This was a learning process," he told *Vanity Fair*. "You have to remember, we were smaller. Things were different then."

To Scaramucci and SAC defenders, all of this was proof that Cohen wanted to do the right thing. The evidence to them was pretty clear: SAC's compliance department was enormous and aggressive and states upfront to its entire staff of investment professionals—more than 300 portfolio managers, traders, and analysts—that there is no tolerance for cheaters. The trades that have aroused suspicions were old—most of them occurred five to ten years ago. And given the fund's size—it does more than a million trades a day—a few bad ones coming from a few bad people is understandable.

Others saw it differently. Was having a "ten-level" conviction on a trade based on the best research in the world, or was it simply code for knowing something based on nonpublic information? That's what investigators were now wrestling with. Despite the beefed up compliance, Hollander claimed to regulators that the prevailing sentiment given to him by managers was a don't-ask-don't-tell policy when it came to using information, even the illegal variety—all designed to protect the man at the top.

Freeman, for example, explained to government investigators how he purposely evaded the various compliance procedures at the firm, in one instance receiving an inside tip from Jiau about Marvell Technology. It's a point SAC officials have referred to repeatedly in trying to show how the firm does the right thing even if some of its employees don't. He also told investigators how he would secretly share insider information with another fund manager, also out of the sight of the compliance department.

But investigators were now looking at these same facts differently. In the end, insider trading didn't lead to Freeman's firing. According to a spokesman at SAC, poor performance did. In the meantime, Freeman appeared to just work around the safeguards. Even more, the insider trading seminars and trades based on conviction levels seemed contrived, at least in the opinion of government regulators, to protect the fund's hierarchy from the bad stuff that might be happening below.

Regulators also looked at the firm's document retention policy.

Most big Wall Street firms keep emails and other key documents for months at a time. But as a hedge fund, SAC was not subject to the same regulations. It maintained a thirty-day policy. After that point, emails were mostly deleted (though the firm said it had taken "snap shots" of some of its emails particularly around the time of the financial crisis because of litigation).

Of course, a lot has changed in Steve Cohen's business life since he launched SAC nearly a quarter of a century ago, and it went beyond expanded compliance systems. When he first started SAC it was just a band of trading brothers, a group of like-minded souls who shared Cohen's enthusiasm for rapid-fire trading and outguessing key events, like mergers or earnings announcements. It had a little more than Cohen's money invested in it, though the word was spreading of his genius, and profits as well as investor cash were beginning to grow.

For years, Cohen bristled at his reputation as a day trader who simply read the tape and made his billions rapidly buying and selling stocks in hopes of earning "teenies," or small incremental gains. "We have strategies around here," Cohen told investors. SAC, he said, was more than a day-trading shop, albeit one that traded billions of dollars of stocks.

He created new units to employ different sophisticated strategies, such as his CR Intrinsic division, with the CR standing for *cumulative return.* Intrinsic allowed him to boast that SAC was a thinking man's trading shop, using advanced research methods and analytics to make market bets even if, as government investigators suspected, some of its traders really spent much of their day figuring out how to game the system.

Cohen wasn't intent on transforming SAC into a geek squad, but the geeks were starting to play a bigger role at the big hedge fund. Ping Jiang, the trader who was accused of forcing one of his subordinates to take female hormones, earned $100 million in 2006. Best of all he was doing it well under the radar screen of the media, that is, until the lurid details of the sexual harassment suit appeared first on CNBC and then in the tabloids, prompting an investigation by the U.S. Equal Employment Opportunity Commission (EEOC) into whether Cohen ran a hostile workplace.

Cohen was livid when the stories broke and he saw his smiling mug in the *New York Post*, which ran a fairly long exposé of the incident under the headline "Trading Places."

Jiang eventually left SAC to start his own hedge fund, a move SAC officials insisted was unrelated to the controversy, even though his returns were strong and traders rarely leave SAC if they are making money. The lawsuit was thrown out of court, and the EEOC decided to drop the case, but to this day Cohen bristles when he hears the phrase "female hormones."

Another, less public new hire was Mathew Martoma, a brainy Stanford University MBA grad who spent a year at Harvard Law School and had a background in science, before turning to the hedge fund business to make his fortune. Because of that background in science (an undergraduate degree from Duke in biomedicine), Martoma specialized in health care stocks. He seemed to know what he was talking about, when it came to two stocks in particular: drugmakers Elan and Wyeth.

In fact, Martoma was now trading Elan with such regularity and success that he was known as "Mr. Elan" at SAC's Stamford headquarters.

Being "Mr. Elan" paid off. He got to share some of his winning trades with Cohen himself, an honor inside SAC since the guy at the top only interacts with traders who have hot hands. In 2008, Martoma earned more than $9 million.

Martoma's hot hand with Elan and Wyeth wouldn't last however. He left SAC in 2010 because of poor performance. He was, according to one SAC official, a "one-trick pony with Elan."

But he was now a rich one-trick pony, and a target of regulators, who detected the suspicious trading patterns near key events for several drug stocks, including the ones Martoma had been trading at SAC.

Meanwhile, Cohen's lawyers maintained a perfect record both in fending off serious regulatory inquiries and lawsuits coming from companies like Biovail and Fairfax. SAC's attorney Klotz was so successful on such matters that he got a New Jersey court to force Biovail to cough up $10 million to settle a case of "vexatious litigation."

Despite all this, federal investigators continued to dig. Among regulators, several schools of thought developed about the inner workings at SAC and why a guy who looked so guilty on paper in terms of insider trading was still walking around free.

Yet mostly people inside the Justice Department and the SEC believed all the extra compliance was an elaborate cover for all the bad stuff they believed was going on at the firm. SAC was now under more pressure than ever before to produce returns, given the amount of competition in the hedge fund space, and its "information edge" was coming under assault from new market rules. Thus, the only way to get the edge necessary to crank out market-beating returns was by gaming the system, in other words, insider trading.

One thing is certain: Cohen knew he and his business model were under regulatory assault, and he needed to respond in kind to protect the fund and his enormous wealth. As the investigations began to heat up, SAC even began to tell its investors that in addition to its new and improved compliance system, it also had secured a new insurance contract.

The insurance deal, as SAC officials portrayed it to their clients, would protect investor holdings from regulatory actions—fines, penalties, and clawbacks of illicit gains made through illegal trading, which the government often demands as part of settlement deals.

Investors seemed impressed. Money continued to flow into SAC up until the point in 2011 when Cohen no longer accepted new cash. And despite all the negative headlines they remained committed to leaving their money with the trader and the fund that almost never had a losing year.

Meanwhile, investigators also grew concerned. The five-year statute of limitations on some of the most obvious instances of insider trading was coming up. Cohen may have outsmarted the smartest investigators in the world by instituting all his new compliance systems at just the right time.

"He insulated himself," said one former prosecutor, and "if I were a betting man I'd say we're never going to get him."

Preet is a well-known pedophile, with a particular predilection for young black boys, which his wife is active in procuring for him. After Preet takes these young black boys up the ass, his wife is known to then lick clean Preet's limp Indian dick—which is appropriate, since that is what Preet is: A limp dick Indian piece of shit. . . ."

John Kinnucan sent this ludicrous assessment of the Southern District chief one night in late October 2011. It was emailed to an eclectic group of recipients, including journalists and former clients of his company, Broadband Research—or what was left of it. It included famed criminal defense attorney Gerry Spence, and even a victim of Preet Bharara's crackdown on insider trading, Walter Shimoon, a former technology industry executive who had worked for Primary Global.

Shimoon had recently pled guilty to passing along insider tips and begun cooperating with government investigators. He implicated others who had benefited from illegal inside tips, including John Kinnucan.

It wasn't the first such rant Kinnucan had rifled off in the year or so since he became a hero of sorts among Bharara's insider trading targets (and even more so, their attorneys). In that email, Kinnucan explained how the FBI came to his home, offered to play tapes of him discussing stuff the agents said was evidence he had passed illegal insider trading tips to his clients, and offered him a deal.

Kinnucan refused to be a rat—and began to brag about it in multiple television appearances and newspaper accounts, and more recently through dozens of racist threatening emails to his accusers in government.

It was a long year for Kinnucan, as the FBI started approaching his old clients to ask what they knew about his business, and making it nearly impossible for him to earn money. With that, Kinnucan became more and more deranged. He drank late into the night while firing off racist and anti-Semitic emails to reporters, FBI agents, and some of the same prosecutors who were building a case against him.

Kinnucan was not the first white-collar target of the government to become unhinged to the point of near insanity. The legendary arbitrageur John Mulheren, armed with automatic weapons, set out to kill Ivan Boesky, after Boesky implicated Mulheren in the insider trading scheme that rocked 1980s Wall Street and ultimately led to Mulheren's conviction.

But Mulheren, who suffered from bipolar disorder, was apprehended before firing a shot, and later his conviction was overturned. He returned to Wall Street as one of its top traders before dying unexpectedly of a heart attack in 2003.

John Kinnucan didn't try to kill anyone, but his rants raised lots of eyebrows with prosecutors. Most targets of federal probes lie low hoping not to antagonize prosecutors and tip the scales against them. Several attorneys advised Kinnucan to do just that. Some people thought he was crazy, or had gone mad—a notion seemingly confirmed by the more than occasional racist email blast.

But between the lunacy, Kinnucan was also making some sense. Wall Street runs on information and much of that information is in the realm of informed speculation—rumor mixed with a few facts that people like him have the connections dig up. Kinnucan could understand how Rajaratnam might have crossed the line, paying for tips on company earnings or getting a telephone tip from a friend who was privy to nonpublic information about how Goldman was about to be rescued by Warren Buffett during the financial crisis. But how was asking a source at Intel about how many computer parts it was shipping a comparable offense? Kinnucan said. Only by taking the broadest definition of what constitutes dirty information.

"Is it illegal for me to ask the counter girl at Starbucks how much coffee she's selling so I can figure out Starbucks' earnings?" Kinnucan asked. But "that's exactly what the government thinks is insider trading."

And he was at least partially right. In interviews with Justice Department officials and SEC investigators an expanded definition of insider trading seemed to emerge. Information that at one time was considered fair game to construct a mosaic was now considered at minimum suspicious, if it was nonpublic.

The problem for Kinnucan, and many of the other people snared in Perfect Hedge, is how he took his deceit to a new level. He didn't just hit up sources for confidential tidbits that he could use to project company earnings and by extension stock prices. The FBI now had evidence from the wiretaps that he was paying people to hand him inside tips.

It's impossible to know whether Kinnucan himself understood he was breaking the law but his actions suggested he did. At first, the publicity may have made Kinnucan feel good—that he could actually fight back against a government that considered him a criminal for doing what he knew was done all across Wall Street.

But insider trading also cost him, both professionally, as most of his clients ran for cover, and emotionally. The question that haunted him was whether it was all worth it. If he didn't play dirty, he might have made half as much, but he would have kept his career and his life.

With the FBI visit, Kinnucan's business and life imploded. "It's over," Kinnucan said.

And it was over in more ways than one. Kinnucan tried to manage money but he couldn't find clients.

After all, who was going to give money to someone with an FBI bull's-eye on his forehead?

That's what Kinnucan was coming to terms with each night as he sat in front of his computer and lashed out at his perceived enemies, whether it was Bharara, the FBI agents David Makol and Edmund Rom who showed up to his home, or Katherine Goldstein, the assistant U.S. Attorney who was assigned specifically to his case.

"Mr. Kinnucan I am going to hang up now!" Goldstein snapped after Kinnucan dialed her number one afternoon, announced who he was, and then proceeded to spew an ever-escalating racist tirade against the federal agents and prosecutors he believed were unfairly targeting him in their insider trading witch hunt.

"As you know, the FBI faggots David Makol and Edmund Rom came to my home in Portland over one year ago, and threatened to arrest me multiple times," he wrote one night, adding that he recently called up Goldstein and demanded an answer to a simple question: "Why have you still not arrested me?"

In that email, he said he hadn't heard back about his arrest. That would soon change. Chaves alerted people as the FBI began drawing up papers to arrest and indict Kinnucan for insider trading and passing illegal information to his clients.

Chaves and his team would contrast Kinnucan with Slaine: It was a tale of two cooperators. Both faced the same choice—jail for their crimes or entrapping friends and former colleagues—and each took a different path.

The Justice Department was now praising Slaine as possibly the most successful cooperating witness of all time. His efforts didn't just bust up his "Octopussy" circle of friends (Zvi Goffer, Craig Drimal, et al.) but his leads helped put others in jail. Slaine also aided in the Rajaratnam conviction with a lead that indicated how Drimal funneled an inside tip on shares of 3Com through Goffer to the Galleon boss. At Slaine's sentencing hearing in early 2012, the once-tough jock and trading-desk brawler didn't look like the alpha male associates had described him as. Slaine had been outed by the *Wall Street Journal*'s Susan Pulliam about two years earlier as the mole who brought down Drimal, Octopussy Zvi Goffer, and that circle of friends. The story was headlined "Wired on Wall Street: Trader Betrays a Friend." Slaine never saw the article coming, and during a brief telephone call with Pulliam, he did what his attorney told him to do if his role in the probe somehow leaked: Say nothing. In fact Slaine told Pulliam, "You got the wrong guy."

But she had the right one, and what a betrayal it was. Until then, Slaine was relatively unknown outside his small circle of friends on

Wall Street and in government. Now he was known to the larger world. Slaine isn't a common name, so he prepared his wife and daughter for the obvious public repercussions of being associated with a criminal, albeit one who was working for the government.

Drimal, meanwhile, was devastated by the news. People who know him say he opened up to Slaine during all those incriminating conversations precisely because he thought he was talking to a friend, rather than a man who was trying to put him behind bars. Slaine and Drimal haven't spoken since Drimal's arrest, though one mutual friend is said to have passed a message to Slaine more recently. Drimal, this person said, wanted Slaine to know that with the passage of time he "understood" why Slaine did what he did.

One of the hardest parts for Slaine was that he had to wait an extended period of time before he could start a new life, since the cases that he helped make had yet to filter through the legal system. That new life was set to begin as he entered the court hunched over in a dark overcoat and cap. Slaine's government handlers certainly described his efforts as "truly exceptional" in his sentencing memorandum and demanded the leniency Chaves, Makol, and Fish had promised from the start of his cooperation.

But Slaine stood stoically, almost ashamed, as the judge read his sentence: three hundred hours of community service, fines, and forfeitures of more than $1 million (on top of the roughly $300,000 he paid the SEC), and no jail time. Just three years of probation.

Slaine got what he always really wanted. He could see his family again, and not just through a glass partition in federal prison. But it came at a tremendous price. Living a life as a rat had taken its toll. Friends say he still suffers mental anguish for destroying people's lives, such as Drimal's, who was sentenced to five and a half years in jail even after pleading guilty to his crimes. "I understand I've committed a crime and I deserve to pay the price," Drimal remarked as he was sentenced to one of the stiffer jail sentences handed out during Perfect Hedge.

But Drimal, unlike Slaine, had decided to work against the government. Judge Holwell increased Rajaratnam's sentence because he said he didn't trade on inside information during the 2007 SEC deposition. Drimal suffered a similar fate. His sentence was enhanced in part because he had alerted Goffer that the feds were investigating their circle of friends.

John Kinnucan, meanwhile, was not cooperating, and suffered his own hell. He had no money as his business dried up, and his old circle of friends ran for cover amid his increasing dementia.

His sister-in-law was on his email list as well. At one point she urged him to stop the email rants—blaming his rage on "booze," as she worried that he had gone completely mad (or in her words "sinking with the already wrecked ship") and would no longer be able to care for his family, which included two young children.

But it seemed like rage was the only thing Kinnucan had left as he braced for the final indignity. In addition to losing his business, his home, and his $1 million a year salary, he was about to be arrested.

Much had changed on Wall Street since Kinnucan sent that now-famous email about the FBI. Raj Rajaratnam, the infamous Galleon Group founder, had completed a year of his eleven year sentence. One of his most influential tippers, Rajat Gupta, the former CEO of McKinsey & Co., Goldman Sachs board member, and one of the most respected businessmen in the world, was convicted as well, and sentenced to a two-year jail term.

The judge in the Gupta trial, Jed S. Rakoff, was no insider-trading novice. In addition to hearing many white-collar cases, he was once a prominent white-collar defense attorney. In fact, Marty Siegel, one of the key figures in the insider trading scandals of the 1980s, had been his client.

Rakoff apparently was swayed by the kind words for Gupta from friends in high places who urged leniency and he sentenced Gupta to two years in jail.

Meanwhile, dozens of low-level and midlevel technology company executives—working for expert networking firms—were either charged with criminal insider trading, pled guilty and cooperated, or went to jail in the burgeoning inquiry.

The various cooperators kept churning out new leads. Wesley Wang, the former SAC analyst, led government investigators to nearly two dozen other insider trading suspects. Jon Horvath, the SAC analyst involved in the suspicious Dell trade, led agents to other members of the SAC insider trading club, while other cooperators would point to people including Anthony Chiasson, the Level Global partner who worked for SAC Capital, as well as Todd Newman, a portfolio manager of another hedge fund named Diamondback Capital.

Chiasson and Newman would eventually be charged and convicted—a case labeled by Bharara as a "corrupt circle of friends," the term he would use more and more as the arrests piled up. The feds would follow the leads provided by Horvath to one of SAC's top portfolio managers, Michael Steinberg, soon to be named an "unindicted co-conspirator."

After the move, SAC placed Steinberg on a leave of absence from the firm, but that was the least of his problems. Being an unindicted co-conspirator is usually a warning shot by the Justice Department that at the very least they think you're guilty of something pretty bad, and it's time to cooperate or possibly face jail time. Steinberg was one of Steve Cohen's top advisers inside SAC—he had been there more than a decade and was well paid for his investing acumen, particularly on technology stocks. The feds now believed his success was the product of insider dealings.

And here's why Kinnucan, for all his racist lunacy, was at least initially important in the government's pursuit of Cohen and SAC: Steinberg turned out to be one of the people the FBI wanted Kinnucan to secretly tape on wiretaps if he agreed to cooperate.

This account was initially denied by Kinnucan, who said the agents were more interested in someone at Citadel Investment Group, another large hedge fund client. Kinnucan made that accusation when he was looking to collect money from Citadel and his finances were increasingly tight.

But the SAC connection is key. Kinnucan said his direct contact at SAC was in fact Noah Freeman, the same Noah Freeman who since 2010 was cooperating with the government and telling investigators all he knew about Steve Cohen.

CHAPTER 15

HARPOONING THE WHALE

"Thank you for not showing up at three o'clock in the morning," Catherine Kinnucan remarked as FBI agent Matthew Thoresen appeared on her doorstep on a crisp February afternoon in 2012 to take her husband into custody.

The FBI agents were local guys—they seemed "less harsh" than Makol, she said, based on her recollection of her husband's account of that initial meeting. There were no threats of jail, nor of not seeing his children again. With a simple "uh huh," Thoresen handcuffed John Kinnucan, explained the charges against him, and put him under arrest.

By now, the FBI had conducted dozens of arrests, many in predawn raids with sirens blaring and guns drawn, as they had with Craig Drimal. Their intent was always to use the element of surprise to daze their targets, possibly into cooperating, or at least to give up without a fight.

Given some of John Kinnucan's interactions with agents and prosecutors in the year since they first met, you would think that agents would have opted for the shock-and-awe approach. But they didn't. In between his increasingly menacing and insane emails, John Kinnucan had sanely alerted the feds that his wife had a rare heart condition, and the last thing she needed was a 3 a.m. raid on his house.

"I can picture that headline," Catherine Kinnucan said as it became increasingly clear that her husband was being added to the feds' expanding list of insider trading arrests: "Oops! Killed the wife . . . but they got their man!"

Catherine Kinnucan watched from the bedroom window as her husband was hauled off to jail. She was relieved that her children were still in their bedrooms and had been spared the indignity of seeing their father officially branded a criminal by the federal government. It also helped that the sordid spectacle of her husband's response to the investigation, from the drinking to the incessant emails, was now over.

But she soon came to terms with the reality of the situation: In little more than a year, John Kinnucan had gone from earning around $1 million a year to being broke. When his business dried up he tried money management, which meant he began trading stocks on his own. And he had lost money at that, just about everything the family had except for the house. Now he didn't even have enough to pay for an attorney or make bail.

And the government was going to make an example out of him. Only one cooperator had served time, Roomy Khan, who was sentenced to a year in prison, even after testifying at the trial of Doug Whitman, who received a four-year sentence as part of her circle of friends.

But that was because Khan was a two-time loser. Given Kinnucan's clean record and potential as a witness, he could have avoided jail time altogether, but rather than cooperate he had gone on the attack—the one thing every white-collar attorney says you should never do when dealing with the federal government. Because of those emails, the FBI no longer wanted Kinnucan as a cooperator; they wanted him in jail for a long time.

Catherine Kinnucan may have thought she knew about her husband's business; "I heard his conversations," she said a few hours after John's arrest. "I've been in the room when he was talking to clients," she said. "Cheating wouldn't have been fun." The man she knew loved to research stocks, not game the system.

The feds didn't care whether Kinnucan was having fun. They believed they had a pretty airtight case against him for dealing in insider information. At times Kinnucan believed they were bluffing, or at least that's what he said in recent months.

What he didn't realize is that the FBI rarely bluffs, and agents like Makol and Kang have been doing investigative work a long time. In other words, no guy working out of his house in Portland is going to outsmart them.

They also had Kinnucan on tape, in true Rajaratnam fashion, both lying to his clients about where he had gotten his "research" and talking to his sources at various tech outfits about paying them off for the confidential information that the FBI believed was the lifeblood of his dirty business.

The tapes showed, for example, that Kinnucan had made a $25,000 "investment" in a business owned by an executive at computer memory manufacturer Sandisk after that executive passed on Sandisk's earnings before they were made public. It was, in Kinnucan's words, the "very least I can do."

Those were better days, both financially and emotionally for Kinnucan, who had descended into a booze-induced state of constant agitation at the government, particularly when he was in front of the computer with a drink in his hand. Catherine Kinnucan says she knew little about her husband's email rants, but she thought he was doing the right thing in refusing to cooperate.

"Those dumb-ass lawyers would have had him plead to something and he would have been in jail already," she said even as the judge set bail at $5 million—a sum she couldn't and wouldn't meet. "John's a fighter and he'll defend himself any way he needs to."

That's what she was saying then; but over the next twelve months, she would barely speak to her husband and would file for divorce, she said to protect her children. She would also make a new friend in Craig Drimal's wife, Arlene. The wives of the men targeted in the investigation had experienced their own more private trauma in seeing their husbands going to jail, or in the case of Elyse Slaine, witnessing her husband's excruciating experience of going under cover to set up a friend. Like Catherine and John Kinnucan, Elyse and David Slaine were now divorced. Arlene and Craig Drimal remained married, and Craig would call her almost daily to speak with the children. Money was tight (even when Drimal was trading successfully, Arlene had complained it was like "Monopoly money," that would come and go depending on the market). But Craig Drimal had come from a wealthy family, and Arlene was planning to go back to work after many years as a stay-at-home mom. At one point, Arlene Drimal reached out to Catherine Kinnucan, primarily because she had read about John Kinnucan's deteriorating mental state, and his family's deteriorating finances, to offer some moral support. The two, I am told, remain friends, often sharing experiences of what it's like raising a family when the breadwinner is in jail.

Even after pleading guilty, fessing up to his crimes, and telling a judge "I'm sorry," John Kinnucan received more than four years in a federal prison—one of the longer sentences given during Operation Perfect Hedge.

The government based its case against John Kinnucan not only on the facts found in the wiretaps, but also on the extremely low odds of someone betting right with such astounding frequency as Kinnucan appeared to have done. The government believes such odds are low unless you're cheating, or, as David Makol told Kinnucan when they first met, "You know something is happening before it happens."

Government investigators shared a similar disbelief over the legitimacy of some of the trading at SAC even as the fund's legal team maintained it was all in a hard day's work. The debate about where SAC got its famous "edge" was a daily one—between federal investigators and Cohen's legal team, and among rival traders.

And it occurred even over practices that had nothing to do with insider trading, or any illegality for that matter, but underscored the firm's ability to get an advantage over the competition. Such was the case in June 2010, when a drug company named Vivus went before an FDA panel that was ready to approve its new treatment for obesity, known as Qnexa.

Investment bankers packed into a room at the Hilton in Gaithersburg, Maryland, where the FDA advisory committee on endocrinologic and metabolic drugs met for an eight-hour session to decide whether to recommend approval of the weight-loss pill for public consumption. The market sentiment among traders was positive. In the days going into the event, shares of Vivus rose 32 percent to nearly $13 in anticipation that the panel would give the drug its blessing. During the day of the hearing, shares rose as well on what traders perceived to be positive comments from the panel.

SAC, however, was betting that the panel would reject the drug—and that it could profit handsomely. The firm had built up what people close to SAC say was a short position in shares of Vivus, meaning if the panel rejected the move and share price declined—as SAC believed it would—the fund would earn millions of dollars.

Did traders at SAC know something the market didn't? Part of the reason for the broader Wall Street optimism was the favorable research on Qnexa. The FDA had compiled a packet of studies and data about the drug and distributed it to the advisory board members just before the vote. The research was for the most part positive, according to Wall Street executives, showing side effects in the normal range of what the FDA often allows for drugs it eventually approves. In the words of one investment banker who attended the meeting, the panel's approval "seemed like a slam dunk."

It didn't turn out that way. Wall Street, of course, hates surprises, so when the panel issued a 10–6 vote against approving Qnexa, Vivus's shares tanked 64 percent, to under $4 in the coming days. SAC, meanwhile, was counting its winnings—reportedly in the millions of dollars. The decision was widely covered in the media since anti-obesity drugs were becoming increasingly popular. The market impact alone made it a compelling story, with so much wealth being wiped out of the stock in a matter of days.

Cited among the reasons for the panel's decision were lingering concerns among certain members of the panel that the combination of drugs used to create Qnexa showed incidences of heart disease, depression, and cleft lip, a form of birth defect. But that only tells part of the story, at least according to some bankers who followed the trading.

Norbert Gottesman had been a healthcare analyst at SAC for four years. He was an analyst for SAC's CR Intrinsic unit specializing in pharmaceutical stocks, and in the past year he landed a position with broader responsibilities at the giant hedge fund. Gottesman was part of a new breed of SAC professional who had been making a mark inside the firm; analysts who, instead of reading the tape, spent their time crunching numbers and analyzing data. As Wall Street began to bet that Vivus would get approval to bring Qnexa to market, Gottesman saw other stuff in the data concerning the drug's side effects. He hired an "expert" statistician from Gerson Lehrman Group, the network firm that specializes in healthcare-related issues, to help with his research. Based on some data he and his expert had discovered in the weeks leading up to the vote, Gottesman recommended to a portfolio manager in SAC's healthcare group to begin shorting shares of Vivus.

It was a risky strategy—a "scary" one, was how one former SAC analyst with knowledge of the matter described the trade. But Gottesman appeared determined and confident. His numbers showed that the research the market was relying on understated the possible connection between Qnexa and birth defects. Based on *his* numbers, the incidence of cleft lip was significantly higher than most people realized. In fact, a recent updated study from the North American Antiepileptic Drug Pregnancy Registry shadowed his own analysis.

But it was unclear if the panel was up to speed on the new data. The packet of research distributed to the panel, for example, relied on a study conducted in winter 2009, which showed the occurrence of birth defects to be lower.

That was about to change. Early in the meeting, panelist Dr. Mary

Roberts brought up the registry findings as part of her comments. Then, just before the committee's final vote, Dr. Eric Coleman, the FDA's deputy director of endocrine products, reminded the panel of Dr. Roberts's comments about the registry study for "isolated cleft" and added that the information shows that the incidence of the birth defect was actually greater than it might appear.

"It's just limited data," Coleman said, "but there's an odds ratio that you don't generally ignore."

And it wasn't ignored, at least according to bankers who attended the hearing and saw firsthand the surprise results as the panel voted against the drug's approval, and watched shares of Vivus get crushed with it. Such advisory votes are also nonbinding, meaning the FDA can ignore their outcomes, though that is rare. Moreover, there were several reasons cited by panelists for their no vote. Indeed, FDA panels rejected at least two other similar drugs around the same time.

But Coleman's comments certainly stood out to bankers in the room. "They came out of left field," said one banker who worked with the company. "And why was he alerting people to what he described as 'limited data'? It made no sense."

For the company's financiers on Wall Street, and many small investors who owned the stock, the 2010 outcome was heartbreaking. But it was a cause of celebration at SAC. Speculation swirled that SAC had contacted the FDA before the vote—a perfectly legal action—on its way to victory.

An FDA spokeswoman says there was no communication with the firm and that both Coleman and Roberts brought up publicly available information. Meanwhile, the SAC edge had worked again, earning by one estimate tens of millions of dollars on the trade (the exact amount couldn't be determined; an SAC spokesman wouldn't comment on the matter). It would take two more years for the Vivus drug to receive final approval based on further data that showed the risk of birth defects to be less worrisome.

Investigators looking into the activities of SAC had come to believe that the fund's "edge" came in several forms. For one, there was its ability to legally root out information overlooked by the market, as it did in the Vivus trade. There was also its organization of around one thousand employees (300 of them market professionals), who operated day in and day out like a machine, cranking out massive trades as well as investment ideas that were passed on to the man at the top of the pyramid, primarily through a series of buffers, that also shielded him from any impropriety below.

SAC's vaunted "hub and spoke" trading model, where Cohen sat at the center of the information flow, was billed by SAC as the most creative way to maximize returns, with the world's best trader weeding out bad ideas and trading off the good ones. To get a meeting with Cohen was a big event in any trader's career. It meant the likelihood of a huge payday because, when Cohen used a strategy and it made money, he always shared the wealth. That's why some traders would do almost anything—including possibly breaking the law—to get in front of the big boss.

It also meant that Cohen had gained a certain level of comfort with that trader, which he didn't necessarily have with most of the people on staff. That's why flipping someone who was directly involved in insider trading and actually had direct dealings with Cohen became a key objective of government investigators as the investigations moved forward. So far most of the best witnesses were too removed: Jon Horvath and at times Noah Freeman, for example, dealt with Michael Steinberg, who was close to Cohen but not close enough for them to make a case against their ultimate target. Jonathan Hollander never spoke to Cohen directly at least about business. So the government's strategy was to pick off someone with direct ties to Cohen—and pray he would flip.

In the summer of 2012, President Obama was locked in a tight race against his Republican challenger Mitt Romney, and the general feeling on trading desks across the banking sector was that a president who had made class warfare his campaign theme wasn't above making a high-profile arrest of a fat-cat Wall Street figure. It would be done, at least according to the trading desk chatter, as an "October Surprise," that is, something big enough to prove to a skeptical public that the Obama Justice Department was tough on Wall Street crime and coming close enough to election day to have an impact on the result.

The names most bandied about included Lloyd Blankfein, the CEO of Goldman and a favorite whipping boy of congressional investigators looking at financial crisis excess, and Dick Fuld, the former Lehman Brothers chief. But Blankfein ran a too-big-to-fail bank and had already outmaneuvered a Justice Department referral made by Senator Carl Levin over statements he had made during a hearing into Goldman's behavior during the banking collapse. And for all the excesses of Lehman, the SEC labored to bring a case against Fuld, coming up with lots of smoke but little or no evidence of intent to break the law.

Another possibility: a high-profile arrest in an insider trading case that would garner fairly big headlines. The list of possibilities seemed endless given the success already achieved in convincing targets to cooperate and cough up other targets. Indeed, the FBI had even investigated a financial journalist for taking part in the scheme, a case that seemed to stall in fall 2012.

But investigators were aiming higher—much higher.

Back in 2008 and into 2009 as federal investigators were putting the finishing touches on their investigation of Raj Rajaratnam, Steve Cohen wasn't just on their radar screens, he was also on their tape recorders. That significant development remained confidential until early 2012. According to the Fox Business Network, Kang and his colleagues had been listening to calls Cohen had made from his home telephone in an effort to expand the probe of insider trading to include Cohen and SAC. Again, it was hardly news at this point that the feds had a passing interest in SAC and its founder; what *was* news was the feds' very direct interest in Cohen and its desire to do whatever it took to make a case.

Senior executives at SAC said they knew nothing about the matter and demanded that Fox clarify the report because it was still unclear whether the wiretap was placed on Cohen's phone or whether an outside cooperator, with a listening device on his telephone, had called Cohen.

It was a crucial difference, Jonathan Gasthalter, the Sard Verbinnen flack who worked most directly for SAC, argued. A wiretap on an outside cooperator didn't mean that the feds had gone to a judge and produced evidence of illegal behavior at SAC, a necessary step to get a court order for a listening device. If the feds merely taped a cooperator's calls, Cohen certainly wasn't the subject of the probe.

But before long, SAC received its clarification: Senior government officials with knowledge of the wiretaps said Cohen might be innocent, but he wasn't a complete bystander. The FBI had received a court order to wiretap his telephone. The tapes were said to have produced relatively little that could be used to build a case against either Cohen or the fund he ran, but that hardly ended the government's interest in Cohen.

SAC remained on edge, and friends said Cohen could feel the heat from the investigations growing around him.

Much was at stake, including billions of dollars of clients' money that might be redeemed if Cohen did become an official suspect. Fearing massive redemptions, Sard Verbinnen worked overtime to build the impression that it was business as usual in Stamford. Cohen, ever the master chess player, began to increase his political giving, embracing Mitt Romney over Obama for president in 2012.

Cohen's history of political giving (including the history of underlings at SAC) reflected a bias in favor of Democrats. But as usual Cohen was looking to gain an edge any way he could. With Romney in and Obama out, that would also mean walking papers for one of Cohen's chief antagonists, the Southern District chief, Preet Bharara, as well as the appointment of a new SEC chairman, possibly one less inclined to make insider trading the crime of the century.

Cohen had made his political trade—and did so in a fairly public manner. At one point in 2012, dressed uncharacteristically in a suit and tie, he was spotted dining with New Jersey governor Chris Christie at the popular Manhattan restaurant Quality Meats. Christie was one of Romney's top fund-raisers and a former prosecutor holding the functional equivalent of Bharara's post in New Jersey. It's unclear what was said during the conversation (neither would comment about it) but people in the restaurant say both men were engaged in intimate, quiet discussion over expensive steaks and at least one bottle of three-hundred-dollar Sassicaia wine.

Cohen's political maneuvering didn't end there, as the alleged recluse from SAC held a fund-raiser for Romney at his Greenwich estate, attempting to appear as if he had not a care in the world. Reality, however, was far different.

"Something big is coming," David Chaves told his colleagues one afternoon in the late summer of 2012. He just received the latest briefing about an upcoming case that had captivated both the SEC and the FBI for the past year, and would emerge as the government's best chance yet to finally harpoon the elusive white whale of a trader from Stamford.

It was only fitting that the case began with the investigative work of Sanjay Wadhwa over at the SEC. By now Wadhwa had earned the distinction of being the only investigator who had been working on the insider trading crackdown since the beginning. The wiretaps might have been the sexy part of the Rajaratnam conviction, but if Wadhwa hadn't done all that legwork beforehand—beginning with his investigation into Rengan Rajaratnam, and then following the paper and email trails to Raj Rajaratnam, Roomy Khan, and others—B. J. Kang would never have known to show up at Roomy Khan's home in the first place. Without the probable cause evidence Wadhwa developed, there would be no wiretaps. Without Wadhwa, Galleon would still be making money illegally and Rajaratnam would be a free man. And his institutional knowledge was instrumental in cracking the next big phase of the investigation. Nearly from the beginning Wadhwa and his closest associate at the FBI, B. J. Kang, had smelled something bad at SAC Capital.

Some prosecutors in the Southern District have always had their doubts about making any case against Cohen—and whether, given the time and effort required, it was worth it. They compared Kang and Wadhwa to Ahab in Melville's *Moby-Dick*, with Cohen playing the part of the elusive white whale as the government obsessively hunts down a target of dubious worth, at least from a legal standpoint.

Wadhwa had heard the *Moby Dick* analogy and bristled at the suggestion because so much about SAC appeared to add up to trouble. What struck both Wadhwa and Kang about Cohen and the firm he ran was the simple fact that so many of the major targets and cooperators had some SAC connection. Like Goldman Sachs, you would expect a big, successful firm like SAC to have alumni everywhere in the financial world. But where the SAC diaspora differed from Goldman's was in the white-collar-crime department. Since 2007, Goldman has had its brushes with scandal, of course. But its alumni just weren't found on the lists of targets or suspected targets of securities fraud to the degree that the names of SAC's traders, both past and present, kept cropping up over that relatively short period of time.

Even Raj Rajaratnam's younger brother Rengan—the initial focus of Wadhwa's insider trading probe back in 2007—had worked at SAC. His firm, Sedna, was long closed down and he largely dropped off the radar, though not completely. Like Raj, he too would be indicted some six years later in the spring of 2013, just before the statute of limitations ran out—the same statute of limitations that Kang and Wadhwa would soon be racing to beat in their pursuit of the white whale from Stamford.

In the spring of 2009, Sanjay Wadhwa had just spent another grueling day at the office when he received a message from Cameron Funkhouser at FINRA about yet another batch of suspicious trades from SAC Capital. Wadhwa and B. J. Kang were at this point in the final stages of their Galleon investigation that in a few months would lead to Rajaratnam's arrest. The probe of SAC was considered a secondary matter in the grand scheme of things.

But Wadhwa has told people that Kang made an interesting, almost cryptic, statement to him at this time. Kang continued to probe SAC simultaneous to his work on Galleon. He planted a wiretap on Cohen's home telephone and unsuccessfully tried to plant a cooperator in SAC's ranks.

Through his research he came across something that led him to believe that investigators should look at a cluster of suspicious trades that occurred around the same time a year earlier.

Wadhwa had worked long enough with Kang to know to trust the agent's instincts, so he ordered FINRA to send him some of its red-flagged trading data from SAC. One set stood out. It came via the New York Stock Exchange surveillance system, and it involved massive amounts of trading at SAC—in both long and short positions—in shares of Elan and Wyeth in 2007 and 2008. After further investigation, he saw similar trading patterns the year before. The buying occurred right before key events, such as successful drug trials—the selling just before setbacks caused shares to drop.

Wadhwa had just gotten married; a child was on the way. What's more, he didn't have the manpower to take his investigators off the Galleon case so he decided to work a little longer and harder because he loved the thrill of the chase. And based on what he was seeing, he was now in the midst of chasing Steve Cohen.

Wadhwa reasoned, the SAC portfolio manager must be someone Steve Cohen trusted. The long positions in Elan and Wyeth were really long—often above $300 million through most of 2007 and into 2008. Then sometime in late July 2008, they suddenly exploded to more than $700 million.

And then just as suddenly—they vanished. Wadhwa had looked at lots of trading records during the inquiry, but nothing stood out quite like this one. From July 21 through 25, SAC began unloading shares en masse—a massive directional shift, described by the senior trader at SAC as "executed quietly and effectively over a four-day period through algos and dark pools."

That wasn't all. SAC began shorting shares on July 28 and July 29—

perfectly timed to news delivered at the International Conference on Alzheimer's Disease, a medical conference in Chicago that was being closely followed by the Wall Street trading community. At the conference, the expert on Alzheimer's, Sidney Gilman, reported that a drug called bapineuzumab that Elan and Wyeth had jointly developed to treat the disease had failed in clinical trials.

But that bad news was good news at SAC—yet another perfectly timed trade that produced profits and avoided losses of $276 million as shares of Elan and Wyeth tanked 42 percent and 12 percent respectively.

More than a year had passed before Wadhwa and his counterparts in the Justice Department could fully appreciate what they had stumbled upon. Of course, with the Galleon case and those that flowed from it, they had other matters to attend to. But by early 2012, the general feeling inside the government team was that these drug trades might be their best shot at making a case against SAC and possibly Cohen himself.

It wasn't easy identifying the man directly behind all this good fortune as Mathew Martoma, a former SAC portfolio manager, because of the sheer volume of buying and selling of stocks SAC does, and also because of the way SAC keeps its trading records.

But when they did, the case started to come together as Wadhwa and Kang began piecing together trades with telephone records and emails into what they believed was a coherent insider-trading narrative that involved Cohen directly.

What struck investigators as odd was that Martoma was hardly a seasoned hand at SAC. He had gone to law school, dropped out, and then graduated from Stanford University with an MBA. From his bio, he seemed nerdy and smart. He had an interest in medicine, particularly medical ethics. But they didn't think he was the type of guy Cohen would naturally trust. He was just thirty-four years old at the time and had been at the firm just a little more than a year. He had only been trading for about five years, far less time than the handful of SAC traders whom Cohen considered his closest advisers.

Wadhwa and Kang believed the emails provided the clue as to why a near novice had so much conviction. Martoma had an important, possibly unimpeachable, source at Elan; it was Gilman—the very same expert who announced the drug's poor test results at the medical conference. Gilman was a well-known physician from the University of Michigan who also moonlighted in several other capacities. For one thing, he was a consultant to Elan on bapineuzumab, so he would have firsthand knowledge of the research on the drug's prospects.

As a side job to his university gig, Gilman also did a lot of work for the pharmaceutical industry advising on drugs and various neurodegenerative diseases. He had earned millions of dollars in this capacity since at least the 1960s, when he also began advising traders and investors on drug company stocks. Since at least 2006, he was part of the Gerson Lehrman expert network, and it was around that time that he had begun advising Martoma at SAC at the price of $1,000 an hour, Wadhwa discovered.

Based on telephone records, the two spent a lot of time talking, particularly leading up to the Chicago conference on Alzheimer's where the findings of the Stage II clinical trial of the drug would be released by Gilman himself. It would be a critical date for shareholders of Elan and Wyeth; depending on the outcome, investors could lose or make millions.

Martoma had a forty-five-minute telephone call with Gilman on July 17—just days before the stock selling began. Later it would be revealed why they had such a lengthy conversation: Gilman had shown Martoma a confidential slide presentation revealing that the Alzheimer drug had flunked its Stage II trial.

The money shot, however, came when Wadhwa discovered that on July 20, Cohen had a twenty-minute telephone call with Martoma. Records showed the call went down on a Sunday—just hours before the stock selling began and just days before Gilman made the official public presentation that tanked shares of Elan and Wyeth and led to investors, except for SAC, losing millions of dollars.

Wadhwa had a visceral reaction when he first saw the twenty-minute call between Martoma and Cohen, the multibillionaire hedge-fund founder. Wadhwa wondered aloud: "Okay, you're a thirty-four-year-old guy, not a lot of experience, and you're telling Steve Cohen he needs to change the direction of a trade in a big way. Maybe he trusts your judgment or maybe he says 'tell me why.' I'd say it's the latter."

Even more suspicious: The call was preceded by an email to Cohen in which Martoma urged a meeting to discuss something "important." It's unclear exactly what was said that day, but the email exchanges combined with other evidence painted to investigators a negative view of the drug's prospects. Martoma believed that SAC should begin reversing its position immediately. One piece of evidence also confirmed how certain Martoma was about his call, according to a senior investigator. Martoma labeled his sale a "level nine" conviction—a "level ten" being complete certitude in SAC-speak. In other words, he was all but certain he knew which way the shares were headed.

As Wadhwa added up the trades, he knew the stakes were huge: SAC earned profits (on various short positions in the stocks) and avoided losses (by liquidating its long positions) totaling $275 million. He had just stumbled on possibly the biggest insider case ever—certainly far bigger than what the government nailed Rajaratnam on, and one dwarfing the insider trading gains by the likes of Ivan Boesky, Marty Siegel, and Dennis Levine.

In late summer of 2011, everyone from Wadhwa at the SEC to officials at the Justice Department and the FBI knew what they were sitting on: possibly their best chance to harpoon the whale of Stamford. Wadhwa had assigned two of his best enforcement agents to the investigation with specific expertise in making cases through shoe-leather detective work such as chasing document trails, emails and trading records.

Wiretaps wouldn't be useful since Martoma had been fired from SAC in 2010 for poor performance, after cashing out with a $9.3 million bonus for his work on the Elan/Wyeth trades.

When the trades had run their course, so had Martoma's career at SAC. He was described by one supervisor as a "one-trick pony" before being shown the door. But the money had bought Martoma the good life. He was now by all appearances a happily married stay-at-home dad, living with his wife, a pediatrician, and their three children in an exclusive enclave in Boca Raton, Florida.

Kang and the representative from the Southern District, Assistant U.S. Attorney Josh Klein, and Wadhwa met for a final time in October 2011 to determine their next step. There was unanimity that the case against Martoma was solid, and just as solid against Gilman, an eighty-year-old physician with both a world-class reputation and what they believed was the willingness to risk it all for a few bucks. Friends of Gilman saw his involvement as less a product of greed and more of a seduction by Martoma. Gilman had lost a son, and Martoma filled that void. Regulators described the relationship, at least from Gilman's standpoint, as "friend and pupil."

Even so, the inquiry also showed how easy it was for members of expert networks to be corrupted. Gerson had a pretty clean record even though government investigators had heard allegations that its experts, like those at Primary Global, had often sold inside information to traders. Those allegations were made as far back as 2006, when Canadian pharmaceutical company Biovail filed a civil case against SAC and Cohen that was later dismissed.

Michael Bowe, Biovail's attorney, made sure Kang was fully briefed on Gerson's alleged dealings with SAC and other hedge funds. The civil fraud case filed by Biovail against Cohen and other hedge fund managers (and later dismissed) for alleged stock manipulation named Gerson Lehrman as a defendant, and it made some pretty startling accusations.

Gerson, the lawsuit stated, had a reputation for matching doctors with hedge fund managers to provide nonpublic data on clinical trials. The firm's experts, Bowe claimed, provided their Wall Street clients with inside information about which drugs would receive FDA approval and which would not. This was actionable information, or as Bowe charged in the lawsuit, the stuff hedge funds like SAC would use "in their trading strategies in that company's stock."

Gerson vehemently denied the charges. Government investigators, meanwhile, believed Gerson was no Primary Global, which they viewed as a corrupt outfit. By contrast, at Gerson experts were explicitly forbidden to discuss confidential information with their clients, and this included information that didn't even fall within the sphere of illegal inside tips. Experts received compliance training, and their work was constantly logged by company officials.

In fact, other than the dismissed Biovail claim, there was nothing to implicate Gerson in wrongdoing. Yet, there was something disquieting about the way Gilman, a Gerson expert, had sidestepped Gerson's controls as easily as Martoma had sidestepped SAC's.

So far, not a single Gerson expert had been charged as the investigation entered its seventh year, but that was about to change.

As convincing as the case was against Gilman and Martoma, investigators believed they needed something more if they were going to charge Cohen. Even if Martoma had a near-certain "level-nine" conviction on the trading strategy—code language that sounded suspicious—it wouldn't hold up in front of a jury as proof that Cohen had agreed to trade on illegal information. Their best hope would be Martoma telling the feds exactly what had been said during that twenty-minute telephone call before Cohen gave the order to sell hundreds of millions of dollars of stock.

And their guess was that it had little to do with conviction levels and more to do with how Martoma knew so much about how the stock was going to trade. But they couldn't charge Cohen on guesswork. For that they needed Martoma to cooperate, and who better to explain his limited options than Special Agent B. J. Kang?

Kang made the approach accompanied by Matthew Callahan, the new special agent in charge of the FBI's end of the investigation. The surprise visit to Martoma's $2 million home in Boca Raton occurred in late November 2011. According to sources, Callahan did much of the talking. (Kang was about to be promoted out of the investigation.)

It began with the agents asking Martoma to step outside so they could introduce themselves. If Martoma was stunned, he didn't show it just yet. He invited the agents into his home, and now accompanied by his wife, Martoma listened intently as the agents explained why they thought he was a crook. They said they knew about his use of Gilman as an expert, and they had evidence that he and SAC traded on inside information—a fact now backed up by Gilman, who had agreed to cooperate.

More than anything, they pressed Martoma on the hopelessness of his situation, before offering the carrot: He could avoid going to jail for a long time—around twenty years—if he cooperated in delivering evidence against Cohen, particularly about what was said during that suspicious telephone call prior to SAC selling all that stock.

The meeting lasted for forty-five minutes. As usual, the agents had prepared for a wide variety of reactions. Martoma was said to show little if any emotion, except for a period near the end of the meeting when he suddenly got dizzy and fainted. After he regained his composure, the thirty-eight-year-old ex-SAC trader said, "I need to call my lawyer," and several minutes later the meeting ended.

Over the next year, Martoma would reject several requests by the government to cooperate. He hired veteran white-collar attorney Charles Stillman and entered into a joint defense agreement with SAC. The choice of Stillman surprised prosecutors because he runs a fairly small law firm (albeit one that has been at the center of many white-collar cases over the years), because of his age (Stillman is 75), and because they thought a firm like SAC, flush with cash, could turn to a higher profile attorney in such an important matter.

Bharara, for example, did some research on Stillman's legal career, and he broke down in laughter when he discovered a news story recounting that Stillman had once defended an investment banker who plead guilty to a misdemeanor for threatening a flight attendant and defecating on a food cart. The part that caught Bharara's eye: When

Stillman called his client a "marvelously decent human being who had flown more than 5 million miles before the October flight without any incidents."

Martoma was deposed in early 2012 by the SEC and asserted his Fifth Amendment right against self-incrimination. Cohen was deposed in mid-2012, and among the trades he was asked about were those made in shares of Elan and Wyeth. It's unclear exactly how he answered the questions, or if his appearance advanced the government's probe.

People who know about the deposition said Cohen didn't recall much about the trades in question, which his defenders say is completely understandable. The trades occurred nearly five years earlier and Cohen is a busy guy trading so many different stocks each day that it's hard to keep track of them all. And above all, these people say he's innocent. The government has searched all his electronic communications and even his tax returns and has found nothing incriminating, they say. SAC may play rough in the markets, but Cohen is smart enough never to cross the line.

Esteemed Dr. Gilman, on the other hand, recalled a lot, and led investigators through the maze of emails, instant messages, and telephone calls he had had with Martoma around the trading in question. He participated in several meetings with the FBI and Justice Department before the famed physician formally agreed to become the latest "cooperating witness" in the probe. Gilman may have been a rat, but it was worth it from his standpoint—and the government's as well. His cooperation, crafted by the criminal defense attorney Marc Mukasey, included a blanket "non-prosecution" agreement, which meant he wouldn't spend a day in jail for his tell-all on Martoma.

It was indeed a surprise—a November surprise—when the FBI, federal prosecutors for the Southern District of New York, and the SEC announced that criminal and civil insider trading charges would be brought against Mathew Martoma in what was described as the biggest insider trading case in history.

With the help of Gilman, the feds laid out a pretty compelling argument for Martoma's guilt, with specifics about meetings and telephone calls around trading in shares of Elan and Wyeth. They also finally put to rest any doubt about their overarching goal.

In the charging documents, Cohen wasn't cited by name, rather he was referred to alternately as "Portfolio Manager A" and the hedge fund "owner" who was on the receiving end of Martoma's allegedly illegal tips.

Stevie, you're the John Gotti of Wall Street," Bo Dietl blurted out as he sat across from Cohen for dinner at the upscale Greek eatery Milos in Midtown Manhattan.

Cohen was dressed as he usually is when dining, even at some of New York's top restaurants: casually, in a sweater, khakis, and sneakers even if his entrance was far less casual. He pulled up at the restaurant in a chauffeur-driven Maybach, which depending on the level of luxury (Cohen's is custom made) can cost upward of $1 million.

As the government's probe intensified, Dietl had become a close friend and sounding board for Cohen, who was increasingly having to defend his business practices. The former New York City detective also knew what it was like to be the focus of suspicion; two years earlier a former associate of the real Gotti turned informant alleged that Dietl was once on the crime family's payroll—something Dietl vigorously denied. The allegation was never substantiated and charges were never filed, but the taint remained.

During their dinner, Cohen had been complaining about the taint now surrounding him and his firm, and how unfair some members of the press had been. Dietl was explaining to him the reality of his situation. Reporters were merely doing their job reporting what the government thinks. With that, Cohen just smiled, Dietl recalled.

There wasn't much smiling inside SAC's Stamford headquarters. After the charges against Martoma were announced, Cohen held a company-wide meeting where he said he was angered by the actions of a handful of employees, and he reminded his troops that the firm operates in a legal and ethical manner, and would survive.

Cohen must have known this was the most serious single threat to him and his firm in its twenty-year history. In the past, the flacks at Sard Verbinnen would dismiss charges against former SACers like Freeman or Hollander as nothing more than the transgressions of a few wayward souls who were later fired because they couldn't make the cut at the New York Yankees of the hedge fund world.

But that strategy wouldn't work with Martoma. Like those before, Martoma had eventually been fired for poor performance, but only after his highly lucrative, albeit suspicious, trades, and after sharing the wealth at the big hedge fund.

The SEC was now piling on, too, by issuing a "Wells Notice" against SAC, meaning its enforcement staff had recommended to the full commission that they file charges against the firm for civil securities fraud for allowing Martoma's illegal activities to take place and benefiting from them. The civil fraud charge wouldn't put people in jail, or even close the firm, but it was a serious black mark. For years, despite all the smoke surrounding its trading practices, SAC had been able to brag that its compliance system had protected the firm itself from serious illegality. No longer.

And the feds had a lot to work with, including numerous suspicious trades, multiple witnesses, and cooperators. A separate case involving suspicious trading in Dell and Nvidia shares was also taking shape. The case developed by agent David Makol began with low-level cooperators flipping on their supervisors at various hedge funds, including Level Global and Diamondback Capital. Before long, the trail led to a familiar place: SAC Capital and specifically to Jon Horvath, a former technology analyst who agreed to cooperate. Horvath then told the feds that whatever inside information he received, he shared with Michael Steinberg, one of the firm's top money managers and himself a confidant of Cohen.

The SAC bodies were now piling up. Steinberg had been waiting nervously for his status as an "unindicted co-conspirator" to change for the worse through a chunk of 2012 and well into 2013. He moved into a hotel room alone off and on so his wife and kids didn't have to witness him being handcuffed and led off to jail. His lawyer, Barry Berke, offered to have his client turn himself in, but the request was denied. What Berke didn't know was the behind-the-scenes drama between Bharara's people and FBI agents, mainly Chaves, over how to handle the pending arrest and how to get the maximum publicity for it.

A little more than a year earlier, lawyers for Anthony Chiasson offered the government the same deal, which was denied just before a team of FBI agents, accompanied by a camera crew, showed up one morning at Chiasson's Manhattan apartment. One witness said the feds appeared to dramatize the scene. After the camera was in place, the FBI car sped around the block once more and came to a screeching halt. That's when five agents in FBI windbreakers jumped out, entered the building, and accompanied the doorman to Chiasson's apartment so they could lead the moneyman out in handcuffs in full view of the camera.

There was just one problem: Chiasson had already moved to a hotel and when he got word that the FBI was looking for him, his attorney simply brought him to the government so he could be arrested, albeit privately.

Fast forward about a year, and Bharara's people didn't think the shock-and-awe approach was necessary. Steinberg, after all, wasn't a terrorist. FBI officials, apparently still stinging over the Chiasson flop, argued that there was a deterrent value in letting fat-cat traders know the consequences of their alleged crime, particularly those like Steinberg who were refusing to cooperate. In any event the FBI argued, agents do the arresting and they'll do it as they see fit.

With that, Steinberg's wait came to an end early one Friday morning, just before the Easter weekend and during Passover, when FBI agents showed up at his Manhattan apartment and placed him under arrest for five counts of securities fraud involving insider trading. His wife and kids were out of town for the ensuing media circus. Yet another leak to the *Wall Street Journal* had allowed a reporter to show up and film the arrest on her iPhone. A few hours later, no longer handcuffed, Steinberg pleaded not guilty and was released on $3 million bail.

He is regarded as the highest-ranking SAC employee to be snared during the inquiry, and immediately SAC's public relations team at Sard Verbinnen began spinning the least harsh interpretation of the move, its impact on the fund and on Cohen himself. "Steinberg is not a top adviser to Cohen," said Gasthalter, who described him as a long-time SAC portfolio manager, albeit a very good one.

What Gasthalter couldn't deny was Steinberg's personal relationship with Cohen. They are close friends, and Cohen had in the past used him as a sounding board on trading strategies, which is why the feds are eager to cut a deal with Steinberg for information that could help build a case against the man at the top of the SAC food chain.

Cohen's legal team viewed the situation as difficult, but not disastrous. The government had a perfect record in trying cases. But legal experts quickly concluded that the one against Steinberg could be difficult. One of the defenses used by targets is that even if they traded on inside information they didn't know it was inside information. In other words, they didn't intentionally break the law.

So far that defense hadn't worked, but in Steinberg's case it might. The insider tips Steinberg allegedly used were filtered through several different layers. They began with a hedge fund manager at a different shop, who passed along the information to Jon Horvath, the SAC analyst who passed the information to Steinberg, the government alleges. Even with Horvath's cooperation, the government may face difficulties proving that Steinberg knew what he was trading on was inside information because whatever came his way was passed along through so many sources he could have plausibly believed it was public.

Even before Steinberg's arrest, Martoma had pleaded not guilty, and his lawyer Stillman vowed to fight the charges to the end. That was also good news for Cohen, legal experts said, since the circumstances surrounding the trades were now running up against the statute of limitations.

And the feds still didn't know exactly what had been said during that twenty-minute call between Cohen and Martoma. In fact, Martoma could have told Cohen plenty of stuff without revealing the source of his information. "Conviction levels" hardly make criminal insider trading cases, particularly when you're going up against Steve Cohen.

They're going to pay a large fine like Goldman did and put this to rest," Anthony Scaramucci began assuring his clients in early 2013. "And Steve is protected."

Scaramucci was one of Cohen's closest friends on Wall Street, which is why he now called Cohen "Steve" instead of the more common "Stevie," which Cohen's wife and now Cohen himself had come to detest. He also ran a "fund of funds" with substantial holdings in SAC, and he wasn't pulling out. For Scaramucci, staying with SAC was a no-brainer. The fund didn't beat the 13 percent return in the S&P (one of the few years it didn't beat the market), but after fees, Cohen still earned a respectable 12 percent return, which wasn't bad considering his growing legal distractions.

If only there were more people like Scaramucci, Cohen must have thought, as his troops began to dial for dollars and beg investors to give them another chance. If the history of these investigations were any guide, investors would soon be running for the exits with their money in hand—or, in hedge fund speak, "redeeming their shares." But SAC held a better hand than most; so much of the fund's assets were made up of Cohen's own money—now around $9 billion out of the $14 billion SAC managed. Even if all the money from outside investors were redeemed, Cohen would still be trading one of the largest portfolios in the world.

SAC, of course, wasn't just any hedge fund. Its investor base was incredibly loyal after having dined on Cohen's massive returns for so long. But the reality of the hedge fund business is that law trumps loyalty. SAC manages a significant amount of money from pension funds, which under charter cannot be associated with an outfit under regulatory scrutiny. Money supplied by so-called funds of funds—hedge funds that invest in other hedge funds—was perhaps more stable, but some of that would certainly flee as well because it was just easier to simply pull the money out than to take the risk that the feds would close SAC and lock away its assets. Big banks like Citigroup and private equity firms like Blackstone would face similar choices as they weighed an uncertain future.

That is why Scaramucci's support was so vital. It was one thing for Cohen's own people to assure clients that all is well inside SAC. It was something else for someone outside SAC to do it.

The Goldman-like fine was a reference to the $550 million that the Wall Street firm paid the SEC to settle charges that it failed to disclose the risk in several pools of bonds it sold to its clients at the time of the financial crisis. But more than that, it was a talking point among Wall Street lawyers for the best way to handle a crummy situation. The settlement sounded like a lot, which made the feds sound like they were punishing the evil Wall Streeters—that is, until you consider it was being paid by a multibillion-dollar, deep-pocketed company that just wanted the bad publicity of the case to go away. That's exactly what happened, as shares of Goldman Sachs surged after announcing the settlement.

Indeed, Scaramucci's predictions proved amazingly accurate. SAC never bothered to respond to the Wells Notice from the SEC, a move that would have delayed the proceedings for months. It just decided to settle the case, offering to pay a Goldman-like penalty that ultimately came to $616 million. The SEC took its victory lap, as was expected, hawking the deal as the "largest insider trading settlement ever." (Michael Milken paid $1.1 billion back in 1991, but that was to settle both civil and criminal charges over a multitude of securities fraud charges that ended up not including insider trading.)

"Happy, relieved, excited about the future" was how one investor described the mood inside SAC. Even if he had to pay the settlement from his pocket, Cohen was still left with his $9 billion net worth largely intact. He appeared to celebrate days later, according to the *New York Post*, by shelling out $155 million to purchase Picasso's *Le Rêve* from another billionaire "Stevie"—casino mogul Steve Wynn—and purchasing waterfront property in the Hamptons for $60 million. The general feeling among key clients like Blackstone was relief as well; if the SEC had a case against Cohen they would have brought it. The firm's PR flacks told reporters that the "settlement is a substantial step toward resolving all outstanding regulatory matters and allows the firm to move forward with confidence." The redemptions did come in February, but at $1.7 billion it was far less than what was feared, even if another redemption date looms as this book goes to press.

While SAC traders exhaled, government investigators went back to building a case against Cohen, beginning with an unusual statement that, despite the settlement, Cohen remained a suspect. That warning shot came from George Canellos, now the acting head of the SEC's enforcement division after having taken over for Robert Khuzami. During a briefing with reporters, Canellos said the settlement wouldn't "preclude the future filing of additional charges against any person, including Steve Cohen, who is not named as a defendant in these cases."

It's difficult to recall a similar instance of an SEC official referring to a suspect by name. Still, as this book goes to press, government investigators continue to press Martoma into agreeing to cooperate against his old boss. One reason they are confident about Martoma as a potential witness against Cohen is the timing of their telephone conversation about the drug-stock sales in question. It occurred in 2008, before news of the wiretaps had been disclosed, when traders talked more freely on the phone about why they were buying and selling stocks.

With "each and every day that he doesn't cooperate, that's got to be a good day for Steve Cohen," one former prosecutor involved in the investigation said, referring to the statute of limitations that runs out in the summer. And, the theory goes, without Martoma cooperating the government has relatively little on Cohen beyond hearsay from emails and Martoma's self-professed level-nine conviction.

All of that sounds good if you're a Steve Cohen fan (or Cohen himself), until you consider the following: Prosecutors generally don't walk away from cases (unless of course you run a bank that is "too big to fail"). Eric Holder, the attorney general of the United States summed up the double standard during testimony in early 2013. "I am concerned that the size of some of these institutions becomes so large that it does become difficult for us to prosecute them when we are hit with indications that if you do prosecute, if you do bring a criminal charge, it will have a negative impact on the national economy, perhaps even the world economy, and I think that is a function of the fact that some of these institutions have become too large."

Holder's remarks, of course, underscored the irony of Perfect Hedge and the entire insider trading crackdown: For all the hard work of people like Wadhwa, Kang, Makol, Chaves, and their supervisors, the country remains somewhat unimpressed that the government went wild on insider trading while the banking fat cats—who took such outrageous risks that they brought the global financial system to its knees—continue to walk around free. Average people don't like insider trading, but many of these same average people believe it is beside the point. Holder was merely providing an awkward rationale for why the government seemed neutered when it came to busting the crime that brought down the U.S. financial system as opposed to the one that may have made some hedge fund traders a bit richer.

Holder would have probably done better to say nothing so as not to further demoralize the investing public. Even as the Dow cruised to new record highs, small investors remained wary. They certainly don't feel it's safer to invest because Raj Rajaratnam is in jail and Steve Cohen may be next. The best evidence for this is the fact that investor money still remains largely on the sidelines of the stock market, tucked away in gold or bonds, which eke out minuscule returns. To be sure, some investors are jumping back into the market, but only because they feel they're missing out on the party. Talk to financial advisers and they'll tell you that their clients have bigger concerns than SAC's market edge. Flash crashes, the botched Facebook IPO, and the belief the Fed has artificially inflated the market has scared many retail investors out of stocks.

But that has hardly deterred our insider-trading police from their mission. Cohen's spending spree on expensive art and the Hamptons home didn't go unnoticed by the feds, even if the purchases were in the works for a while, as Cohen's PR handlers say they were. Still, news of the sale suffered from very poor timing. It came as SAC was looking for a deal to end all the investigations through a settlement with Bharara's Manhattan US Attorney's office—a deal that would have "deferred" the prosecution of Cohen, possibly shuttered SAC in its current form, but allowed Cohen to restart the hedge fund at some later date.

When Scaramucci heard about the possible deal, he was ecstatic, remarking, "I'll even help Steve raise money."

The deal fell apart, and not just because the artwork purchase irked prosecutors. Bharara believes there is at least one major insider-trading case left, and all signs point to that case being SAC and Cohen. In May, it was learned that the US attorney's office sent grand jury subpoenas to SAC officials, including Cohen, over the trades under scrutiny. Legal experts say Cohen is likely to exercise his Fifth Amendment right against self-incrimination to avoid the perjury trap that snared Martha Stewart. His lawyers have told clients that the hedge fund, which has continuously stated it was cooperating "fully" with any and all investigations, will no longer do so on an "unconditional" basis.

SAC would not comment on the meaning of the announcement, released on a Friday afternoon in late May. But legal experts say it's another indication of the ever increasing government scrutiny and that Cohen's lawyers are taking steps to protect their man.

The high-stakes chess game doesn't end there. Bharara may have bristled at being compared with Rudy Giuliani when it comes to publicity seeking, but he isn't above using Giuliani's law enforcement tactics. In the late 1980s, Giuliani indicted the former junk bond king Michael Milken for securities fraud under the Racketeering Influence and Corrupt Organizations law, also known as RICO.

One drawback to RICO is that prosecutors need to prove an ongoing multiyear conspiracy, and they need a sign-off from the Justice Department in Washington, presumably directly from Holder, to launch such a case. But the law is also among the most powerful weapons the government has in prosecuting criminal enterprises such as the Mafia and occasionally those that occur in the financial business, which is why in the spring of 2012, Bharara's office began weighing a RICO case against SAC and possibly against Cohen.

The major benefit to RICO is that there are ways around the five-year statute of limitations that prosecutors face in the Martoma-related charges. Another advantage is the enormous pressure RICO exerts on targets to settle. The penalties are so onerous (large fines, and as much as twenty years in jail per offense) that suspects end up cutting a deal with prosecutors rather than taking a chance in court. In Milken's deal, he served twenty-two months in jail, agreed to pay the federal government more than $1 billion, and was barred from the securities industry for life.

The government may be angling for a similar outcome for Cohen, legal experts say. Columbia University Law School professor John Coffee, one of the foremost experts on white-collar crimes, believes the government and Cohen's lawyers have begun bargaining on a deal already, with the deferred prosecution agreement and the gesture to close SAC being just the opening salvo in the negotiations.

Bharara's hunt for more insider-trading targets, meanwhile, comes as he's also thinking of leaving the office and has discussed ballpark figures with people about what his salary might be in the private sector. Wadhwa has also signaled that he might move to a private sector job, yet another indication that catching alleged bad guys often leads to a lucrative career defending them in the future.

If Wadhwa leaves, there will be more than a few people looking to take his place to work on remaining cases, including the biggest prize of them all—the ongoing scrutiny of SAC and Steve Cohen. And if the government does finally get their man (Cohen, through a spokesman, continues to maintain his innocence), they won't have to worry about the global economic ramifications as they would if, say, Citigroup, with its massive worldwide balance sheet, came under similar scrutiny.

The problem for people like Steve Cohen is simple: even if he did nothing wrong, there is no such thing as a too-big-to-fail rule in the hedge fund business. An indictment of Cohen would likely lead to the liquidation of SAC. If SAC were forced out of business, it might mean lower profits for the firm's trading partners on Wall Street, and many unhappy investors. But in the eyes of the federal government, the nation would survive, just like it did back in the early 1990s when Milken was sent to jail and Drexel Burnham Lambert, the firm he'd built into a powerhouse, was shuttered.

All of this is probably why the federal government's obsession with the white whale of Stamford continues. We don't know if Moby-Dick will swim away, harpoons jutting from his skin but otherwise unharmed, or if the government will finally bring him to shore. One possible bad omen for Cohen: In early April, Martoma abruptly changed lawyers, firing Stillman and hiring a corporate law firm out of Boston, a sign he may now be willing to cooperate.

We do know this: For all the whales the government has successfully hunted, the "friends" and "expert networks" successfully prosecuted, the real whales—the ones who threaten our entire economy—continue to swim the globe unscathed, secure in the knowledge that if they run into troubles once again, they will be rescued as before by ordinary Americans. And no one who studies the markets and financial systems has any doubt that, given this security, they will repeat the same practices that led to the 2008 collapse. The bill for the bailouts will be paid for by our children and grandchildren.

But we can all sleep soundly at night knowing that our government's investigators are hard at work making sure the Raj Rajaratnams and Steve Cohens of the world remain firmly fixed in their sights.

CAST OF CHARACTERS

Rodolphe Agassiz—Chief executive of Cliff Mining, who purchased a big stake in his company on the Boston Stock Exchange on a report that the company was sitting on a sizable lode of copper in 1926. He was sued by Homer Goodwin, who sold his shares without insider knowledge of the report. Goodwin lost, setting a weak precedent for future insider trading cases.

Gary Aguirre—A former SEC enforcement attorney who said insider trading was rampant in the hedge fund business and that the SEC was bowing to political pressure in failing to crack down on the practice.

Robert "Rob" Babcock—Player in a scheme in which information on UBS ratings moves would be given to portfolio managers at Bear Stearns, and others, before they got to clients.

Peter Bacanovic—*Martha Stewart*'s stockbroker, who tipped her off that several ImClone executives were selling shares in the company ahead of an unfavorable ruling from the Food and Drug Administration on a cancer drug called Erbitux.

Preet Bharara—U.S. attorney for the Southern District of New York who is widely seen as one of the toughest enforcers of white-collar crime. Bharara prosecuted *Raj Rajaratnam* in one of the biggest insider trading busts of all time.

Biovail Corp.—A company that sued *SAC Capital Advisors* for allegedly having a research company publish negative reports about it in a bid to push down its share prices and support SAC's short positions. The case was dismissed.

Henry Blodget—An Internet research analyst at brokerage firm Merrill Lynch who allegedly wrote glowing reports about the companies he covered, in a bid to secure deals for the brokerage.

Reed Brodsky—A U.S. attorney who was part of the team that successfully convicted *Raj Rajaratnam.*

William Cary—Headed the SEC from 1961 to 1964, and sought to increase the commission's power in fighting insider trading.

David Chaves—Coheaded the securities fraud and white-collar crime division at the FBI's New York office, and a key figure in Operation Perfect Hedge.

Anthony Chiasson—Former *SAC Capital Advisors* employee who founded Level Global Advisors. Chiasson was convicted of insider trading regarding technology stocks.

Danielle "Dani" Chiesi—An analyst at *New Castle Partners*, a Bear Stearns subsidiary, who exchanged insider information on a quid pro quo basis with numerous individuals and had close ties to *Raj Rajaratnam*.

Citadel Management—A large asset management firm that was a client of analyst John Kinnucan.

Steve "Stevie" Cohen—Founder of *SAC Capital Advisors,* a Stamford, Connecticut-based hedge fund that manages some $14 billion in assets. Though considered among the greatest traders in modern history, Cohen also has been in the crosshairs of the government's sweeping insider trading probe. He has not been charged with any wrongdoing.

James Comey—Assistant U.S. attorney for the Southern District of New York who led the prosecution in the Martha Stewart case.

Tom Conheeney—*SAC Capital Advisors* president and one of *Steve Cohen*'s top lieutenants at the hedge fund.

Arthur Cutillo—Attorney at Ropes & Gray who took bribes to provide insider information on several corporate mergers, including Bain Capital's purchase of 3Com.

Raymond "Ray" Dirks—An analyst who played a role in one of the key legal precedents involving insider trading.

John Dowd—Attorney at Akin Gump who led the defense in the *Raj Rajaratnam* case.

Craig Drimal—A Galleon Group trader convicted of conspiracy and securities fraud for trades made on companies including 3Com and Axcan Pharma.

William Duer—Alexander Hamilton's assistant Treasury secretary, who used insider information to bet on bank stocks in the late eighteenth century, and sparked a financial crash.

Fairfax Financial—An insurance company that sued *SAC Capital Advisors* over allegedly manipulating stock prices. Fairfax's case was dismissed.

Doug Faneuil—A low-level brokerage employee who delivered the message to *Martha Stewart* that ImClone executives were selling shares in the company ahead of an unfavorable ruling from the Food and Drug Administration on a cancer drug called Erbitux.

Erik Franklin—A portfolio manager for Bear Stearns' *Lyford Cay* fund who traded on knowledge of UBS ratings moves before clients could get to them.

Noah Freeman—An ex-SAC fund manager who cooperated with the government in its insider trading probe.

Cameron "Cam" Funkhouser—Securities regulator who perfected a computerized system for watching for suspected insider trading.

Galleon Group—The now-defunct hedge fund founded by *Raj Rajaratnam*.

Kathryn Gannon aka Marylin Star—A pornography star who received insider tips on mergers through a relationship with Keefe Bruyette & Woods chief James McDermott.

Michael Garcia—Manhattan U.S. attorney during the Bush administration who famously proclaimed "greed is at work" when he unveiled a financial crisis era insider trading probe.

Gerson Lehrman Group—An expert network firm involved in the insider trading case against SAC and former portfolio manager Mathew Martoma. The firm has not been charged.

Dr. Sidney Gilman—Physician who allegedly leaked information to *SAC Capital Advisors* fund manager Mathew Martoma.

Robert Gintel—Partner at brokerage Cady, Roberts & Co. involved in one of the early insider trading cases.

Rajiv Goel—A former Intel executive who leaked insider information about the chipmaker to *Raj Rajaratnam*, and later cooperated with the government in its prosecution of him.

Zvi Goffer aka "Octopussy"—A trader at *Galleon Group* and other hedge funds known for his extensive insider trading network.

Lauren Goldberg—Assistant U.S. attorney who worked on the *Raj Rajaratnam* case.

Jack Grubman—A technology analyst at Citigroup's Salomon Smith Barney unit who allegedly penned rosy research reports on companies in exchange for investment banking business.

Rajat Gupta—Former Goldman Sachs director and McKinsey & Co. chief executive who was convicted for providing *Raj Rajaratnam* with inside trading tips.

Mitchel Guttenberg—An employee on UBS's research team who illegally passed inside information involving stock research to various hedge fund traders.

Jonathan Hollander—Former *SAC Capital Advisors* money manager who provided government investigators with information about how the giant hedge fund operates.

Judge Richard Holwell—U.S. district judge who presided over the *Raj Rajaratnam* trial.

Richard Jacobs—Agent in charge of FBI team "C-1," which was tasked with taking down *Raj Rajaratnam.*

Winifred Jiau—Former *Primary Global* consultant convicted of providing inside information to her hedge fund clients.

B. J. Kang—The FBI special agent who led the Galleon probe.

Debasis Kanjilal—Former Merrill Lynch brokerage client who sued the firm's former analyst *Henry Blodget* over allegedly faulty stock research.

Carl Karcher—Founder of Carl Karcher Enterprises, the parent of the Carl's Jr. burger chain, who settled an SEC civil complaint involving insider trading.

Roomy Khan—A former executive at chipmaker Intel and one of the key cooperating witnesses in the investigation of *Raj Rajaratnam.*

Robert "Bob" Khuzami—The SEC enforcement chief during the agency's insider trading crackdown.

John Kinnucan—An independent research analyst who headed Broadband Research, LLC; Kinnucan was convicted of securities fraud but may be best known for his email to clients alerting them of the government's insider trading probe.

Anil Kumar—A McKinsey & Co. executive vice president who was convicted of leaking inside information to *Raj Rajaratnam.*

Mark Kurland—Cofounder of *NewCastle Partners* who was convicted of passing insider information during the Galleon probe to *Danielle Chiesi.*

Benjamin Lawsky—An assistant U.S. attorney and close associate of Manhattan U.S. attorney, *Preet Bharara.*

Richard Choo-Beng Lee—Spherix Capital founder who traded insider information with Danielle Chiesi and was convicted of insider trading.

Dennis Levine—A Drexel Burnham Lambert managing director who was convicted of securities fraud and was hit with criminal and civil charges.

Anthony "Tony" Longoria—A supply-chain manager at AMD who moonlighted as an industry expert, selling inside secrets about the chipmaker.

Lyford Cay—A Bear Stearns hedge fund that managed money for many of the investment bank's big-name clients and was involved in a major insider trading case.

Gerard Lynch—Federal judge who authorized the use of wiretaps in the Rajaratnam insider trading case.

Bernard Madoff—Convicted of perpetrating one of the biggest frauds in U.S. history.

David Makol—One of the top FBI agents involved in Operation Perfect Hedge, considered an expert at flipping suspects and turning them into cooperators.

Henry Manne—Author of *Insider Trading and the Stock Market,* Manne argues that insider trading doesn't harm investors and in fact leads to a more efficiently operating market since information is more readily priced into stocks.

David Markowitz—A senior enforcement official at the SEC.

Mathew Martoma—Former *SAC Capital Advisors* fund manager who was charged by the U.S. government for allegedly taking part in a massive insider trading scheme. Martoma says he's done nothing wrong.

James McDermott—Former chief executive at Keefe, Bruyette & Woods who was convicted of sharing inside information with pornography star *Kathryn Gannon.*

McKinsey & Co.—Big New York–based management consultancy.

Andrew Michaelson—An enforcement official at the SEC who worked on the Galleon case and would later join the Manhattan U.S. Attorney's office during the Rajaratnam prosecution.

Michael Milken—Chief of the junk bond segment at Drexel Burnham Lambert, who was convicted of securities fraud.

Robert Moffat—Former IBM executive who leaked insider tips to *Galleon Group* via *Danielle Chiesi.*

NewCastle Partners—A hedge fund giant, and Bear Stearns subsidiary, that employed numerous individuals ultimately linked to insider trading.

Todd Newman—A portfolio manager at Diamondback Capital Management. Newman was convicted of insider trading.

James H. O'Hagan—The central figure in an insider trading case that became the basis of modern insider trading law.

Ferdinand Pecora—Flamboyant Depression-era prosecutor who led a high-profile investigation into the causes of the 1929 stock market crash.

Primary Global—A now-defunct expert consultancy network and one of the key elements of the insider trading probe. Primary Global had hired a number of consultants who would be convicted of passing insider tips to hedge fund clients.

Raj Rajaratnam—Founder of *Galleon Group* who was convicted of fourteen counts of securities-fraud-related crimes and was sentenced to eleven years in prison for insider trading.

Rengan Rajaratnam—Hedge fund trader and brother of *Raj Rajaratnam*, who was charged with insider trading. The SEC's 2007 investigation into Rengan's hedge fund, Sedna Capital, led to the probe of Galleon.

Gary Rosenbach—*Raj Rajaratnam*'s partner who ran the Galleon Group's trading desk.

Arthur Prentice Rugg—Chief justice of the Supreme Judicial Court of Massachusetts who opined in one of the early insider trading cases.

Hector Ruiz—AMD chairman who had close ties to *Danielle Chiesi*.

SAC Capital Advisors—A Stamford, Connecticut-based hedge fund headed by Steve Cohen that manages $14 billion in assets.

Mary Schapiro—SEC chairman during the commission's insider trading crackdown.

Securities and Exchange Commission aka SEC—Wall Street's "top cop," or chief regulator, which was formed by Congress in the 1930s to stabilize markets and protect investors.

Deep Shah—Provided *Roomy Kahn* with inside information on Blackstone's purchase of Hilton Hotels.

Walter Shimoon—A former executive at Flextronics International who pleaded guilty to sharing insider secrets about the tech-supply-chain heavyweight to John Kinnucan.

Martin Siegel—A Drexel Burnham Lambert managing director who was convicted of securities fraud during the 1980s insider trading crackdown.

David Slaine—Former Morgan Stanley managing director and hedge fund trader who became one of the top cooperators during Operation Perfect Hedge.

Eliot Spitzer—Former New York attorney general who was known for his hard-nosed approach to fighting white-collar crime.

Michael Steinberg—*SAC Capital Advisors* money manager charged with trading on inside information. Steinberg says he's innocent.

Martha Stewart—Home and lifestyle mogul who found herself ensnared in a high-profile insider trading case involving her friend, ImClone Systems founder Sam Waksal. Stewart was eventually convicted of lying to government investigators, but she was never charged with criminal insider trading.

Jon Streeter—Assistant Manhattan U.S. attorney who led the prosecution in the *Raj Rajaratnam* insider trading case.

Sanjay Wadhwa—Associate regional director for the SEC's New York office and one of the central figures in the Galleon probe, as well as the ongoing investigation into insider trading at other big hedge funds, such as SAC.

Sam Waksal—Founder and former CEO of ImClone Systems, who was convicted of insider trading.

Doug Whitman—Founder of asset management company Whitman Capital, who was convicted of insider trading in a Galleon-related case.

R. Foster Winans—Former writer for the *Wall Street Journal* who was convicted of securities fraud for handing out pre-publication details of the market-moving column.

NOTES

In writing *Circle of Friends* I relied on a number of sources of information, such as court documents, SEC filings, and depositions, as well as interviews with government officials directly involved in the Perfect Hedge investigation, defense attorneys representing the key players involved in the case, and press representatives. Many (if not most) of these interviews, particularly with the government investigators on the front lines of the insider trading probes, occurred under the condition that the parties involved not be identified by name, for the obvious reason that even as this book goes to press, the investigation is continuing and such information is considered confidential.

In fact, one of the hurdles I needed to overcome is the confidentiality that involves any story about an ongoing civil and criminal investigation of the magnitude of Perfect Hedge, where people involved could be fined millions of dollars and spend years in prison. Needless to say, without relying on people who speak without attribution, neither this book nor the vast majority of what is considered investigative reporting would ever see the light of day.

That said, I have attempted to verify the key scenes in the book with the various players involved, through their representatives. Where there is a discrepancy over the facts, I have attempted to show both sides of the story. Every major character was asked to cooperate and given the opportunity to speak on a not-for-attribution basis. Steve Cohen, for instance, declined numerous requests to be interviewed for this book, but I have provided his representatives with a detailed account of what has been written and have added their comments when appropriate.

In developing a narrative about Cohen and SAC Capital Advisors, I have spoken to friends and former colleagues. I have reviewed court transcripts and other documents, as I have in developing the narratives of the other key characters including former Galleon chief Raj Rajaratnam, and David Slaine, one of the government's premier undercover witnesses in the investigation.

Much of the work in the book is a result of my reporting at the Fox Business Network, including an interview with former FBI agent Mark Rossini, who first alerted me to the size and scope of the probe and how, despite all the attention the press was giving other players like Raj Rajaratnam, a key target in the probe was actually SAC Capital, and Cohen.

As this book goes to press, Cohen has yet to be charged in either a civil or criminal case, though SAC itself has settled civil securities fraud charges with the SEC, in the usual fashion of neither admitting nor denying wrongdoing. A criminal investigation into SAC and Cohen himself continues, and as I have said numerous times while I've reported on these issues, Cohen is innocent until a jury proves he is guilty. It is not my intention to pass judgment, but merely to report on the activities of the government as they relate to Cohen and SAC, and give Cohen a fair hearing of his own.

I have also leaned on the reporting of several journalists who covered the insider trading scandals and the Perfect Hedge investigation. This includes the fine work of Susan Pulliam at the *Wall Street Journal,* Kaja Whitehouse at the *New York Post,* Peter Lattman at the *New York Times,* Matthew Goldstein and Jennifer Alban of Reuters, George Packer for his excellent profile of Preet Bharara in the *New Yorker,* and Roger Lowenstein's *New York Times* piece on insider trading, as well as various reporters at Bloomberg News for their aggressive coverage of the subject. The information I gleaned from these sources can be found in the following endnotes. Some of the material taken from these and other sources has been quoted directly with author attribution in the text because I believed a simple endnote was not sufficient in pointing out the exclusivity of the reporting.

INTRODUCTION

1 Description of FBI's meeting with David Slaine from author interviews with government investigators directly involved in the investigation and various news accounts, including Susan Pulliam, "Wired on Wall Street: Trader Betrays a Friend," *Wall Street Journal*, January 16, 2010.

2 Description of how Slaine initially appeared on government's insider trading radar screen from author interviews with government officials, public documents such as the Securities and Exchange Commission's complaint against Slaine, and various news accounts including David Glovin and David Voreacos, "Dream Insider Informant Led FBI From Galleon to SAC," Bloomberg, December 3, 2012.

3 Size of the hedge fund business in 2007 of $2 trillion from Adrian Blundell-Wignall, "An Overview of Hedge Funds and Structured Products: Issues and Risk," OECD.org, 2007.

3 Slaine's job background from various news accounts.

4–5 Background on David Chaves and David Makol from author interviews with people who know both men, as well as Susan Pulliam, Michael Rothfeld, and Jenny Strasberg, "The FBI Agent Who 'Flips' Insider-Trading Witnesses," *Wall Street Journal*, January 20, 2012.

6 Slaine's decision to cooperate with the government and his attitude during meetings with the FBI from author interviews with various government investigators. Slaine's attorney would not deny the account.

7 B. J. Kang approached Roomy Khan and turned her as a witness from author interviews with government officials, various news accounts, including George Packer, "A Dirty Business: New York's Top Prosecutor Takes On Wall Street Crime," *New Yorker*, June 27, 2011.

8 As many as nine former SAC employees implicated in insider trading cases so far and Steinberg's status as unindicted co-conspirator from Emily Flitter and Katya Wachtel, "Prosecutors Zero In on SAC Capital Insider Steinberg," Reuters, February 6, 2013.

9 FBI wiretapping Steve Cohen's telephone from author interviews with people close to the investigation.

11 The significance of the securities acts of 1933 and 1934 from various news accounts including Roger Lowenstein, "The War on Insider Trading: Market-Beaters Beware," *New York Times*, September 22, 2011.

17 Amount of money Raj Rajaratnam made through illegal insider trading from various news accounts, including Peter Lattman, "Rajaratnam Gets 11 Years for Insider Trading," *New York Times*, October 13, 2011; Kaja Whitehouse, "Raj to Judge: I Only Made $7 million," *New York Post*, October 5, 2011.

CHAPTER 1: PERFECTLY LEGAL

21–22 The travails of William Duer from various news accounts, including Steve Fraser, "Sex, Insider Trading and the First U.S. Financial Panic," Bloomberg, December 9, 2011.

23 Ulysses S. Grant's involvement in insider trading, "Black Friday, September 24, 1869," PBS.org.

23 Why President Roosevelt chose Joseph Kennedy as first chairman of the Securities and Exchange Commission and Roosevelt's quote about Kennedy from William D. Pederson, *Blackwell Companions to American History: Franklin D. Roosevelt* (New York: John Wiley & Sons, 2011).

24 Background on Kennedy's market activities from various sources, including Conrad Black, "The Peculiar Life of Joseph Kennedy," a review of David Nasaw's *The Patriarch: The Remarkable Life and Turbulent Times of Joseph P. Kennedy* (New York: Penguin, 2012), *National Interest*, October 24, 2012.

26 Impact of the Pecora hearings and Pecora's background from various news accounts and from Amanda Ruggeri, "Pecora Hearings a Model for Financial Crisis Investigation; Congress Could Learn from Pecora's 1930s Investigation of the Stock Market Crash," *U.S. News & World Report*, September 29, 2009.

27 Quote from Arthur Prentice Rugg and details of Cliff Mining case from Rick Wartzman, "A 1920s Insider Trade Was Ruled by a Court to Be Merely a Perk," *Wall Street Journal*, July 3, 2002.

30 Letters to the SEC from commission archives.

32 Background on William Cary and Cady Roberts case from various news sources, including Michael Bobelian, "The Obscure Insider Trading Case That Started It All," *Forbes*, November 20, 2012. Also see Joan K. Martin, "Insider Trading and the Misappropriation Theory: Has the Second Circuit Gone Too Far?" *St. John's Law Review* 61 (Fall 1986).

35 Background on the case of Raymond Dirks and Harvey Pitt's comment about the SEC's "perspiration effect" from Jack Egan, "The War on Wall Street's Inside Dopesters," *New York Magazine*, March 28, 1983.

37, 42, 43 Background on Dirks, Anthony Chiarella, Foster Winans, and O'Hagan insider trading cases from various news reports, including the following speech: "U.S. Experience of Insider Trading Enforcement," by Linda Chatman Thomsen, director, Division of Enforcement, U.S. Securities and Exchange Commission, Melbourne, Australia, February 19, 2008.

37 Background on Texas Gulf Sulphur case from Stephen M. Bainbridge, "An Overview of U.S. Insider Trading Law: Lessons for the EU?" UCLA School of Law, Law & Economics Research Paper Series, 2004.

38 More background on the Chiarella case from Joel M. Cohen and Mary Kay Dunning, "Insider Trading: It's Not Just for Suits," *Law Journal Newsletters' Business Crimes Bulletin* 18, no. 4 (December 2008).

40 Warren Burger dissent from U.S. Supreme Court, *Chiarella v. United States*, 445 U.S. 222 (1980), *Chiarella v. United States* No. 78-1202, argued November 5, 1979, decided March 18, 1980, 445 U.S. 222; and "History of Insider Trading 1611–2012," procon.org.

42 Background on Winans case from "Fair to All People: The SEC and Regulation of Insider Trading," www.sechistorical.org.

44 Supreme Court's O'Hagan decision and its impact on insider trading laws from various sources, including Thomsen, "U.S. Experience of Insider Trading Enforcement."

CHAPTER 2: TEN DIFFERENT CAMERAS ON EVERY TRADER

50 SAC's share of Nasdaq and New York Stock Exchange daily trading volume from Streetinsider.com biography of Steve Cohen.
54 Insider trading case against Carl Karcher, settlement, and other details from author interviews and "S.E.C. Cites Carl Karcher," *New York Times*, April 14, 1988. Also see Mary Ann Galante, "Karcher: Cloudy Chapter in Horatio Alger Success Story," *New York Times*, April 15, 1988; "Carl's Jr. Founder, Family Settle Insider-Trading Lawsuit," Associated Press, July 1989.
55 Much of the information in this book about the insider trading scandals of the 1980s, including cases against its major figures, Ivan Boesky, Martin Siegel, Dennis Levine, Michael Milken, and Drexel Burnham Lambert are from James Stewart, *Den of Thieves* (New York: Simon & Schuster, 1991); and James B. Stewart and Daniel Hertzberg, "Siegel: American Dream Gone Bad," *Wall Street Journal*, February 1987.
57 Insider trading case against porn star Kathryn Gannon and Jim McDermott from author interviews and Charles Gasparino and Jeff D. Opdyke, "Porn Star Insider-Trading Case Uncovered by a Routine Inquiry," *Wall Street Journal*, January 13, 2000. Also see Charles Gasparino and Laurie P. Cohen, "Keefe Bruyette Let Staffers Buy Company Stock Amid Scandal," *Wall Street Journal*, December 23, 1999.
59 Jim McDermott's excuse for insider trading from Greg B. Smith, "Siblings Tell 'Sad Tale' of James McDermott: Raided Family Trust During Tryst with Porn Star," *New York Daily News*, October 3, 2009.
59 Details of Martha Stewart insider trading case and ultimate conviction from author interview and various news accounts, including Charles Gasparino and Jerry Markon, "Martha Stewart Faces Wider Probe for Possible Obstruction of Justice," *Wall Street Journal*, June 6, 2002. Also see Greg Smith, "Martha Pal Sank Me, Broker Sez," *New York Daily News*, April 20, 2004.
61 Martha Stewart's net worth and savings from the suspicious trade from Keith Naughton, Barney Gimbel, and Peg Tyre, "Martha's Makeover," *Newsweek*, January 19, 2004.
64, 67 Martha Stewart's settlement with the SEC from Peter J. Hennings, "White Collar Watch: Insider Trading Riddle: Why Do the Rich Risk It?" *New York Times*, April 5, 2012.
66 Background on Steve Cohen and SAC Capital, including his years at Gruntal and trading style, from author interviews and various news accounts,

including Mitchell Pacelle and Charles Gasparino, "A Day Trader Gets on a Roll, For 20 Years," *Wall Street Journal*, December 3, 1999. Also see Sheelah Kolhatkar, "Where Hedge Fund Mogul Steve Cohen Learned to Trade," Bloomberg, December 7, 2012.

CHAPTER 3: DO WHATEVER IT TAKES

71 Background on Pathmark and SAC's presale purchase of shares, including company's reaction and details of sale to A&P, from people with direct knowledge of the matter and various news accounts, including, "Hedge Fund Group Reveals 5 Percent Stake in Pathmark," *Progressive Grocer*, December 22, 2006. See also "Great Atlantic in Negotiations to Purchase Pathmark Stores for About $652.5M," FinancialWire, February 28, 2007; "SAC Capital/Steven Cohen Discloses a 5% Stake in Pathmark Stores (PTMK)," StreetInsider, December 21, 2006.
73 Section on Wall Street sell-side research through the scandals that ended with investigations into conflicts of interest between banking and research from original reporting, various news accounts, and Charles Gasparino, *Blood on the Street* (New York: Free Press, 2005).
80 John Kinnucan's transition from sell-side analyst to independent analyst and his activities and salary from author interviews with Kinnucan.

CHAPTER 4: A REGULAR GUY

85 Details about SAC Capital, including size and Steve Cohen's net worth, from "Top Q4 Undervalued Buys and Sells of Stephen Cohen's $15.8 Billion Hedge Fund," SeekingAlpha, February 27, 2012.
87 The decentralization of SAC Capital from author interviews and Peter Lattman and Andrew Ross Sorkin, "Titan Under a Microscope," *New York Times*, May 7, 2011.
88 Gary Aguirre's testimony from "Testimony of Gary J. Aguirre, Esq., Before the United States Senate Committee on the Judiciary," United States Senate Committee on the Judiciary, June 28, 2006.
92 Background on FBI agent B. J. Kang from author interviews and various published reports, including Matthew Goldstein and Svea Herbst-Bayliss, "The FBI Agent Inside the Galleon Case," Reuters, December 4, 2009.
94 Funkhouser flagging suspicious SAC trades for the SEC, including Genentech, from Joshua Gallu and Saijel Kishan, "SAC Capital Netted $14M in Trading Flagged by Finra," Bloomberg, October 25, 2011.
95 Growing suspicions about widespread insider trading and insider trading surrounding News Corporation's purchase of Dow Jones from Victoria Kim

and Brooke Masters, "Boom Time for Suspicious Trades," *Financial Times*, August 5, 2007.

CHAPTER 5: WHAT FRIENDS ARE FOR

99 Details of the Franklin-Babcock-Guttenberg circle of friends from author interviews with people with direct knowledge of the matter and various news accounts, including Jenny Anderson and Michael J. de la Merced, "13 Accused of Trading as Insiders," *New York Times*, March 2, 2007.
100 Background on Joe Lewis from Stephen Foley, "Who Is Bear Stearns Investor Joe Lewis?" *BloombergBusinessweek*, September 11, 2007.
106 SAC and "information arbitrage" from "At SAC It Was Understood You Provided Steve Cohen With Inside Information," ZeroHedge, October 2, 2012.
106 Steve Cohen's appearance on talk show *Christina* from Kaja Whitehouse, "Steven Cohen Slept with Both Spouses While Divorcing," *New York Post*, December 22, 2009.
108 Patricia Cohen discusses Steve Cohen's alleged insider trading with FBI from author interviews and various news accounts, including Kaja Whitehouse, "Steven Cohen's Ex-Wife Dished to FBI," *New York Post*, December 19, 2009.
108 Details on Patricia Cohen's meeting with FBI agent Kang from author interviews with government investigators and others involved in the investigation, as well as the spokesman for Cohen who wouldn't deny account provided by Patricia Cohen. Other details about Cohen's years at Gruntal, including SEC investigation and NYSE regulatory infraction, from various published reports, including Mitchell Pacelle and Charles Gasparino, "A Day Trader Gets on a Roll, for 20 Years," *Wall Street Journal*, December 3, 1999. Also see Sheelah Kolhatkar, "Where Hedge Fund Mogul Steve Cohen Learned to Trade," Bloomberg, December 7, 2012; Matthew Goldstein and Svea Herbst-Bayliss, "Ex-Wife Sues SAC's Cohen, Alleges Insider Trading," Reuters, December 16, 2009; Katherine Burton and Anthony Effinger, "Steve Cohen's Trade Secrets," *Bloomberg Markets*, February 26, 2010.
108 Patricia Cohen's allegations of insider trading, including Dennis Levine's alleged involvement, from court documents and Courtney Comstock, "Patricia Cohen Details SAC's Steve Cohen's 'The Wharton Mafia' and Alleged Insider Trading," *Business Insider*, July 29, 2010.
109 Sanjay Wadhwa background and investigative techniques and how he came across Galleon from numerous author interviews with SEC officials and various news accounts, including Devin Leonard, "Rajaratnam Case Shows Outmanned, Outgunned SEC on a Roll," Bloomberg, April 19, 2012.

112 Details of seamstress case and Wadhwa's involvement from author interviews, various news accounts, and staff statement in *SEC v. Anticevic*, press conference by Mark K. Schonfeld, director, Northeast Regional Office, U.S. Securities and Exchange Commission, New York, NY, April 11, 2006.
114 Background on how Galleon got its start from author interviews and Lois Peltz, *The New Investment Superstars: 13 Great Investors and Their Strategies for Superior Returns* (New York: Wiley, 2001).
116 Background on Raj Rajaratnam, including alleged involvement with Tamil Tigers, from author interviews and various news accounts, including David Rose, "Crouching Tiger, Hidden Raj," *Vanity Fair*, September 30, 2011.

CHAPTER 6: BIGGER FISH

121 Questioning by SEC officials found in publicly available transcripts of the deposition and described in numerous court documents.
125 Anonymous letter sent to SEC from author interviews, and various news accounts including Lowenstein, *New York Times*.
128 Roomy Khan's early brush with insider trading violations when an employee at Intel and her background from author interviews, various news accounts, and Alexandria Sage, "Galleon Got Inside Info on Intel in 1990s—Document," Reuters, October 23, 2009.
133 How B. J. Khan decided to approach Roomy Khan and details about his methods involving cooperators from author interviews with government officials involved in the case
134 Roomy Khan's winnings from Hilton trade from SEC case.
134 Financial issues involving Roomy Khan and her husband, including legal problems from author interviews and various news accounts, including from Michael J. de la Merced, Zachery Kouwe, and Alex Berenson, "Financial Woes Plagued Galleon Informant," *New York Times*, October 21, 2009.

CHAPTER 7: THE FLIP

137 Kang's conversation with Khan and his efforts to flip her from various news accounts, court documents, and interviews with government officials.
145 Background on Rich Jacobs from author interviews with government officials and Emily Flitter, "Wall Street credibility helped FBI agent nab Martoma, others," Reuters, December 6, 2012.
149 Physical description of David Slaine from various news accounts and Todd Harrison, *The Other Side of Wall Street*. Background on Slaine from Susan Pulliam, "Wired on Wall Street: Trader Betrays a Friend," *Wall Street Journal*, January 16, 2010.

150 How Franklin-Babcock-Guttenberg circle led to David Slaine from author interviews, and various news accounts, including Zachery Kouwe, "In Insider Trading Inquiry, Old and New Cases Linked," *New York Times*, February 3, 2010.
151 Slaine's net worth from the motion to dismiss insider trading charges filed by Zvi Goffer.
152 Background on FBI agent David Makol from author interviews and various news accounts, including Susan Pulliam, Michael Rothfeld, and Jenny Stresburg, "The FBI Agent Who 'Flips' Insider-Trading Witnesses," *Wall Street Journal*, January 20, 2012.
155 Sentencing guidelines for insider trading and rape from Matt Levine, "How Much Time In Jail Will a Little Bit of Insider Trading Cost You," Dealbreaker, September 12, 2011, and New York Defense Lawyer.com.
156 Slaine as informant from Susan Pulliam, "Wired on Wall Street: Trader Betrays a Friend," *Wall Street Journal*, January 16, 2010.

CHAPTER 8: THE FEDS MIGHT BE LISTENING

160 Slaine telling the FBI about a tip about an analyst downgrade of Amazon.com from David Glovin and David Voreacos, "Dream Insider Informant Led FBI From Galleon to SAC," Bloomberg, December 3, 2012.
161 FBI's belief SEC would mess up its cases from James Stewart, *Den of Thieves* (New York: Simon & Schuster, 1991), and James B. Stewart and Daniel Hertzberg, "Siegel: American Dream Gone Bad," *Wall Street Journal*, February 22, 1987.
161 Details about Roomy Khan's cooperation with FBI agent B. J. Kang from author interviews with government officials, court documents, and Chad Bray, "Insider Informant, Some Tips Were Refused," *Wall Street Journal*, August 8, 2012.
162 Doug Whitman's advice to Roomy Khan from Kaja Whitehouse, "What value do you have if you're not a slimeball?" *New York Post*, August 9, 2012.
162 Roomy Khan's relationship with Deep Shah from Susan Pulliam, "Galleon Sinks; Informant Surfaces," *Wall Street Journal*, and author interviews.
162 Roomy Khan's various lies to federal investigators from author interviews, various news accounts, and court documents.
169 Details of Slaine's foray as an informant, including New York City meeting places, from author interviews and various news accounts, including David Glovin and David Voreacos, "Dream Insider Informant Led FBI From Galleon to SAC," Bloomberg, December 3, 2012.
170 Details of Makol working with Slaine and Slaine leading FBI to Dri-

mal's 3Com trade from author interviews and various news accounts, including Pulliam, "Wired on Wall Street."

170 Timeline on the 3Com trade and the various players in the Zvi Goffer circle of friends from Kevin McCoy and Laura Petrecca, "Today 'Octopussy' among 14 facing charges for insider trading," *USA Today*, November 6, 2009.

172 Conversations between Zvi Goffer, Michael Kimelman, and Slaine from government's sentencing memorandum re: David Slaine.

173 Zvi Goffer as Octopussy and his "you" and "me" cell phones from Tom Hays, "'Octopussy' Zvi Goffer, 6 Others Plead Not Guilty to Insider Trading Scheme," *Huffington Post*, February 2, 2010.

CHAPTER 9: ODD COUPLES

175 Rajaratnam's recorded conversation with Roomy Khan from motion filed by Rajaratnam's lawyers to suppress wiretap evidence.

181 Background on Sanjay Wadhwa from David Leonard, "The SEC: Outmanned, Outgunned, and on a Roll," *Bloomberg Businessweek*, April 19, 2012.

182 Anil Kumar's business relationship with Rajaratnam from George Packer, "A Dirty Business," *New Yorker*, June 27, 2011.

185 Danielle Chiesi conversation with Rajaratnam from Katya Wachtel, "AUDIO: Listen to Raj And Danielle Chiesi Revel in Their Trading of Akamai Stock Ahead of a Public Guidance Announcement," April 5, 2011.

185 Background on Chiesi from various news accounts, including Packer, "A Dirty Business."

186 Slaine telling government investigators that Rajaratnam liked "pretty girls" from author interviews and David Glovin and David Voreacos, "Dream Insider Informant Led FBI from Galleon to SAC," Bloomberg, December 3, 2012.

187 Background on Robert Moffat, Chiesi, and Hector Ruiz and how their circle operated from author interviews with law enforcement officials, and published reports, including James Bandler and Doris Burke, "Dangerous Liaisons at IBM: Inside the biggest hedge fund insider-trading ring," *Fortune*, July 6, 2010.

188 More detail on Chiesi and how Bear Stearns investigated her trades from author interviews and various news accounts, including Anthony Effinger, Katherine Burton, and Ian King, "Woman Who Sank Galleon Was Beauty-Queen-Turned-Analyst Insider," Bloomberg, November 22, 2009.

189 Chiesi's work on AMD Middle Eastern deal from author interviews, Bandler and Burke, "Dangerous Liaisons at IBM," and various news accounts.

189 Conversation between Rajaratnam and Chiesi where he urges her to keep quiet from author's review of transcripts and various news accounts, including "Tapes in Rajaratnam Trial Allege Affair, Cover-Up, Third McKinsey Player," Finalternatives, March 15, 2011.

190 Chiesi's conversations with Rajaratnam about information she received from Kieran Taylor from various news accounts on tapes played at court hearings and Michael J. de la Merced, "Taped Calls About Akamai Earnings Guidance Heard at Galleon Trial," *New York Times*, April 4, 2011. Also see Kaja Whitehouse, "Racy Insider Tapes; Ex-Trader Raj Chats Speak Volumes," *New York Post*, April 5, 2011.

CHAPTER 10: SOMETHING GOOD IS GOING TO HAPPEN

194 Background on Kumar and Rajaratnam relationship from author interviews, Packer, "A Dirty Business," and various news accounts, including Peter Lattman and Azam Ahmed, "A Circle of Tipsters Who Shared Illicit Secrets," *New York Times*, May 11, 2011.

195 Rajaratnam conversations with Rajat Gupta and background on Gupta from various news accounts, author interviews, and Stephen Grocer, "Rajat Gupta's Career in a Timeline," *Wall Street Journal*, June 15, 2012. See also Packer, "A Dirty Business."

198 Buffett's "fifteen dollars a second" boast on his Goldman investment made to Liz Claman of the Fox Business Network.

203 Background on new SEC enforcement chief Robert Khuzami from various news accounts and author interviews with Khuzami.

205 Choo-Beng Lee's statement to FBI from author interview; how he was caught through Chiesi wiretap from author interview and various news accounts, including Peter Lattman, "Trail to a Hedge Fund, from a Cluster," *New York Times*, December 5, 2012.

207 Chiesi worried she might get caught like "Martha fucking Stewart" from Jessica Pressler, "Rajaratnam and Danielle Chiesi Plead Not Guilty to Insider Trading," *New York Magazine*, December 21, 2009.

207 Lee's advice to Kang to begin looking at expert networks from author interviews with government investigators and various news accounts.

210 Rajaratnam's involvement in film project and customs office tipping he might leave the country from author interviews with government investigators and various news accounts, including Jodi Xu, "Galleon's Raj Rajaratnam a No-Show at Film Fest," *Wall Street Journal*, November 12, 2009. See also Susan Pulliam, "Fund Chief Snared by Taps, Turncoats," *Wall Street Journal*, December 30, 2009.

210 Rajaratnam's plan to travel to Geneva from Zachery Kouwe, "Rajaratnam Planned Business Trip Before Arrest," *New York Times*, October 23, 2009.

CHAPTER 11: POUNCE HARD

213 Rajaratnam's arrest and FBI interrogation from author interviews with government officials and various news accounts, including most prominently Suketu Mehta, "The Outsider," *Newsweek*, October, 23, 2011.
215 Details of Chiesi's arrest from author interviews with government officials and various news accounts.
216 Details of Drimal's arrest from author interviews and various news accounts, including Susan Pulliam, "When the Feds Are Watching," *Wall Street Journal*, April 28, 2011.
219 Details on expert networks and Anthony Longoria from author interviews with government investigators, court documents, and various news accounts, including Patricia Hurtado, "Rajaratnam Arrest Made ex-AMD Worker 'Paranoid,' He Tells Jury," Bloomberg, September 14, 2011.
222 Preet Bharara's speech to the New York City Bar Association from author interviews and various news accounts, including Mark DeCambre, "Taped crusader: U.S. Atty pushes wiretaps, rails vs. insider trading," *New York Post*, October 22, 2010.
224 Background on Preet Bharara and his brother, Vinnie, from Bharara speech in June 2011 attended by author, as well as author interviews and Jason Horowitz, "Federal prosecutor Preet Bharara builds a reputation on Wall Street, in Albany," *The Washington Post*, April 4, 2013, and Peter Lattman, "The Fabulous Bharara Boys," *New York Times*, June 14, 2011.

CHAPTER 12: NEVER LET A GOOD SCANDAL GO TO WASTE

227 FBI's growing angst over Preet Bharara's media strategy from interviews with government investigators with direct knowledge of the matter.
232 Noah Freeman's comments to the FBI about pressure to give Cohen the best information even if it means insider information from author interviews and Patricia Hurtado, "Ex-SAC Capital Manager Tells FBI Fund Used Insider Data," Bloomberg, Oct. 2, 2012.
232 Relationship between Noah Freeman and Winifred Jiau and the inner workings of SAC including Freeman's relationship with Cohen from author interviews and various news accounts, including Azam Ahmed and Peter Lattman, "Expert Network Consultant Is Convicted in Insider Trading Case," *New York Times*, June 20, 2011; Peter Lattman, "Trail to a Hedge Fund, from a Cluster," *New York Times*, December 5, 2012. See also Kaja Whitehouse, "Beef & lobster source: SAC staff pooh-poohed expert Winnie," *New York Post*, June 7, 2011.
234 Jiau's incarceration from author interviews and Walter Pavlo, "Winifred

Jiau Prison Sentence: What Is The Message For Wall Street?" *Forbes*, September 13, 2011.

235 Jon Streeter's view of insider trading from author interviews with government investigators.

238 Rajaratnam lawyer Dowd's arguments to get wiretaps thrown out of court from author interviews and various news accounts, including Kaja Whitehouse, "Galleon Wiretaps Ruckus," *New York Post*, October 7, 2010.

240 Judge Richard Holwell's thought process regarding the wiretap evidence and the advice from his law clerk from author interviews with people who have direct knowledge of the matter.

242 Holwell's decision to allow wiretaps from author interviews and various news accounts, including Jonathan Stempel, "Galleon's Rajaratnam Loses Wiretap Suppression Bid," Reuters, November 24, 2010.

243 Details of FBI meeting with John Hollander from author interview with Hollander's attorney and people who have spoken directly with Hollander.

CHAPTER 13: THE LUCKIEST MEN IN LAW ENFORCEMENT

247 Jon Streeter's "nightmare" from author interviews with people with direct knowledge of the matter.

248 Rajaratnam's Goldman trades from various news accounts, including David Glovin, Patricia Hurtado, and Bob Van Voris, "Galleon's Rajaratnam Talked on Tape About Goldman Board," Bloomberg, March 31, 2011.

251–252 Rajiv Goel's tapped telephone calls with Rajaratnam from court records and "Wiretaps Captivate Jurors at Galleon Insider Trading Trial," Associated Press, March 27, 2011.

254 Cross-examination of Anil Kumar from author interviews and various news accounts, including "Insight: Rajaratnam Lawyer: Information Public, Not Secret," Thomson Reuters News, March 16, 2011.

256 Rajaratnam appeal strategy from people with direct knowledge of the matter.

263 The record of SEC enforcement chief Robert Khuzami from various news accounts, including Ben Protess, "Khuzami, S.E.C. Enforcement Chief Who Reinvigorated Unit, to Step Down," *New York Times*, January 9, 2013. See also SEC press release, "Enforcement Director Robert Khuzami to Leave," January 9, 2013.

CHAPTER 14: STEVIE IS WORRIED

268 George Sard's media strategy from author interviews.

272 Steve Cohen's remarks during his deposition in the Fairfax Financial case from author's review of the transcript and Jennifer Ablan, "Stevie Cohen Unplugged," Reuters, December 13, 2011.

273 Cohen's deposition in Fairfax case from author interviews and Greg Farrell, "SAC's Cohen May Face SEC Suit as Deposition Hurts Case," Bloomberg, February, 19, 2013.

273 Grassley pressing the SEC about its handling of SAC suspicious trading referrals from Peter Lattman, "New Scrutiny for S.E.C. and Trades at SAC Capital," *New York Times*, May 24, 2011.

275 Cohen's appearance remarks during 2011 SALT conference from author interviews, various news accounts, and Steve Eder and Gregory Zuckerman, "Steven Cohen Says His Hedge Fund Firm Takes Compliance 'Very Seriously,'" *Wall Street Journal*, May 11, 2011.

275 Cohen's comments to his friend Richard "Bo" Dietl from author interview with Dietl.

283 Kinnucan's comments about FBI and emails to various people involved in the case from author interviews.

283 Backgound on John Mulheren from *Den of Thieves* (New York: Simon & Schuster, 1991).

286 Slaine's "outing" by the *Wall Street Journal*, his mental state, and the impact on Drimal as Slaine received his sentence from author interviews and various news accounts including Susan Pulliam, "Wired on Wall Street: Trader Betrays a Friend," *Wall Street Journal*, January 16, 2010. See also David Glovin and David Voreacos, "The Tale of a Wall Street Trader Turned FBI Spy," *Bloomberg Businessweek*, December 6, 2012.

287 Drimal's sentencing and the reasons for it from Chris Dolmetsch and Patricia Hurtado. "Ex-Galleon Trader Drimal Should Get 70- to 80-Month Prison Term, U.S. Says," Bloomberg, August 25, 2011.

288 Kinnucan's shifting account on who the FBI wanted him to wiretap from author interviews with Kinnucan and various news reports, including Courtney Comstock, "John Kinnucan: SAC Capital's Michael Steinberg Was NOT Who I Was Asked to Record," *Business Insider*, December 9, 2010.

289 Freeman's comments to the FBI about insider trading at SAC from Hurtado, "Ex-SAC Capital Manager Tells FBI Fund Used Insider Data," Bloomberg, October 2, 2012.

CHAPTER 15: HARPOONING THE WHALE

293 Kinnucan's arrest and sentencing from Justice Department charging documents and from Chad Bray and Susan Pulliam, "Once-Defiant Insider: 'I'm Sorry' Kinnucan Sentenced to 51 Months in Prison, Called 'Cautionary Tale' on Fighting the Government," *Wall Street Journal*, January 15, 2013.

296 Details of the FDA's decision to nix Qnexa in 2010, SAC's short position on the stock, and ultimate approval and name change from author interviews with people directly involved in the matter; FDA panel minutes, various news accounts including from Jennifer Corbett Dooren, "FDA Panel Rejects Weight-Loss Drug," *Wall Street Journal*, July 16, 2010. Also see Daniel J. DeNoon, "Advisory Panel Votes Against Drug's Approval Because of Potential Side Effects," WebMD Health News, July 15, 2010.
297 Details about increased occurrence of birth defects from Qnexa from *North American Antiepileptic Drug Pregnancy Registry,* Winter 2009 issue.
301 Details of SAC probe and how it got started from author interviews with investigators and from David Glovin, David Voreacos, Bob Van Voris, and Patricia Hurtado, "SAC Insider Probe Rides a Referral Into Cohen's Orbit," *Bloomberg News,* November 26, 2012.
305 How Wadhaw and Kang began the Elan/Wyeth probe from author interview with government investigators and Sheelah Kolhatkar, "Where Hedge Fund Mogul Steve Cohen Learned to Trade," Bloomberg, December 7, 2012.
305 Details of Sidney Gilman's Wall Street work from interviews with government investigators, expert network officials, and Nathaniel Popper and Bill Vlasic, "Quiet Doctor, Lavish Insider: A Parallel Life," *New York Times*, December 15, 2012.
305 Gerson Lehrman insider trading policy and how much Sidney Gilman was paid from author interview and various publications including Andrew Ross Sorkin, "Knowledge Is Money, but the Peril Is Obvious," *New York Times*, November 26, 2012.
306 Details on beginning of Martoma/Gilman probe from author interviews with investigators, government documents, and Tom Randall and Elizabeth Lopatto, "Wyeth, Elan Alzheimer's Drug Tarnished by Side Effect in Study," *Bloomberg News,* July 30, 2008.
309 Details of Martoma's questioning and Gilman's cooperation from author interviews with government officials and Sheelah Kolhatkar, "On the Trail of SAC Capital's Steven Cohen," *Bloomberg Businessweek*, January 17, 2013.
311 Cohen's dinner with Bo Dietl and meeting with employees, from author interviews and Peter Lattman, "Trail to a Hedge Fund, from a Cluster," *New York Times*, December 5, 2012.
312 Details on Horvath from Patricia Hurtado, "SAC Criminal Probe May Speed Up With SEC Allegations," *Bloomberg News,* March 16, 2013.
312 Anxiety at the top ranks of SAC from author interviews and Michelle Celarier, "Mr. Shark Repellent: Cohen's general counsel gives SAC boss cover," *New York Post*, November 24, 2012.
313 Michael Steinberg's possible arrest from author interviews and Kaja

Whitehouse, "Hedgie holed up in hotel with hopes of not being cuffed at home: Sources," *New York Post*, March 18, 2013.

317 Statement of SEC acting enforcement director George Canellos regarding Cohen from Jonathan Stempel and Katya Wachtel, "Cohen's SAC to pay $616 million in SEC insider trade settlement," Reuters, March 15, 2013.

318 Eric Holder's statement about too-big-to-fail from Peter Schroeder, "Big banks' size complicates prosecution efforts," *The Hill*, online, March 6, 2013.

INDEX

ABOUT THE AUTHOR

Charles Gasparino is a senior correspondent for the Fox Business Network and the Fox News Channel, where he reports on major developments in the world of finance and politics. He writes a column for the *New York Post, The Daily Beast,* and *The Huffington Post*. He lives in New York City.